UNDERSTANDING DEFEAT

UNDERSTANDING DEFEAT

How to Recover from Loss in Battle to Gain Victory in War

Col. T. N. Dupuy

U . S . A R M Y , R E T .

A G I N I G E R B O O K

PARAGON HOUSE

New York

First edition, 1990
Published in the United States by
Paragon House
90 Fifth Avenue
New York, NY 10011

for

The K. S. Giniger Company, Inc.
250 West 57th Street
New York, NY 10107

Library of Congress Cataloging-in-Publication Data

Dupuy, Trevor Nevitt, 1916–
Understanding defeat : how to recover from loss in
battle to gain victory in war / T. N. Dupuy.—1st ed.
p. cm.
"A Giniger book."
Includes bibliographical references.
ISBN 1-55778-099-4
1. Combat.   2. Military art and science.   3. United States—
Military policy.   I. Title.
U104.D862   1990
355.4'2—dc20   90-31504
CIP

Manufactured in the United States of America

10 9 8 7 6 5 4 3 2 1

The paper used in this publication meets the minimum requirements of
American National Standard for Information Sciences—Permanence of Paper
for Printed Library Materials, ANSI Z39.48-1984.

Contents

Introduction

This book was written in order to force myself—and the reader—to focus on the unpleasant subject of defeat, which is too often ignored because of its unpleasantness. The underlying assumption of the book is that the nation and military force that better understands defeat in battle is more likely to be able to avoid it, or at least to mitigate its effects when such defeat is unavoidable. I had come to the conclusion that military planners and their supporting analysts in the United States do not adequately understand defeat, a matter of great concern if my basic assumption is correct.

The problem, in brief, is that our military planners and civilian analysts of military affairs in and out of government tend to avoid analysis of defeat in battle by mindless assumptions about its significance. In particular, they either ignore or fail to evaluate consistently the relationship, the similarities, and the differences between defeat in battle and defeat in war. I have made the two principal consequences of this state of affairs the parallel themes of this book.

The more important of these themes, and the one governing this book's principal thrust, is that—if we understand the relationship—defeat in battle need not necessarily result in defeat in war. The other theme is that we cannot understand defeat in battle unless we can properly represent it in the modern planning process.

As described in Chapter 12, ever since modern military planning has come to rely upon computers and computer simulations of combat, planners and analysts have avoided the necessity for understanding defeat by arbitrarily, inadequately, and improperly representing it in the planning process. We tend increasingly to rely upon computerized models of combat in planning today. This is not necessarily bad, but it fosters a tendency to ignore the *reasons* for what happens in battles because computers give us the answers without need for thought. If the computers could truly represent combat processes, they could save us the necessity for wasting time and effort in thinking unnecessarily about matters the computers can handle better and more quickly than our slower but more flexible brain cells. But if the computers are not programmed to represent combat processes adequately, then we must use our brains to adapt the computer outputs to the real world.

Unfortunately, there has been a consistent failure on the part of analysts to do anything about the inability of most combat models in use today to simulate defeat. Particularly seriously, this results in an arbitrary approach to the representation of defeat that ignores the fundamental fact that defeat is one side of a coin, the other side of which is victory. This simple relationship of victory, defeat, and the planning process appears to me to be logical. But it is a relationship that has been virtually ignored by planners and military analysts in this country for at least thirty years.

Probably they ignore the relationship because of a questionable assumption that they take for granted: The United States will be victorious in war even if in the process we suffer some defeats in battle. They fail to recognize that defeat in battle is inevitably a step to what I describe early in this book as "the slippery slope to defeat in war."

Barbara Tuchman once quite accurately described her biography of General Stilwell as "an egg with two yolks." This book might also be described that way, even though its two themes are both related to defeat, the unifying phenomenon ever implicitly present in war or battle. Through these themes I hope that I can achieve my unitary objective, fostering improved understanding of the defeat phenomenon. This understanding, however, can ultimately be useful to us only if we realize that the fundamental objective in battle is to lead to victory (which might better be stated as avoiding defeat) in war.

T. N. Dupuy
McLean, Virginia

Part I

THE CONCEPT OF DEFEAT

Chapter 1

Winning and Losing in Battle and War

"NO DISGRACE TO BE DEFEATED"

History tells us that only two of the so-called Great Captains never knew defeat: Alexander the Great and Julius Caesar. And history may be partially deceiving us about both of those great leaders. As Frederick the Great once remarked, with the benefit of some bitter experience: "It is no disgrace to be defeated. . . ."

Englishmen are almost proud to say that "Britain loses every battle but the last one." In World War I the British actually commemorated a defeat with a service medal that was worn proudly by the few survivors of the Retreat from Mons. However, one of Britain's greatest generals did not look upon defeat with such equanimity. Three interesting quotations suggest the attitude of the Duke of Wellington:

In his dispatch after the Battle of Waterloo he wrote: "Nothing except a battle lost can be half so melancholy as a battle won."

In later life he commented to a biographer about Waterloo: "The next greatest misfortune to losing a battle is to gain such a victory as this."

Then there was the time at a party in London when a gushing woman said to the Duke: "What a glorious thing must be a victory, sir." Wellington is reported to have responded: "The greatest tragedy in the world, Madam, except a defeat."

The Iron Duke obviously remembered his relatively few defeats with considerable bitterness.

But perhaps the most interesting comment about defeat in battle from a soldier who had tasted it was uttered by a tough, wiry, bespectacled, gray-haired American general at the end of a retreat longer and more galling (if possible) than that from Mons: "We got a hell of a beating. We got run out of Burma and it is humiliating as hell. I think we ought to find out what caused it, go back, and retake it."

That matter-of-fact acknowledgment of the humiliation of defeat, combined with a professional statement of determination to learn from defeat how to achieve ultimate victory, expresses succinctly what this book is all about. And there can be no better object lesson. Because Joseph W. Stilwell—"Vinegar Joe"—did just what he said should be done: He studied the defeat, learned from his study what should and could be done to turn the tables on the original victors, and went back to retake Burma in one of the more brilliant campaigns of World War II.

But, even though it can be experienced by the greatest generals and the best armies, defeat in battle is terribly costly, and it has often been the beginning of the slippery slope to defeat in war. That is perhaps the most important reason why military men, and the thinking citizens of a democracy, should understand the implications of defeat, should seek ways to avoid it if at all possible, but should also learn the secret of converting an unavoidable defeat on the battlefield into a stepping stone toward ultimate victory in war.

In the United States there are two particular reasons why we need to understand defeat better than we do. In the first place, as Winfield Scott once said: In the first half of many of our wars "more defeats than victories have fallen to our share."[1] This has been the price we have paid for groundless optimism and unwillingness to gird ourselves in peacetime to a reasonable state of readiness for our wars. It is all well and good to tell ourselves that we must be ready in the future. But we probably won't be.

That being the case, we must at the very least understand defeat. And, since most military planning these days is based upon computer models and simulations, we must be able to represent defeat objectively and realistically in such media.

It is evident that currently we do *not* understand defeat. We neglect it in our military thinking, probably for fear of appearing "defeatist." Until very recently, we could not come close to representing defeat in computer simulations, and very few people were concerned about it. Now that some progress has been made toward using computers to represent defeat, it is still generally ignored by operations research analysts and planners.

What is defeat? Do we really need to worry about it? Since the United States always wins its wars, aren't we justified in accentuating the positive—victory—and ignoring or taking "in stride" the occasional defeats that preceded inevitable victory?

DEFEAT "IS HUMILIATING AS HELL"

The United States has fought ten wars (if we ignore the numerous minor, bitter, and not always successful conflicts against American Indians). Of these ten, we have won seven and lost three; one was a draw. (My arithmetic may be peculiar, but it is correct; remember, we fought one of those wars against ourselves, and though some Americans won that war, some Americans also lost it.)

We have been luckier in our unsuccessful wars than is usually the case for defeated nations. Although they won most of the battles and briefly occupied and burned our capital in the War of 1812, the British were satisfied simply to teach us a lesson and to return to the *status quo ante* after signing a peace treaty favorable to them. That part of America that

Figure 1.1.   Victory/Defeat Record
Wars of the United States

War	Victory	Defeat	Draw
American Revolution	X		
War of 1812		X	
Mexican War	X		
Civil War	X	X	
	(Union)	(Confederacy)	
Spanish–American War	X		
Philippine Insurrection	X		
World War I	X		
World War II	X		
Korean War			X
Vietnam War		X	

was defeated in the Civil War was occupied by the victorious army, but it was a benign occupation (victorious American occupying armies have always been benign). Although the citizens under that occupation considered themselves downtrodden, actually they were probably better off in most respects than they had been in four brief years under their own government. As for our defeat in Vietnam, while we recognized that we had lost the war, that was the way the American people wanted it; furthermore, we knew that we had won practically all of the battles. So we simply undeclared the war and withdrew, leaving our reasonably faithful allies to the not-so-tender mercies of the victors.

Because of our luck, because of geography, and because of the unprecedented grace bestowed upon our nation by a very kind and merciful God, we have never really had to pay the full price of defeat in the wars we have lost. At least not up until now. But we are not invincible. We can be defeated in war as well as in battle. We *have* been defeated in war. It *could* happen again, and the chances are that if it did we would not be so lucky as we have been in the past.

What could happen to us if we not only were defeated but also had to suffer the fate of most defeated nations? We do not have to go back to ancient history to recall that the defeated Carthaginians were sold into slavery as their city was razed by the victorious Romans. We merely need to remember what happened—during the lives of many of us now living— to the peoples of Europe under Nazi terror from 1939 to 1945 and under Stalinist terror from 1939 to 1953 and later. Certainly Hitler and his henchmen ultimately paid the price for their deeds—but that does not return to life the millions who died in gas chambers and other millions who died in concentration camps and elsewhere from starvation and torture, or who (like much of the Polish officer corps) died before Communist firing squads.

If "war is hell," as General Sherman said while teaching that as a lesson, then defeat can be an inferno or holocaust which suggests that "the coolest rooms in Hell" can be moderately comfortable. The humiliation, even the carnage, of defeat in battle pale into insignificance beside the potential disaster of defeat in war.

We know from history that defeat in battle has sometimes been unavoidable for the defeated side. But whether avoidable or unavoidable, we also know from history that defeat in battle can be retrieved. Finally, we know from history that retrieving victory from defeat in battle does not come easily and can happen only as the result of desperate and dedicated efforts to understand what caused the initial defeat as well as to take the actions (always difficult) to rectify those causes.

SOME BASIC CONCEPTS

Before going further, it will be helpful for the reader to understand exactly what is meant in the frequent use of the four terms *success*, *defeat*, *failure*, and *termination of combat*. The reader need neither agree nor disagree with the definitions of these words as used in this book. But it will be helpful if we are all reading from the same sheet of music.

Let's start with *success*. This is a better word than "win" or "victory" since these are often used loosely. Success—military success in combat—means the unequivocal accomplishment of an assigned or perceived combat mission. A few years ago we were treated to the spectacle of a celebration by the people of Libya, a year after the event, of their "victory" over the American air forces that struck their country on 14 April 1986 in retaliation for Libyan involvement in international terrorism. It is doubtful that many Americans would claim that strike as an American "victory." But, in terms of battle outcome, the Americans accomplished their mission, the Libyans did not.

Defeat is the other side of that coin and is synonymous with *failure*—failure to accomplish a combat mission.

It is possible (though rare) for both opponents to be successful in a combat encounter. For instance, a force with a delaying mission may give up territory and still accomplish its mission. If the attacker's mission was to seize the territory thus ceded, he also was successful.

There do not appear to be any historical combat encounters in which *both* sides failed to accomplish their missions, though it may theoretically be possible. If an attacker fails, the defender almost automatically succeeds. If a defender fails, this almost certainly means the attacker was successful. And if a delaying defender is pushed back more rapidly, or pushed back farther, than contemplated in his mission, he also has failed.

Termination of combat, or battle termination, is something that can be done by either a successful or a defeated combatant. However, the term is usually used by American planners and analysts to describe the action of a defeated force in bringing its unsuccessful combat efforts to a conclusion.

That is the way the expression is used in this book. It is worth noting that the battle-termination action of a defeated force, particularly a defeated defender, may itself be unsuccessful. In such case the battle will continue until the defeated force is destroyed, until it is finally able to break contact, or until the successful side halts its pursuit.

ORGANIZATION OF THIS BOOK

In the remaining two chapters of the first part of this book we examine the concept of defeat from two different perspectives: first from the somewhat Olympian standpoint of some of the most successful generals of history; second from the viewpoint of soldiers who suffered the agonies of defeat on the battlefield.

Part II examines in some detail the theoretical aspects of defeat and why and how military forces and commanders are defeated.

Part III looks at a number of historical examples of defeat in the past two centuries. This cross-section examines the experience of Napoleon, who won more battles than any other general in history but who also lost more campaigns than most generals have an opportunity to fight. We look at the defeats suffered by two great American generals of the Civil War: Robert E. Lee and Ulysses S. Grant. Next is a critical and analytical examination of four twentieth-century defeats. That part of the book closes with the experiences of two World War II divisions: one a German division suffering bitter defeat in Russia, the other an American division decisively repulsed on the western frontier of Germany.

Part IV looks at how defeat is examined and represented in the modern processes of planning and analysis. Since these processes rely extensively on the use of computers, this examination focuses on computer simulations of defeat and battle termination.

Finally, in Part V we see how defeat in battle is not necessarily terminal. Historical examples show us that defeat in battle *can* be converted into success—and here the word *victory* can be appropriate—in war.

There are three appendices. The first discusses the Principles of War, often used for battle analysis, and explains why a somewhat different analytical approach is used in this book. The second lists 138 significant defeats in history. The third describes the relatively recent study in which, as noted earlier in this chapter, "some progress has been made toward using computers to represent defeat."

Chapter 2

The Experience of the Great Captains

B Y   C U R T   J O H N S O N

With few exceptions, each of history's Great Captains has experienced defeat on the battlefield and, in many cases, those defeats have been crushing—even decisive.

For example, of Napoleon's eight Great Captains (and the Corsican's list may be regarded as near-definitive—for Europe, at least—up to his own era) only two did not know defeat in battle. Napoleon's list included Alexander, Hannibal, Julius Caesar, Gustavus Adolphus, Turenne, Eugene of Savoy, and Frederick the Great.[1]

The undefeated (or most successful) in that group were Alexander and Caesar. Alexander, in his relatively brief but remarkable military career, conquered the world from the Balkans to the Himalayas. He is arguably history's greatest soldier. Caesar had his share of "near-run things" and profited greatly from the quarrels and political divisions of his enemies, but his greatness is undiminished thereby. He ranks not far behind Alexander among history's greatest military leaders.

To Napoleon's list of greats may be added many others, whose individual accomplishments perhaps equaled (and in two cases may even have exceeded) those of some of the emperor's short list of greats—save Alexander.[2] Among them: Napoleon himself, Heraclius, Genghis Khan, Tamerlane, Edward I, Babur, Montrose, Condé, Charles XII of Sweden, Moltke the Elder, and Ludendorff. (Obviously, others will have other candidates.)

Yet few of these greats were strangers to defeat, and those whose profession is war best understand the ubiquity of failure and defeat. After crushing the Russian fleet at Tsushima (1905) Japanese Admiral Togo Heihachiro reminded his captured adversary, Admiral Zinovi Rozhdestvenski, that defeat is the "common fate" of military men, and that "there is nothing to be ashamed of in it." Togo was echoing a sentiment of Frederick the Great, who well knew whereof he spoke. If defeat, then, is relatively commonly the lot of even the best of captains, it behooves those who would analyze the phenomenon to examine it in the context of how it befell the best. This chapter addresses how some of history's greatest military leaders have been defeated.

GREAT CAPTAINS IN DEFEAT

HANNIBAL

Hannibal (247–183 B.C.), author of a string of victories that includes one of history's greatest (Cannae, 216 B.C.), was finally defeated by Scipio Africanus at Zama, in North Africa, in 202 B.C. This Scipio was the son of P. Cornelius Scipio, whom Hannibal himself had defeated at the river Ticinus in 218 B.C., at the outset of the Second Punic War (one of Rome's three great struggles with Carthage).

Including the Ticinus and Cannae, Hannibal had four great battlefield victories—the others being the Trebia (218), scene also of Suvorov's 1799 defeat of the French, and Lake Trasimene (217). However, before Zama, he had not been uniformly successful. His chesslike encounters with Marcellus in the Campania (216–214) had resulted in one repulse under the walls of Nola and two stalemated engagements at the same place. But these were minor clashes, not great battlefield encounters. Ignoring the three Nolas and Hannibal's successes against barbarians in Spain, his success rate in battle was 80 percent (four of five), making him the third most successful of the great captains who *were* defeated. (Napoleon was first, with 92 percent, Genghis Khan was second, with 90 percent.)

All things being equal, it is probable that Hannibal would have been the victor at Zama, because he was the greater of the two generals. Scipio, however, was a formidable opponent. When Scipio and Hannibal met in conference before the battle they were, in Livy's words, "not only the greatest soldiers of their time, but the equals of any king and commander in the whole history of the world."[3] But Scipio, besides his military skill, had a great advantage in cavalry and—most important—in overall troop quality, and he was able to utilize these advantages to win. Hannibal's veteran infantry fought heroically under adverse circumstances, but his cavalry was swept from the field, and the Roman cavalry under Masinissa (Hannibal's former ally) and Laelius was able to envelop the infantry center and strike it from the rear. The result was a disastrous defeat for Hannibal—the only one he ever suffered in a great open-field fight. Hannibal survived the defeat and fled, living out the rest of his days in exile among Rome's enemies in western Asia.

GENGHIS KHAN

Napoleon included in his list of Great Captains two excellent European generals (Turenne and Eugene) who are omitted from some lists of later military historians and did not include three names that are contained in the list of at least one contemporary military historian.[4] One of these three was Admiral Lord Horatio Nelson, who won three great sea battles and never suffered a defeat and is therefore omitted from this discussion of Great Captains who have been defeated. Another was Napoleon himself, who—though never one to hide his light under a bushel—recognized the impropriety of including himself in his list. The third was Genghis Khan, whose career was probably not adequately known by Napoleon.

A later chapter focuses on the victories and defeats of Napoleon, so it seems appropriate to round out our treatment of Great Captains who tasted one or more defeats by including a discussion of the career and defeats of Genghis Khan in this chapter.

Genghis Khan (1162–1227) was without doubt the greatest conqueror in history; he is, with Alexander and Napoleon, one of the three men for whom a serious case can be made as the single greatest general who ever lived. His conquests were accomplished through skillful employment of an army he created, applying a doctrine he formulated. As an organizer and conceptualizer of doctrine, he was at least the equal of Gustavus Adolphus. Yet he never learned to read or write.

The military career of Genghis can be summarized in terms of four major periods of war. The first and longest of these, from about 1179 to

1204, was the Mongolian Wars period, in which Genghis first consolidated his control over the Borjigen Mongols and then expanded his dominion over all of Mongolia as a result of a great victory at Chakrimont. It was during this period that he developed his system of warfare by establishing a simple but flexible organization completely of horsemen, adding a shock element to the traditional Mongol horse archers and molding the hitherto undisciplined tribesmen into an efficient and disciplined army.

The second period was the conquest of northern China, in which Genghis Khan fought and defeated first the Hsia Hsia Empire of northwestern China, suppressed an uprising in western Mongolia, and then began a six-year campaign against the Chin (or Kin) empire of eastern China. During this period, after repeated attempts, he finally captured the Chin capital of Peking in 1215, and consolidated his control of all China north of the Yellow River by 1217. Militarily, he conscripted a contingent of Chinese engineers into his army and adapted Chinese techniques to develop the most efficient siege warfare capability of all history. Never again was he to be frustrated by the strong walls of cities like Peking.

The third period was one of campaigns in Central and Western Asia, begun by the conquest of Kara-Khitai by one of his principal subordinates, Chepe-Noyon, in 1218. In 1219 Genghis Khan himself took the field with the largest army he ever raised and commanded—200,000 men—to respond to a challenge from Mohammed Shah, ruler of the Khwarezmian Empire, which included modern Iran, Afghanistan, northern Pakistan, Iraq, and the southern Soviet Union as far as the Caucasus Mountains and the Aral Sea. In two campaigns he swiftly conquered Transoxiana, Khurasan, Afghanistan, eastern and central Persia, and northern India. This brief period culminated in a great victory over Mohammed's son, Jellaluddin, in the Battle of the Indus River, 24 November 1221. While he consolidated his control over the annexed regions of the former Khwarezmian Empire, Genghis Khan sent his two most able subordinates—Chepe and Subotai—on a long-range reconnaissance through the Caucasus to southern Russia. This two-year expedition, in which the Mongols defeated a far larger Russian army, set the stage for Subotai's later conquest of Russia and eastern Europe in 1240–1242.

Genghis Khan returned home in 1223 intending to spend the rest of his life in peace. However, less than two years later the Chin and Hsia Hsia empires—nominally vassals of Genghis Khan since their earlier defeats at his hands—joined forces and invaded their former domains north of the Yellow River. Genghis Khan took the field again, for the last time. In the largest pitched battle of his career—about 150,000 Mongols against nearly 300,000 Chinese—Genghis Khan defeated the rebel allies on the banks and frozen surface of the Yellow River, December 1226. He forced the Hsia Hsia to make peace, then turned south and east against the Chin. However, he fell ill and, with a premonition of death, left his army and returned to Mongolia. He died en route and was buried secretly on the slopes of Mount Burkan-Kaldun, where he had lived as a fugitive in his youth.

The records suggest that Genghis Khan fought at least twenty, perhaps as many as twenty-five, major pitched battles, more than any other Great Captain except Napoleon. Since he lost two of these, his success rate in battle is between 92 percent and 90 percent, second only to Napoleon among Great Captains who have been defeated.

The first of Genghis Khan's two defeats took place in 1203, when he was still known as Temuchin, chief of the Borjigen, one of the several Mongolian tribes. This was at the hands of the Kerait Mongols under Toghrul Khan, former protector and ally of Temuchin, in the hard-fought battle of Gupta Hill, apparently midway between Onon and Karakorum (the respective capitals of the Borjigen and Kerait Mongols). The defeat was due to the overwhelming strength of the Keraits, probably more than 20,000 to Genghis' 5000. Genghis and about half of his army survived only because of hard fighting, excellent choice of a hillside defensive position, and an audacious Borjigen envelopment of the larger Kerait army. This caused the surprised Keraits to slacken the intensity of their attack and enabled Genghis to hold his positions until nightfall, after which he withdrew.

The second, and last, defeat of Genghis Khan took place near Peking in 1213, the third year of his war against the Chin Empire. The previous year he had been frustrated by the strong fortifications of Peking, the Chin capital. He was able, nevertheless, to overrun most of the Chin domains north of the Yellow River. Now, while he was campaigning to the west and south, Genghis Khan learned about a palace coup within the Chin capital. The eunuch general Hu Sha-hu had rebelled against Emperor Wei-wang, killed him, seized power, and installed another Chin prince on the throne. Learning about these events, Genghis Khan marched on the Chin capital in expectation of taking the city easily. Approaching Peking, while crossing a river, his army was ambushed and defeated by a larger Chinese army under General Hu Sha-hu. Genghis withdrew in good order and the Chinese slowly followed. A few weeks later Genghis turned and defeated them in another great battle, then returned to blockade Peking.

In both these battles—as, indeed, in most of the battles of his career—

Genghis was outnumbered by his opponents. In the Battle of Peking he was also surprised—probably because, expecting easy success without the necessity for a battle, he did not exercise his usual care by covering his front with a screen of light cavalry.

GUSTAVUS

Sweden's King Gustavus Adolphus was one of two of Napoleon's Great Captains who died in battle (the other was Turenne).

Among the Great Captains, the organizational ability of Gustavus was matched only by that of Genghis Khan.

Gustavus was unique in that he alone created a new system of warfare: modern linear tactics. That system persisted until recently, and many of its forms are still with us.[5]

Ignoring many victories gained in minor combats, Gustavus had six major successes:

Wallhof (17 Jan 1626) v the Poles under Sapieha
Dirschau (17–18 Aug 1627) v the Poles under Koniecpolski
Werben (8 Aug 1631) v the Leaguers under Tilly
Breitenfeld I (17 Sep 1631) v the Leaguers under Tilly
The Lech (15–16 Apr 1632) v the Bavarians under Tilly
Lützen (16 Nov 1632) v the Imperials under Wallenstein (in which battle
     Gustavus was killed in action)

He was defeated twice:

Stuhm (27 Jun 1629) by the Poles and Imperials under Koniecpolski and
     Arnim
Alte Veste (3–4 Sep 1632) by the Imperials under Wallenstein

Thus Gustavus's success rate in major battles was 75 percent (six of eight), about the same as that of Turenne, Eugene, and Frederick.

At Stuhm Gustavus was beaten by a formidable opponent (or, rather, a formidable opposing team). The opposing commander was the Polish hetman Alexander Koniecpolski, who has been described as:

Gustavus' foremost instructor in the art of war. He not only taught him strategy, but he greatly contributed to the development of the king's genius as a battlefield tactician. He was unquestionably the most able opponent that Gustavus ever faced.[6]

And, in this instance, Koniecpolski was aided by a force of Imperial cavalry sent to Poland by Wallenstein and commanded by the "Lutheran Capuchin," Hans Georg von Arnim, one of the most skilful soldiers of the age (Arnim fought on Gustavus' side against the Imperials at Breitenfeld I).

The Battle of the Alte Veste was another instance in which Gustavus tried issues with a redoubtable adversary. His opponent, the Imperial generalissimo Albrecht von Wallenstein, a Czech, was a consummate professional who was feared and envied by friend and foe alike. In the battle Gustavus attacked Wallenstein's force, entrenched on the Alte Veste plateau near Nuremberg. In severe fighting in broken terrain the Swedes, attacking uphill, were unable to employ their artillery, which negated much of their usual firepower advantage. Moreover, the approaches to Wallenstein's camp were narrow and the Swedes were unable to maneuver, another advantage they usually possessed. All their lodgments at the summit were erased by timely Imperial counterattacks. Finally, Gustavus admitted defeat and drew off.

In both instances Gustavus was defeated by highly skilled opponents. It may be doubted that anyone could have won Alte Veste under the circumstances that prevailed. It is interesting to speculate whether Gustavus might have "won" Lützen had he lived. The battle was "won" and "lost" several times, and it appears that it was finally won for the Swedes when Bernhard of Saxe-Weimar led the Swedish infantry in one last supreme effort to drive the Imperials off by inspiring them to avenge the king's death.

TURENNE

With the single exception of Napoleon, Henri de La Tour d'Auvergne, vicomte de Turenne (1611–1675), was perhaps the greatest soldier France has produced—modest, self-effacing, and diligent, yet anything but methodical and predictable. Turenne's guiding principles in a military career that spanned five decades were: "Nothing ought to be reckon'd done, while any thing remains undone," and "make few sieges, give battle frequently. . . ."[7]

Turenne and his gifted, impetuous companion in arms (and sometime adversary), Louis II of Bourbon, Duke of Enghien, and Prince de Condé (the "Great Condé"), were largely responsible for the establishment and early maintenance of a century of French military predominance on the Continent following the defeat of the Spanish at Rocroi (1643).

In his military career Turenne won seven battles and lost three, a success rate of 70 percent. His victories were:

Zusmarshausen (17 May 1648) v the Bavarians under Melander
Faubourg St. Antoine (2 Jul 1652) v the Frondeurs under Condé
Arras (25 Aug 1654) v the Spanish under Fuensaldana and Condé
The Dunes (14 Jun 1658) v the Spanish under Don John and Condé
Sinzheim (16 Jun 1674) v the Imperials under Caprara
Enzheim (4 Oct 1674) v the Imperials under Bournonville
Turckheim (5 Jan 1675) v the Imperials under Bournonville

Not included in the enumeration above are French victories at Freiburg (3–9 Aug 1644) and Allerheim (3 Aug 1645), both over Franz von Mercy's crack Bavarian army, in which Turenne seconded Condé (then Duke of Enghien), who in both instances held the command of combined armies by virtue of his station as a prince of the blood. The victory of Allerheim was most certainly due to Turenne, the Weimar cavalry, and the auxiliary troops of Hesse, led by Generalmajor Geiso—though a French victory might have been impossible had not the brilliant Mercy been killed instantly by a musket ball in the head after destroying the French right wing of cavalry and crippling Condé's infantry in the center.

Zusmarshausen is included, even though Turenne shared the overall command of allied armies with the Swede Wrangel, as the concept and execution of the operational plan were largely due to Turenne's genius.

Turenne's three defeats were:

Mergentheim (5 May 1645) by Mercy's Bavarians
Rethel (Champ Blanc; 15 Dec 1650) by the Royalists under du Plessis-
    Praslin (César de Choiseul)
Valenciennes (16 Jul 1656) by Condé's French and Spanish forces

The principal reason for Turenne's defeat in these battles was different in each instance. At Mergentheim, perhaps the most embarrassing case, and, for Turenne, the most instructive, Mercy surprised Turenne's army at a time when it was dispersed over the Swabian countryside, Turenne having permitted his run-down cavalry to forage widely in search of spring grasses. Turenne permitted the dispersal of his troops against his better judgment, because of his "compassion for the troops, which were very much fatigued," and his "complaisance for the Officers," who had been persistent in their requests to be allowed to forage widely.[8] His defeat was complete, but Turenne could console himself with the knowledge that his rapid recovery and brief but stubborn resistance to the Bavarian onslaught prevented Mercy from reaping much benefit from his brilliant stroke.

At Rethel, during the Fronde, Turenne commanded a small, poorly trained army of Spaniards and French Frondeurs. Maneuvering near Mézieres, in the Ardennes, he was caught by du Plessis-Praslin and administered a "thorough beating" (in the words of General Maxime Weygand[9]). Du Plessis-Praslin was a skillful soldier in command of a large, well-trained force. Turenne's troops failed him miserably. This was one of two battles in history in which the opposing commanders were both marshals of France, the other being Castelnaudary in 1632.

The defeat at Valenciennes must be attributed entirely to the rashness of Turenne's co-commander, the duc de La Ferté-Senneterre, politically well connected but one of the worst generals of an age that produced some appallingly bad ones.

Weygand comments:

> Condé attacked the headquarters of La Ferté [undoubtedly a mistranslation for "quarters," meaning that part of the line of circumvallation La Ferté was responsible for], who had had the presumption to destroy the entrenchments thrown up by Turenne's order, on the pretext that he did not need them. He was taken prisoner with 4000 of his men.[10]

The one positive result of this episode was that La Ferté's capture removed him from his position as co-commander of the Royal Army. Again Weygand: "Turenne was delivered from the collaboration, with equal rights, of the other marshals."[11]

EUGENE

Eugene, Prince of Savoy (1663–1736)—was by one statistical and superficial accounting—one of the least successful of the Great Captains. Inspection of the comprehensive table of "Major Land Battles and Capitulations [1688–1746]" at Appendix Two of Chandler's *Art of Warfare in the Age of Marlborough* shows that of the eleven battles during 1697–1717 in which he alone was in command, Eugene won eight and lost three, a success rate of 73 percent.[12]

Eugene's successes include:

Zenta (11 Sep 1697) v the Turks
Carpi (9 Jul 1701) v the French and Italians under Villeroi
Chiari (1 Sep 1701) v the Allies under Villeroi
Luzzara (15 Aug 1702) v the French under Vendôme
Turin (7 Sep 1706) v the French under Burgundy
Peterwardein (5 Aug 1716) v the Turks
Kissoda (23 Sep 1716) v the Turks
Belgrade (16 Aug 1717) v the Turks

Thus, Eugene himself had eight battle successes in twenty years' campaigning, not including the fruits of his remarkable cooperation with Marlborough: victories of Blenheim (1704), Oudenarde (1708), and Malplaquet (1709), the last a costly, hard-fought success (Eugene was in Italy in 1706 when Marlborough won Ramillies). Since he was at least equally responsible for each of these great allied victories, his success rate should be recalculated by relating eleven victories to three defeats, a rate of 78.6 percent, fourth highest of the Great Captains who tasted defeat.

Of Eugene's successes, it may be said that two were triumphs (to use Chandler's term for a first-order success)—Zenta and Belgrade, both won against long odds. Another three (Chiari, Peterwardein, and Turin) were military masterpieces that were among the great victories of their time. (Napoleon most admired Eugene's Turin campaign, which he pronounced a "most brilliant success.") Carpi was a minor fight, with few battle casualties, and Luzzara was a stalemate, but with the advantage to Eugene's Imperials.

But Eugene also knew defeat, including:

Cremona (1 Feb 1702) v the French and Spanish under Villeroi
Cassano (16 Aug 1705) v the French under Vendôme
Denain (24 Jul 1712) v the French under Villars (Eugene had only a
    50 percent success rate against French generals whose names began
    with V.)

At Cremona Eugene attacked Marshal Villeroi in his headquarters in a daring (and at the time celebrated) assault that achieved complete surprise and resulted in Villeroi's capture. But one of Eugene's two assault columns was unaccountably hours late and the other column, led by Eugene himself, was finally defeated and withdrew unmolested after eleven hours of bitter street fighting. A major factor in the French success was the stubborn resistance of two Irish battalions (fewer than 600 men) that defended the Po Gate. Of 1500 French casualties the Irish sustained 350.

It is apparent that in this instance Eugene was defeated by the fighting qualities of his opponent and the failure of his subordinate, the young Prince de Vaudemont, who commanded more than half the attacking force, to coordinate with him. In essence, the defeat resulted from partial failure in the execution of a brilliant plan. Eugene must share the blame, since he entrusted such an important role in the enterprise to an inexperienced officer.

Villeroi was succeeded by Marshal Vendôme, who was made of sterner stuff. Eugene bested Vendôme at Luzzara but later was defeated by him at Cassano. This was an obstinate soldiers' battle, in which both sides fought for four hours in serried ranks at murderous ranges and in which Eugene was narrowly but plainly defeated. The defeat was of no great consequence. It seems likely that, as was thought at the time, the Imperial troops were much hampered by wet muskets and powder, as they had to ford a canal to get to their enemies. This fact too might account for the great disproportion in casualties among apparently equally matched forces. Moreover, Vendôme was a formidable opponent; in the words of one of Eugene's biographers, he was "a tactical genius, and a fighting soldier, in addition to his strategical qualities."[13]

However, Eugene's most daunting opponent was his friend and sometime comrade-in-arms, Claude Louis Hector de Villars, a French marshal risen from common beginnings. Villars and Eugene had been fast friends since they had served together against the Turks in 1683, but it was Villars who defeated Eugene at Denain. The basis of the defeat may be sought in the military apostasy of Eugene's British allies, operating under the infamous "Restraining Orders," but nonetheless Eugene was completely surprised by Villars' maneuver at Denain and was a largely impotent spectator to the destruction of the Dutch corps of his subordinate Albemarle.

FREDERICK THE GREAT

Frederick II, King of Prussia (1712–1786), was the foremost practitioner of the art of war in his age. It may be doubted that any of his contemporaries even approached his genius, although France's Marshal Maurice de

Saxe occupied the next rung pretty much by himself. Frederick's nine victories were:

Chotusitz (17 May 1742) v the Austrians
Hohenfriedberg (4 Jun 1745) v the Austrians
Soor (30 Sep 1745) v the Austrians
Lobositz (1 Oct 1756) v the Austrians
Prague (6 May 1757) v the Austrians
Rossbach (5 Nov 1757) v the French and Allies
Leuthen (5 Dec 1757) v the Austrians
Leignitz (15 Aug 1760) v the Austrians
Torgau (15 Aug 1760) v the Austrians

Not included above are Mollwitz (1741) and Zorndorf (1758). Mollwitz was Frederick's first battle and a Prussian victory in which, when things looked bad in the early going, Frederick was in effect sent off the field at the insistence of Field Marshal Kurt von Schwerin and other officers who feared for his life. While this was not exactly a "Lee to the rear" episode such as occurred in the Battle of the Wilderness (1864), it was similar. Frederick was deeply humiliated in the aftermath of the incident and never forgave Schwerin.

Zorndorf, the bloodiest major battle of the century in terms of percent losses,[14] resulted in a stalemate, and Frederick was quite content to see the Russians march off.

Frederick's defeats included:

Kolin (18 Jun 1757) v the Austrians
Hochkirch (14 Oct 1758) v the Austrians
Kunersdorf (12 Aug 1759) v the Austrians and Russians

Frederick's success rate, then, was 75 percent, the same as Gustavus' and slightly greater than Eugene's (smaller if Eugene is given credit for his role in "Marlborough's victories," as in justice he must be).

Napoleon had the greatest admiration for Frederick, particularly for the Prussian king's boldness, strength of character, and resolve. Napoleon believed that Frederick's masterpiece, Leuthen, was itself "enough to immortalize [him]" and "place him among the greatest generals."[15] Indeed, it may be doubted if any military leader before or since achieved so much so quickly as Frederick did in the month in which he won Rossbach and Leuthen. But, as startling and awe-inspiring as Frederick's victories are, his defeats too were remarkable and illustrate a defect of character that has been all too apparent in many of those who have overcome long odds and experienced extraordinary success—overconfidence and its corollary, contempt for the enemy. This is what the Japanese, after Midway, termed "the victory disease." Napoleon, as we shall see, suffered from this malady, and undoubtedly it was at the root of Lee's miscalculation on 3 July 1863 at Gettysburg.

Not surprisingly, this defect led Frederick to believe that, with his superbly drilled troops, he might always achieve "a Leuthen" even under the most adverse circumstances. Thus, even though invariably numerically inferior, he always seized the initiative (his opponents invariably obliged) and, usually by means of a turning movement, attempted to bring the mass of his force against his enemy's flank or rear, thus seeking to achieve superiority at the critical point. He ought to have been able to bring it off every time, but his confidence on occasion begat a kind of fatuous neglect that negated all his plans and resulted in his being surprised—the one unpardonable fault, to quote Frederick himself.

Thus, at Kolin he marched across his opponent's front in order to turn his right. But, having failed to reconnoiter, he had no knowledge of the extent of the Austrian position, and his plan miscarried badly, degenerating into a series of piecemeal frontal attacks. When the Austrians counterattacked, the Prussians were surprised and driven off in confusion with heavy losses. Frederick's subordinates (including one unfortunate cavalryman nicknamed "the anvil" because he had been beaten so often), failed miserably, but their performances only mirrored that of the king himself.

Hochkirch witnessed a remarkable, willful failure on the part of Frederick to observe the fundamental principle of security. Overconfident and perhaps arrogant (he was facing the ordinarily sluggish Austrian Field Marshal Daun), he camped on low ground close by the entrenched camp of his enemy. Warned by Field Marshal Keith that his army was so vulnerable that "the Austrians deserved to be hanged if they don't attack us here," Frederick had replied that "they fear us worse than the gallows." When, the Austrians struck in the predawn darkness of 14 October 1758, the Prussians were completely surprised and suffered a humiliating defeat. The loss was due entirely to Frederick's poor judgment.

At Kunersdorf as at Kolin, Frederick again failed because he had no concept of the form or extent of his enemy's position. In a situation remarkably similar to that of Zorndorf the previous year, he attempted to pass around the flank of an entrenched enemy force and attack it from the rear. And, as at Zorndorf, he discovered too late that his enemy had no rear and was disposed to meet him in an all-around defense. (In both instances, the foe was formed in a rectangular "army square"; in both instances he faced Russians, who, having much experience against the highly mobile armies of the Turks, customarily formed in that fashion to offset an adversary's advantage in mobility.)

It was the perfect counter to the Prussian king's propensity for turning movements. When the Prussian army attacked it found its enemy entrenched and waiting. The battle that followed was practically a butchery, and the Prussian army was literally destroyed. Indeed, Frederick might have lost the war if the Allies had followed up their victory, but they did not (the so-called Miracle of the House of Brandenburg) and Prussia was somehow preserved.

It should be evident from the above, then, that the principal cause of Frederick's defeats was surprise, brought about in one instance by arrogant self-delusion and twice by a failure to reconnoiter the enemy's position before setting complex turning movements in motion. Yet even these failures pale beside the magnificence of Rossbach and—particularly—Leuthen.

SUMMARY

This examination of Great Captains in defeat has focused on the battlefield losses of Napoleon's Great Captains and Genghis Khan (other greats, including Napoleon himself, are discussed elsewhere in this book). It will probably not surprise the reader to learn that most of the greats were defeated. In fact, besides Alexander and (possibly) Caesar, the number of undefeated generals in history is quite small. Scipio, Marlborough, Suvorov and Moltke (the Elder) come to mind; there is probably a handful of others. But, except for Suvorov, few of these uniformly successful generals fought many pitched battles. Those greats we have examined were successful 70 percent to 90 percent of the time.

Figure 2.1 summarizes the causes of their defeats. Most often there were multiple causes, but the most prominent cause, in terms of frequency, were an encounter with an excellent opponent, and unfavorable odds. Ordinarily, the genius of the Great Captain would be sufficient to overcome the exceptionally skillful opponent, but when that exceptional opponent had an

Figure 2.1. Causes of Great Captains' Defeats*

Great Captains	Excellent Opponent	Unfavorable Odds	Surprise	Poorly Served	Troop Quality	Poor Judgment	Totals
HANNIBAL (1)							
Zama	X				X		2
GENGHIS KHAN (2)							
Gupta Hill		X					1
Peking		X	X				2
GUSTAVUS (2)							
Stuhm	X	X					2
Alte Veste	X	X[a]				X	3
TURENNE (3)							
Mergentheim	X		X	X			3
Rethel	X	X				X	3
Valenciennes	X		X		X		3
EUGENE (3)							
Cremona				X			1
Cassano	X						1
Denain	X		X		X		3
FREDERICK (3)							
Kolin		X	X	X		X	4
Hochkirch		X	X			X	3
Kunersdorf		X	X			X	3
NAPOLEON (4)[b]							
Aspern-Essling	X	X					2
Leipzig	X	X		X			3
La Rothière	X	X			X		3
Waterloo	X	X	X	X			4
TOTALS (18)	12	12	8	5	4	5	46

* Undefeated Great Captains: Alexander the Great, Julius Caesar, Horatio Nelson

[a] The numerical strengths were about equal, but this gave Wallenstein an overwhelming advantage in a near-impregnable position.

[b] See Chapter 7.

overarching advantage of another sort, such as surprise (Denain) or qualitative and quantitative superiority (Rethel), the Great Captains revealed
their human limitations.

Surprise was the third most frequent cause, and, interestingly, in the six
cases recorded here, four resulted from culpably poor judgment. Three of
these cases involved Frederick, who said it was unforgivable to be surprised!

The enumerations of successes and failures have ignored sieges, because
they were relatively systematic undertakings that required a different sort
of genius than that displayed in the open field. But—with the exception of
Alexander and (late in his career) Genghis Khan—few of the Great Captains displayed exceptional skill at siege warfare and some, like Gustavus at
Pskov (1615) and Eugene at Toulon (1707), had some rather remarkable
failures.

Chapter 3

Losing Battles: The Experience of the Combat Soldier

B Y G A Y M . H A M M E R M A N

Some time ago, a group of scholars had an opportunity to look at defeat from the standpoint of soldiers and junior officers who had been through the experience. We were part of a study team examining the reasons for "forced posture change" by American units in some operations in World War II and the Korean War.

The study we were carrying out was not intended to be an examination of defeat.[1] Our general objective was to determine when and why a combat engagement ends, and to learn more about why an attacking force stops attacking or a defender stops holding a position and begins to pull back. We were looking at historical examples of failed attacks, and unsuccessful defenses, in order to try to find answers to such questions as: Did this happen because casualties had reached a certain level or were being incurred at some critical rate? If so, what were the levels or the rates that caused the failure? Were other factors as important as casualties? More important?

Part of this examination was to talk with veterans of specific engagements in which we believed that a clear-cut forced posture change had taken place—that is, engagements in which one side had been forced by enemy action to shift posture from attack to defense or defense to withdrawal. We wanted the observations and judgments of people who had been there, to help us form *hypotheses* on why and when forced posture change takes place; there was, of course, no thought that talking with a few veterans could produce statistically significant *answers* to these questions. Since we wanted to talk to people who had themselves experienced the forced change in posture, each of these cases was an example of U.S. troops being forced to shift posture. So, although the concept of defeat had absolutely no part in our study, the roster of military operations for which we were interviewing veterans might nevertheless have looked to the casual eye like a list of the most dramatic defeats of U.S. arms in the past forty years.

We talked with men who had crossed Italy's deep and swift Rapido River on a black night in January 1944, found themselves caught in a net of withering German crossfire, and managed to make it back cross the river, among the few who escaped either death or capture. We talked to seventeen men from the completely green 106th Division, which in mid-December 1944 had been sent to a "quiet sector" for gradual introduction to combat; these men had been hit by the onslaught of the great German Ardennes offensive just three to five days after they arrived at the front. We also talked to men who had struggled through the dense Huertgen Forest with the Pennsylvania National Guard's 28th Division, attacking Schmidt and nearby towns, and then been forced to withdraw. They had pulled back under overwhelming German artillery bombardments while skillful German infiltration brought them under fire from behind and hacked at their fragile supply lines.

Among the veterans we interviewed was an officer who had been in the retreat from Kunu-Ri—the six-mile march through a gauntlet of Chinese fire immortalized by S. L. A. Marshall in *The River and the Gauntlet*. And there was an enlisted artilleryman whose battery was overrun, its guns lost, near the Kum River, and who spent many days moving south, cross country, in territory held by the North Koreans, down the Korean peninsula, before finding and rejoining his division.

Altogether we spoke with thirty-nine men from eight different operations in individual face-to-face discussions or in groups of from two to seven men, or, in three cases, by telephone. Thirteen of these men had been officers, the other twenty-six were enlisted men. Their ranks at the time of the battles varied from brigadier general down to private. One was the commander of an armored division combat command, another commanded a battalion, and another a company, while others led platoons, rifle squads, a machine-gun squad, and a cavalry squad. There were two medics, a radio operator, regimental and battalion staff officers, artillery forward observers, a mortarman, an armorer-artificer, and many others. All had fought in Europe or North Africa in World War II and/or had fought in Korea.[2] Most of the men we reached were willing to talk with us; many were eager. They were moved by two chief purposes: They wanted to get the truth as they had seen it into the historical record, and they wanted to identify mistakes they felt had been made, so that the Army might fight more effectively in the future and fewer American soldiers might experience what they had.

REASONS FOR DEFEAT—THE SOLDIER'S VIEW

These veterans were not discussing defeat as such, or reasons for defeat. They were asked to talk about the factors they felt were crucial in bringing about the "forced posture change." Nevertheless, since these forced posture changes meant that a U.S. force had failed to achieve its mission, and in some cases failed dramatically, what the men said is highly relevant for an understanding of defeat.

As to what went wrong, what brought about the defeat, no strong pattern, no agreement emerged from the discussions, and the men's judgments differed from battle to battle. Thirty factors were listed as crucial by one group or another. These factors included lack of prior training for the kind of operation being attempted, high casualties, a much larger enemy force, poor communications, poor leadership, lack of air support, low ammunition, and many less obvious factors—like poor maps, poor staffwork, and confusion among the troops as to their orders and objectives. Figure 3.1 shows the factors and the frequency with which they were cited.[3]

One category of factor was cited in almost every operation: tactics. While a high casualty rate was seen as crucial by veterans of only two of the operations, men from seven of the eight operations commented about the tactical situation—an enemy flanking movement, for example, or the U.S. forces placing themselves "out on a limb," ready for plucking. Here are some of the veteran's comments.

A retired four-star general—then a brigadier general—asked why he made the decision to stop defending an important road center during the Battle of the Bulge and to pull back, replied, "To keep from being surrounded."[4] He had conducted a mobile defense, controlling valuable

Figure 3.1. Key Factors in Breakpoints as Judged by Veterans

OPERATIONS

Factors	A 36 Div Rapido	B 45 Div Anzio	C 28 Div Schmidt	D 106 Div Schnee Eif	E 2 Div Krink-Roch	F 7 Amd Div St. Vith	G 24 Div Taejon	H 2 Div Kunu-Ri
Force Strength Factors								
High enemy-friendly force ratio		X						X
Low troop-frontage ratio				X				
High casualty rate			X	X				
Tactical Factors								
Enemy maneuver/flank/envelop		X	X	X		⊗	X	X
Force tactically vulnerable	X	X						
High-level intelligence failure				X				X
Environment Factors								
Terrain broken by crevasses				X				
Terrain hilly/heavily forested			X					
Poor roadnet			X					
Means and Materiel Factors								
Poor communications			X	⊗	X		X	
No antitank weapons				X	X			
Low ammunition			X	⊗	X			
No air support				X				
No/poor artillery support					X			
No air supply				X				
Poor/no maps				X				
Low/no food				X				

Human Factors	#3	#14	#8	#1,4,6,11	#5	#2,7,12	#10	#13
Poor leadership				X				
Poor staffwork				X				
Poor cohesion/esprit				X				
Inexperienced officers for inexperienced troops								
Poor training and fitness				X				
Poor training for specific operation	X			X				
Poor joint engineer/infantry training and coordination	X							
Little/no unit combat experience				⊗				
High personnel turnover/replacements	X			⊗				
Little time in position before operation				X				
Troop expectations of quiet sector				X				
Confusion among troops as to orders and objectives	X			X				
Exhaustion/time in combat in current operation						X		
Source Descriptors								
Number of groups	1	1	1	4	1	3	1	1
Total participants	3	1	2	17	1	10	1	1
Group identification number(s)	#3	#14	#8	#1,4,6,11	#5	#2,7,12	#10	#13
Level at which operation seen	pltn/bn	div	pltn/co	co/bn/regt	co	pltn/co/cmbt cmd	btry	regt
Participant(s) at command level	no	yes	no	yes	yes	yes	no	yes

X = Factor cited by at least one group.

⊗ = Factor cited by at least three groups in this multigroup operation.

ground as long as he could, but repeatedly trading ground for time. When it became clear that his command would be cut off if it held out longer, he got permission to order the withdrawal. He added a quotation from his German opponent in the battle, who had written him after the war: "Withdrawal is not a disgrace but a way of fighting."

The study research team debated whether or not such a deliberate withdrawal was really a forced posture change and not a defeat. They decided that it was not.[5] But in any event, that American commander and his troops had been driven from their positions by superior enemy strength, and so in a sense had been defeated.

There was also such debate about the failed 1944 Rapido River crossings. Here, although there was no withdrawal from the positions that had been held at the beginning of the operation, there was surely a repulse so decisive that it was a defeat by any name. In the push up the boot of Italy, and in an attempt to divert German forces that would otherwise oppose the Anzio landings, the 36th Infantry Division was ordered to force a crossing of the Rapido. The river was deep and as fast as its name, with banks that swelled up from the flat terrain and then dropped abruptly to the water. The ground on the far (northern) side of the river was equally flat and was overlooked by German positions on much higher ground, including the commanding height of Monte Cassino. The men of the 36th Division had not trained for crossing a river like the Rapido, and they had not trained with the engineer troops who were responsible for their bridges and boats. The division's commander questioned his orders, but was told to carry them out.

Even though the 36th Division, a Texas National Guard unit, was experienced, and although its men heavily outnumbered the Germans—by more than four to one in one sector—relatively few of them reached the German side of the river, and all who survived the withering enemy fire there were ordered back across. Some made it. The two infantrymen we talked to did, under fire, over a shattered bridge, its right side trailing in the water and only the left guiderope for a handhold.

The men had no doubt that the reason they had to be pulled back was that they had been placed in an untenable situation. The enemy had not surrounded them, but they had been inserted into the midst of the enemy, caught in a cage of enemy crossfire, unable to see any targets for their own fire, isolated from reinforcements and supplies by the swift-flowing river, linked to their base by only the most fragile of escape routes. One of our veterans reported that back in the hospital afterward, when talk turned to the river crossings, the consensus was that the whole operation was "kind of a dumb thing to have done to begin with."[6]

Something very like defeat was also experienced by a member of the crew firing a 105mm towed gun in B Battery, 52d Field Artillery Battalion, in Korea in July 1950.[7] They had only been in Korea two weeks. These were the first weeks following the North Korean invasion, and the outnumbered, tankless United Nations forces—Americans and South Koreans—were being pushed steadily down the peninsula. These gunners were proud of the artillery, which they felt was the only thing holding off the North Koreans, and they felt the enemy was making a special effort to eliminate them. This battery was the last one still effective when it was hit on 16 July.

The men were lined up for breakfast when the attack came—as our veteran remembered it, about a thousand North Korean infantry with machine guns and mortars. Because of the much greater enemy strength, there was never any possibility that the battery could fight off the attackers. What made the difference between a fighting withdrawal and what actually happened was the fact that North Korean troops, indistinguishable to the Americans from South Korean farmers, had been digging in on B Battery's left flank for days and held a strong roadblock across their withdrawal route. B Battery held its position all day and into the night, using its guns in direct fire, but took about 70 percent casualties. The men were then ordered to destroy their equipment and withdraw on foot up the mountain behind their position and move to Taejon cross-country. Traveling on foot in small groups, some of the men got to Taejon, whose defenses were crumbling. As the front collapsed, most of them made their way to the Pusan perimeter in the southern tip of the country.

There was no doubt in the mind of the cannoneer that the key factor in the destruction of their unit was tactical: The enemy roadblock, cutting off retreat, made it impossible to hold the battery together, to fight a delaying action, or to get the guns out.

Men from other battles said the same kinds of things: "They were moving in behind us." "They cut us off." "There was nobody [no friendly troops] on our flanks." Speaking of Schmidt, which a U.S. force had reached by penetrating the dense Huertgen Forest along narrow trails and across bridges not meant for tanks, one man said: "We never should have been out there." An officer who was at Anzio said: "If a more aggressive corps commander had . . . seized key terrain [immediately], *that* would have made a difference [in the outcome]." We were looking at only nine operations, and no conclusions can be drawn for wider applications. But in these battles, whether high-ranking officers or ordinary soldiers are speaking, the theme of tactics is consistent: Errors that placed men in vulnerable places or successful enemy maneuvers to outflank, infiltrate behind, or encircle—these were key factors in defeat as seen from the battlefield.

Among other factors cited as crucial, the failure or breakdown of communications was one that appeared several times, and in every case in which it was believed by veterans to have been present, it was judged to have been crucial. Without good communications, commanders could not order attacks or withdrawals and could not locate either their own units or the enemy. Artillery and air support could not be called in. Soldiers who were willing and able to follow orders—who, for example, were trapped in the Battle of the Bulge and did not want to surrender to the Germans—were neutralized, and uncertain of what to do. The regimental commanders of those trapped forces were cut off from communication with their division commander; messages took six, eight, ten hours to get through. As one officer said: "Things were better in the Civil War. *We* didn't have horsemen."

One of the officers interviewed, discussing causes of defeat, said that sometimes the circumstances are such that defeat can't be avoided, and that the key point is to forge the best possible outcome for it. He stressed the importance of a commander's always controlling at least *two* roads to the rear—one for bringing forward supplies and reinforcements and one for taking out, in time of crisis, service and support units that are then only an encumbrance.[8]

High casualties are another factor commonly assumed to be responsible for failed missions and defeat. Casualties were not often cited by these veterans, but one veteran of Schmidt, asked why his unit had to pull back, gave just one factor and gave it without hesitation: casualties. This man's unit had been subjected to extremely heavy enemy shelling over a period of days. "It came down like confetti," he said. "I didn't know the Germans had that many shells."

One of the officers interviewed had been with his regimental commander during the period when that officer made the decision to surrender his force, surrounded in the Battle of the Bulge. Casualties seem to have significantly influenced that decision, but it does not seem to have been either a rational assessment of the casualty rate or the emotional impact of the wounded men that affected the commander. Rather it was the knowledge that, with his command cut off, there was no way to evacuate or properly care for casualties, and that further resistance would mean more and more casualties who could not be evacuated or cared for.[9]

It may well be that in other cases, where casualties were not so visibly present, or in which commanders did not think they were deciding on the basis of casualties, the casualties nevertheless were an important factor— in weakening a flank, for instance, and permitting an enemy breakthrough. But on the role of casualties in determining conscious decisions to abandon an attack or to withdraw, no one spoke more firmly than an Anzio veteran who was a 45th Infantry Division intelligence staff officer when the Germans launched their counterattack of 16–17 February 1944. The Germans threatened to split the Allied lines and push through to the shoreline, and casualties were extremely heavy. Yet the officer does not recall that any unit of the division gave up, stopped fighting, or withdrew without orders, even those whose strength was cut in half. Likewise, commanders did not make decisions to withdraw solely on the basis of casualties; these decisions were made primarily because of the tactical situation—to reestablish the division line and prevent a German breakthrough to the sea.[10]

"You can't just call off the game at a certain level of casualties," he said. This officer later commanded an infantry battalion of the division at Anzio and in France and after the war rose to the rank of four-star general. He told us of an incident in southern France, when he was concerned about the casualties his battalion had taken over several days of heavy fighting, felt doubt about being able to take his objective the following day, and expressed his concerns to his corps commander, Maj. Gen. Lucian Truscott, who was visiting the battalion. Truscott told him "The time to cry over your soldiers is after the battle is won."

This officer also said that he himself had not been concerned about casualties, or even aware of their extent, while combat was actually taking place. By implication, he could not have made a decision in the midst of action on the basis of casualties. The conversation with General Truscott came at the end of the day, when he had had a chance to see the casualty figures for his companies.

EARLY SIGNS OF DEFEAT

We asked the veterans to talk about what first made them realize that things were not going well, that they would not be able to accomplish their mission, that (again, we did not use the word) defeat was likely or imminent.

KUM RIVER

For B Battery, 52d Field Artillery Battalion in Korea, the enemy attack itself was a complete surprise, but as we listened to our veteran's account, defeat—or at least massive withdrawal—seemed in the air from the first. He arrived with his battalion from army-of-occupation duty in Japan— where *they* had been the victors in a defeated land. They had received good artillery training there, he felt, but they were far from prepared, militarily or psychologically, to enter combat on a few hours' notice, which is what they did.

The unit arrived in Suwon, South Korea, on 3 July 1950 as part of the poignantly small U.S. vanguard responding on behalf of the United Nations to the 25 June invasion by North Korea. No one seemed to know whether the town in which they had arrived was in American or North Korean hands, and the unloading of the troops was delayed until this could be clarified. The unit was then immediately committed to action and began to be pushed steadily southward, along with the whole UN front. As one U.S. battery after another was attacked and destroyed and the men of B Battery believed theirs was the last effective artillery facing the North Koreans, there was pride—the artillery was the only thing holding off the enemy— and also awareness that their turn could not be far off.

RAPIDO RIVER

As for the Rapido River operation in Italy, one of the participants could pinpoint the beginning of trouble there. A rifle squad leader, he was a veteran of earlier combat, including the hard battle of San Pietro. In these previous operations he was always briefed before the attack by his platoon leader or platoon sergeant on the specific objectives of his squad—what route they would take, what position they were to reach, what building they were to seize. This time there was no briefing. The orders were to cross the river; nothing was said about what to do on the other side. "I knew right *then* something was wrong," he said.

There were other signs, too. The attack in which our veterans took part was actually the second crossing attempt. On 20 January crossings had been tried in two locations, with heavy casualties but no success. By the time of the second try, on the night of 21 January, word had gotten around of what things were like on the other side of the river. The men were also under fire as they assembled for the attack. Our squad leader had the feeling that men were "wandering away" before the crossing, purposely losing themselves in the dark landscape. Earlier in the day he had passed the foxhole of two men he'd known in basic training, and stopped to talk. They may have been joking, but both said they were going to shoot themselves in the foot to avoid the crossing, and they sounded as though they meant it.

Interestingly, the official division orders for the crossings fit well with these impressions. The orders seem almost perfunctory, are couched in general terms, and do not give the instructions for the crossings and the specific objectives that would be expected for an operation of this complexity. It seemed surprising to the study team that the orders for the second night had no instructions for correcting problems that presumably had led to the initial failure. Fletcher's missed briefing seems to have reflected an emptiness higher up.[11]

THE BULGE: KRINKELT-ROCHERATH

One of the veterans with whom we talked was the distinguished military historian Charles B. MacDonald, who writes elsewhere in this book about the experience of the 28th Division in the Huertgen Forest. In his first book, *Company Commander*, MacDonald told about his own experience with defeat when his company of the 2d Infantry Division was hit at the beginning of the German Ardennes offensive. It was about this experience that he spoke with us.

When MacDonald led I Company of the 23d Infantry Regiment into a dense fir forest forward of the twin Belgian villages of Krinkelt and Rocherath, it was nightfall of 16 December 1944. He expected to lead his men in an attack at dawn the next morning to regain positions just lost by a battalion of the 99th Division in what was thought to be a local German counterattack. No one realized that the 99th had been struck by the opening of the largest German offensive in Western Europe since the campaign of 1940.

As MacDonald's company prepared to attack, its orders were changed: Defend in place to protect the withdrawal of the crumbling 99th Division battalion. This MacDonald and his men did for almost four hours, and the battered men of the 99th did pull back through their positions. But it became clear that MacDonald's men could not hold indefinitely. What were the signs that they would have to pull back?

Platoon leaders were calling for more ammunition, but battalion headquarters said there was no more. MacDonald called for artillery support, but the 99th Division, which was providing it, had little ammunition left and allotted it scantily—"four measly rounds" per request instead of the "reassuring volley" that was needed. Finally, German Mark V Panther tanks appeared; the company had absolutely nothing to use against them. MacDonald became aware of men falling back. It was his machine gun section, out of ammunition. A rifle platoon reported it was almost out of ammunition and that German tanks were firing directly into its foxholes.

MacDonald then ordered a withdrawal to a firebreak that lay behind him, where he hoped to build a new line. This line held only briefly. As he had said, "I know now that I was asking the impossible: When men start falling back under heavy fire, there is no stopping them." MacDonald and his men were soon "running for our lives."

This commander had an experienced, cohesive unit and, unlike many others in our study, it had excellent communications. It was not out-flanked—yet. The signs, and unavoidable causes, of defeat were sim-ple: no more ammunition, no artillery support, no weapons of any kind that could touch the enemy's deadliest weapons—its tanks. The withdrawal began even before it was ordered, and once begun, could not be stopped.

THE BULGE: ST. VITH

While MacDonald's company of the 2d Infantry Division was fighting its battle about twenty miles to the north, the men and tanks of the 7th Armored Division were moving into St. Vith to begin theirs; they had been pulled down from Holland to try to stop the Germans.

Under the command of Brig. Gen. Bruce Clarke, Combat Command B of the 7th Armored fought a five-day mobile defense of St. Vith, an important road center, and then pulled back. Whether their fight was a victory or a defeat can be debated and depends, in the last analysis, on what their mission was. The division was originally tasked with attacking to relieve the surrounded 106th Division. But when General Clarke arrived at St. Vith and assessed the situation, he judged that mission to be unrealistic and took responsibility for assigning a new one to his command: to delay the Germans for as long as possible. His force held the St. Vith area for five days; as a result, a major thrust of the German offensive was blunted and time was gained to stabilize the Allied front. After careful research and analysis and long deliberation, the study research team judged that this operation was not an example of forced posture change.[12]

Nevertheless there was a point at which these men stopped defending the St. Vith area and began a withdrawal, and their perceptions of the signs of this time, whether it can be correctly called a defeat or not, can tell us something about the harbingers of defeat.

Unfortunately, none of the men we talked with about the St. Vith battle was a "shooter"—a combat infantryman or a member of a tank crew who would have been in the thick of the action and could have told us first-hand about the casualties his unit was taking and the pressure they were under from the enemy. Our veterans included General Clarke, two artillery officers, a reconnaissance platoon leader, a reconnaissance squadron adjutant, a tank battalion adjutant, a personnel sergeant major, a motor sergeant, a sergeant in a reconnaissance platoon, and a jeep driver. Except for Clarke, the commander, they were on the fringes of the action. Here are some of their comments on how they learned that withdrawal was imminent.

The tank battalion adjutant first learned about the withdrawal when his battalion received its orders; nothing had happened earlier to alert him. Then, as his unit got under way and he saw the commanding general directing traffic, he realized that things were serious.

An artillery forward observer said his unit was "having a good day." A day or so earlier they had been completely out of ammunition, reduced to firing propaganda shells—shells carrying printed flyers urging the Germans to surrender and not likely to have that effect under the circumstances! However, they had since been resupplied, and it was his impression that their position was not in jeopardy and that they were "ready to go"—to continue their support mission. The orders to withdraw were a surprise to him.

Another artillery officer was in his fire-direction center when he got the word that batteries were displacing rearward to cover a withdrawal. When he learned that one battery had been assigned to cover the demolition of a bridge, he knew things were serious. Blowing a bridge, he well knew, is "not a cheerful sign."

One enlisted man, in a tank battalion, said he was surprised that things weren't going well. His reconnaissance platoon had seen no severe action, had received no direct fire up to that point. He had not even heard much of the battle: the broken terrain and dense forest had deadened the sound. He himself had never fired a shot in the defense of St. Vith—there had been no opportunity to.

Meanwhile, of course, General Clarke knew that his forward elements defending the high ground in front of St. Vith had been overwhelmed a day earlier (21 December), that the weight of the German offensive had moved on—around and beyond his force—and that even if it was able to hold out longer it would inevitably be cut off, isolated, and unable to play any useful future role.

THE BULGE: THE SCHNEE EIFEL

The men of the 422d and 423d Infantry regiments of the 106th Division (the regiments that were surrendered to the Germans on the fourth day of the Battle of the Bulge) were in good positions, well dug in, on a commanding ridge—the Schnee Eifel—at the beginning of the German assault. The mood of the Allied forces, including these newest combat soldiers on the front, was one of optimism, of anticipation of a final Allied offensive. Although most of the seventeen men of the 106th Division with whom we talked had heard the roar of many German motors and other sounds of massive enemy movements, signs they had reported, none of them could have guessed what was in store. Some of the officers knew of the German attack soon after it began and were involved in the efforts to deal with it, especially in the struggles to establish communications with their division headquarters and to get orders, supplies, and reinforcements. For most of the enlisted men and junior officers, however, the first hint of disaster was the news that the enemy had surrounded them.

One medic, who had little good to say about the leadership or general condition of his company, said that "panic and disorganization" followed this news, and he apparently was not surprised by the destruction of the company in its attempted breakout. Others, with different units, saw a different picture. Most saw no panic. One battalion staff officer says: "I didn't think we were going to be defeated until I was told to surrender." He knew the force was in trouble, running out of ammunition and seemingly surrounded, but his battalion and his regiment were still functional. The question was simply what to do next. A platoon leader says that he had no idea the battle was being lost when he was badly wounded on 18 December, less than twenty-four hours before the surrender. The first indication he had of serious trouble was the voice of a chaplain telling him how sorry he was that the regiment would have to leave its wounded, including him, in the care of a medic who had volunteered to stay with them. In other words, they had to be abandoned to the Germans because there was no way to evacuate them.

THE TASTE OF DEFEAT

After talking with these thirty-nine veterans, one thing was clear to us: Defeat can leave an aftertaste that lasts for decades. This is as true for the private soldier who has little or no control over events as it is for the commander. Later, when we talked again with some of these men, this time focusing specifically on defeat, something else became clear: Many soldiers who have been in operations that may look like defeats do not feel that they were defeated. The circumstances of defeat make a great deal of difference, as does the nature of the individual soldier.

In the original study we talked to men who had withdrawn with their units in good order, unwounded, and gone on to fight again and win. We talked with men who had been wounded, evacuated, and returned to fight again with their units. We also talked with men who had been captured at the conclusion of a decisive defeat and had undergone a prisoner-of-war experience. It was for some of these men that defeat seems to have been the bitterest.

The men of the 7th Armored Division, pulling back from St. Vith after a five-day mobile defense, did not feel defeated, to judge by the memories of the men we talked with.

These men had thought well of themselves as a division before they went into St. Vith. According to the officers with whom we spoke, their hard combat in the Netherlands had been good for esprit. They had been transferred up and down the front from one army to another, prompting *Stars and Stripes* to call them "the oft-orphaned waifs of the Western Front," and they took the tag as a badge of pride. They thought of themselves as firemen, troubleshooters. Two enlisted men, meeting in another group of 7th Armored Division veterans, said that they had felt glad to be moving against the Germans and glad the Germans had attacked: "Good. Now we can get at them." Seeing other U.S. troops moving back from the front, seemingly in confusion, surprised them but did not shake them. Rather, it increased their pride.

Moving to the rear after five days of combat, two enlisted veterans said they were tired to the point of numbness, to the point where they were operating on instinct, where "training takes over—training and loyalty," but not too tired to know what they were doing. They insisted that the withdrawal did not surprise them, that they understood it was part of a plan. They were falling back to regroup and make a final push into Germany. They did not feel defeated or disappointed.

The officers meeting in the first group said substantially the same thing: There had never been any expectation that St. Vith would be held indefinitely. The 7th Armored Division had been given a delaying mission and had accomplished it. They also felt that after five days of combat everyone was exhausted to the point that nerves were on edge and efficiency was going down. Tactically it was the right time to withdraw, and from the standpoint of human resources it was also the right time.

These veterans' picture of the 7th Armored was, for the most part, so rosy that some may read about their recollections with wry wonder and some skepticism. Because their division had failed in its original mission to relieve the 106th, and because they did, after all, carry out a substantial withdrawal, it might well seem that they were a bit defensive, that they protested too much. However, research staff members present at the discussions were convinced that the men's comments reflected their true judgments and memories. And their recollections were not all rosy. There were strong criticisms of poor division staffwork, the inadequate training and orientation that replacements received, and the weakness of many of the replacement junior officers. One enlisted man, in particular, was glad to have a chance to get his negative comments into the historical record: the poor quality of the training he and other replacements had received, the shamefully poor handling of replacements, and the high casualties that resulted. He also spoke feelingly about the inferiority of U.S. vehicles to German vehicles, especially for winter fighting—for example, no windshields, tops, or heaters on U.S. vehicles.

But when these men were ordered out of St. Vith they seemed to pull back without feeling defeat. Their chief complaint today seems to be that St. Vith is forgotten in the shadow of Bastogne, and no one else remembers what they did.

Some of the other men we talked with were also upbeat in their recollections. The division staff officer at Anzio felt that there was no defeat; the division line had held despite the extremely heavy casualties.

Even when the defeat is real and bitter, as it was for the 106th Infantry Division, it seems to be easier for professional soldiers to deal with. They study the defeat as they are trained to do, looking for lessons learned, working out ways to correct mistakes that they or others made, and look to do better the next time. They go on to fight other battles. Two of the officers who were surrounded on the Schnee Eifel and spent the rest of World War II as prisoners went on to serve in the Korean War, to teach at West Point, and to retire after proud careers. Their defeat experience is seen in perspective. And yet there is still, perhaps more for professional soldiers than for others, the endless wondering "What if we had. . . . If only we could have . . ." The men of the 106th Division with whom we talked were junior officers, at most, at that time. Yet each wondered what he himself might have done that could have brought a better outcome. "We were so close. . . . We were on that road. . . . If only . . ."

One veteran who was not a professional soldier found a uniquely effective professional way of processing his military experience and coming to terms with defeat. As a young veteran Charles MacDonald wrote a simple, straightforward account of his war experience, including his retreat of 17 December 1944, in *Company Commander*, a book that is still in print and has given a feel for the reality of combat to more than a million readers. In the book he describes graphically the feeling of defeat, his conviction that he had failed, betrayed the trust placed in him, should turn in his captain's bars at the first opportunity. Only when he met his battalion commander and was told "Nice work, Mac" did he begin to realize that he had actually done well in holding as long as he had in the face of a massive enemy offensive.

After the war MacDonald joined the staff of what is now the U.S. Army Center of Military History, later became its Deputy Chief Historian, and authored three of the official histories of World War II. He also has written a number of other books on military history, including a comprehensive history of the Battle of the Bulge (*A Time for Trumpets*). Despite all this, when MacDonald opened his presentation at a recent symposium on defeat by saying that of the speakers present, "I am probably the only one who personally has been defeated in battle," there seemed a tinge of pain to the joke.

Oliver Patton is another writer who has processed his defeat experience through his work. In *The Silent Snow* he combines his own experience, careful historical research, and imagination to tell the story of a man who was, like Patton, a young lieutenant with the 106th Division when the Germans struck in December 1944. The book is a well-crafted, suspenseful story, full of authentic details of combat and the events of the Bulge. But it is impossible not to see also—in this story of a young officer who doesn't surrender, who survives behind the German lines and even helps kill a few Germans, and who finally leads men successfully in battle—the author's creation of a happier outcome for his own first experience in combat.

It would be no surprise to find a sense of guilt accompanying defeat, especially for commanders who made decisions that contributed to it. We did not talk to any such commanders, but we did hear reflections of guilt from those who held positions of responsibility down to the lowest levels, especially in the case of surrenders. The one man who seemed most deeply and lastingly affected by the defeat experience said that what bothered him most was that, as the ranking noncom (he had been a squad leader), he had made the decision to surrender the little group of men he was with.

Gaining an understanding of what happened beyond the microcosm of war within their vision is important for many veterans, and this may be especially true for those involved in a defeat. Many of our veterans had tattered copies of official documents, read widely in published works on their campaigns, and revisited the sites of the battles. Lee Fletcher, one of the Rapido veterans, has read the testimony from the congressional hearings on the Rapido attack and kept copies of the parts that are significant for him. For several of the men, one of the satisfactions in participating in our study was going over large-scale maps with a staff historian, seeing just where the enemy positions were, or getting authoritative answers to such questions as *"Did* those Germans have tanks?"

In the circumstances, it was not surprising that the search for understanding sometimes shaded into the search for a scapegoat. Some officers of the 106th Division observed that there were no artillerymen in their discussion group. That's who we'd like to see, they said, in effect. "Where was the artillery" when they were trying to break through the German net? "We theoretically had a lot—where was it?" This was a reasonable question, the kind to which one of our historians, meeting with the group, could offer answers—in this case showing that neither corps nor division artillery was at fault.

Others spoke of the help they'd been promised from the 9th Armored Division, or the 8th Armored Division, and which never came. Still others carried this a step further, blaming Brig. Gen. Bruce Clarke for not immediately counterattacking when he arrived at St. Vith and making him responsible for the disaster that befell the 106th Division. Another man thought that perhaps the green 106th had been deliberately placed in the line to draw the Germans into a counteroffensive, and still another man in a different discussion group expressed the same idea with much more bitterness—the 106th had just been hung out on the line and left there. Intellectually, this man accepted the fact, readily determined from German records, that the Germans had planned and prepared their offensive well before there could have been any knowledge that the 106th Division would be there to receive it. But he said that he felt he would never really be able to believe this.

It is not only veterans of the 106th Division who have been bitter and have directed their anger at specific villains, who may or may not have been guilty. The division at the Rapido crossings, the 36th Infantry Division, was (as noted) a Texas National Guard unit, and it has often been said that if General Mark Clark, the Fifth Army commander who ordered the crossings, had ventured into Texas he would have been ridden out on a rail. However, the Rapido veterans with whom we talked did not express bitterness. "It was kind of a dumb thing to have done," one of them said, but "You have to take orders." Tactically, they felt, the operation was impossible and could only be justified as a diversion for the Anzio landings—where, as events fell out, it seems to have done no good.

As already suggested, of the veterans we spoke with, those who were taken prisoner reflected the most painful experience of defeat. Since the prisoner-of-war experience played no part in our study we had to discourage discussion of it, but it inevitably came out. For example, when asked whether hunger was a factor in the forced posture change, the men generally said it was not, but made it clear that they experienced a great deal of hunger after being taken prisoner. One man lost close to fifty pounds in three and a half months of captivity. There were wry smiles in recounting the German captors' usual announcement: "For you, the war is over." Actually, for these men, most of whom had seen only a day or two of combat, the war was just beginning.

One of the veterans with whom we spoke gave us much insight into the prisoner-of-war experience. Dr. Charles Stenger, retired chief psychologist for the Veterans Administration, had been a very young company medic with the 106th Division on the Schnee Eifel. His company had lost communication with its battalion, had attacked a German force on its own in an effort to break out, and, in his perception, had been wiped out—most of the company was dead or wounded when the engagement stopped. He had been taken prisoner along with the wounded.

Stenger emphasized the extreme stress captivity places on the combat soldier. To be a prisoner is traumatic for anyone, but Stenger, a medic, had a role to play as a prisoner. He could continue his military occupation— tending the wounds and illnesses of the men. If anything, he was more needed and more valued than before. But for a combat soldier to be without any power, to be completely vulnerable, completely under the control of others who are hostile, with no way to take any action, is psychologically devastating.

An outcome of Stenger's defeat experience was a decision to become a psychologist and, later, to make his career in working with veterans. He told us that throughout his service with the Veterans Administration he tried to act as an advocate for prisoners of war, working, for example, to get counseling for *all* returning prisoners of war as a matter of routine and right, not just for those who showed "symptoms." In retirement he continues to act as a POW advocate, helping former prisoners gain government benefits.

Another 106th veteran, Steve Augerinos, reenlisted after being discharged and later finished his college education. He ties the reenlistment to the 106th's failure and surrender. "I guess I wanted to prove something to myself," he says. "And I wanted to use that four and a half years' training for something" other than an unsuccessful three days in combat. Augerinos had enlisted before Pearl Harbor, but his assignment to the 106th gave him his only combat experience.

Other former POWs have found support and acceptance of their experience in establishing bonds with others who shared it, through membership in American Ex-Prisoners of War. Like many combat veterans, they have joined their division association and, looking around at other 106th veterans, they can note the caliber of the men they were with—two diplomats of the rank of ambassador and at least three Ph.D.s, as well as a general and two colonels among the men with whom we talked. A combat veteran on our research team was impressed that in one group of seven 106th men with whom we met there were three holders of the Expert Infantryman's Badge, demonstrating very high soldierly competence following infantry training. One of our veterans summed it up as he saw it: The 106th was a division of men with greatly varying levels of training but with a core of highly competent soldiers. With stronger leadership—and a little luck—it could have made a fine division. As he pointed out, the third regiment of the division, the one not caught on the Schnee Eifel, was made up of the same kind of men and units, and it performed well.

UNDERSTANDING DEFEAT

As we gathered material from our research study and refocused it on the concept of defeat we found that it was not only the men of the 7th Armored Division who didn't feel defeated even though they had lost a battle.

Paul Elliott, veteran of the Kum River and the retreat down the Korean peninsula, said that he never felt he was involved in a real defeat. "We had confidence in the Army, in the United States. We remembered World War II. We had no doubt that we would eventually win." What happened to the 24th Division in the early days in Korea was in a sense "a planned defeat." At least in retrospect he saw its mission as to hold out, to delay, until somebody got there, until "the Cavalry got there," so to speak. And, sure enough, as it happened, it was the 1st Cavalry Division that did come. His battery, his division, had held long enough. They had done their job.

Michael Davison took command of the 1st Battalion of the 179th Infantry, 45th Division, soon after it had been hit and pushed back by the German counterattack at Anzio. This battalion had taken "a hell of a beating." A couple of the rifle companies were at less than half strength. The men had suffered an exhausting, traumatic experience and had seen a lot of close friends killed. But they certainly didn't feel defeated. They had stopped the Germans, held the Allies' line, done their job.

One of the veterans we had originally spoken with seemed to have become, through accidents of history, something of an involuntary specialist on defeat. Alan Jones had participated in two of the operations we were studying. He was a young battalion staff officer with one of the regiments of the 106th Division encircled and captured in the Battle of the Bulge, and he was the regimental G-2 of the 9th Infantry when it passed through the gauntlet of Chinese fire in its withdrawal from Kunu-Ri. We were impressed with the thoughtfulness of Colonel Jones' analysis, and he returned as an expert witness to provide a full discussion of defeat as seen by a combat soldier.

On the objective reasons for defeat, Jones' judgments agreed well with what we had concluded from our discussions for the study with all thirty-nine veterans: "The major cause of defeat, of course, is the tactical element . . . just as it is the major cause of victory." After tactics he listed communications, lack of the capability to fight (weapons, ammunition, fire support, reserves), and casualties, in that order. Not only are tactics the most important element in objectively causing defeat, Jones felt, they are also the most important element in the commander's *sense of defeat*. Since tactics are a factor over which a commander exerts control, failure resulting from tactical errors really comes home to him. "No one I know of gets upset [feels guilt and remorse] over communications," a mechanical matter for which the commander has less responsibility. And the supply of ammunition, quality of weapons, and availability of reserves are also often beyond his control.

Speaking of first signs that defeat is imminent, Jones bore out our impression that soldiers in action of whatever rank, at least up to the level of regimental staff officers, are generally not aware that a defeat is going to occur until it starts happening. In the Bulge, "I knew we were in trouble. . . . It was a nasty, mean situation. But I had no feeling that there wouldn't . . . be a solution." The orders to surrender were the first sign that there would not.

At Kunu-Ri, he knew the 2d Division had to withdraw; the enemy was just too strong. But, he said, echoing the general we'd talked with earlier, "Withdrawal I've never considered defeat." It was only when word came that the first units going through the pass were taking "such very heavy fire, and I knew there was an awful lot more ahead of us than we had seen—because we thought we'd pretty well cleared it" that he realized "not many of us were likely to get out."

As we went on to discuss the aftermath of defeat, the feelings it engenders, Jones seemed uncomfortable about paying much attention to this. Like many or most soldiers, he could see the value of identifying and analyzing mistakes, learning lessons, modifying doctrine, strengthening training—but not of examining emotions. And yet one thing that seemed to emerge from our discussion was the subjectivity of defeat. *Failure* to accomplish a mission is objective and can be measured by comparing orders with outcome. *Defeat* is subjective and is, basically, how you feel about it.

In order to feel defeated, one has to have had some control over the outcome of an engagement or battle. As Jones said, it depends so much on where you stand in the ranks: "A squad leader can do everything right, be totally successful, and suddenly be told to surrender. To him, this is not a defeat in any way. To the colonel or general who has to make the *decision* to surrender, it's a massive personal defeat." The most devastating defeat experience "would be to realize that *you* had the authority, *you* had the assets, and *you* failed to accomplish the mission. But this is only given to a handful of people."

The men of the 2d Division who survived the retreat from Kunu-Ri felt a tremendous pride. They had carried out a wonderfully successful withdrawal, felt a great sense of achievement in having gotten through at all. Similarly, the Marines who withdrew from the Chosen Reservoir are intensely proud of being among the "Chosen Frozen." Such misfortunes may have been defeats for Gen. Douglas MacArthur or Eighth Army commander Lt. Gen. Walton H. Walker, but not for the officers and men who withdrew. Kum River veteran Paul Elliott and the men of General Davison's Anzio battalion would agree.

Then there is the special experience of being a prisoner of war. "Yes, there is a great sense of defeat that comes if you are captured," Colonel Jones said. He generally agreed with Dr. Stenger's analysis of the impact of captivity on the combat soldier, and he added to it. Not only is the soldier deprived of his role as a fighter and placed under the total control of others who are hostile, but he is given *time*, a tremendous amount of time, in which he is virtually forced to think about what led to his present situation. A unit that suffers a minor defeat and goes back into combat gives little attention to the defeat; there's no time for it, and more recent events replace it. Not so for captured troops. There is nothing but time, plus the stress of fear and pain, and one tends to place blame, either on oneself or on others.

Jones himself never felt that the war was over for him when he was captured. World War II soldiers, although not trained for captivity as thoroughly as soldiers since Korea have been, knew that their mission as prisoners was to survive and to escape to fight again. Jones was able to escape briefly at the time a rescue attempt was made on the camp where he was held. Although he was not rescued, during the confusion he was able to leave on his own and evaded recapture for two days, a great source of satisfaction.

But he also asked his questions about what he, personally, could have done wrong, and found his answer in his obedience to the order to surrender. He wished he had made a break into woods, toward U.S. lines. He had been held back by some feeling, later seen as foolish, that he could be of help to the men in captivity. "Bad decision."

Jones also spoke about another kind of defeat reaction. The soldier who finds himself a prisoner of war and asks himself how he got there may feel—even if he himself was doing his job successfully to the moment of surrender—a kind of guilt for the unit. After all, something has gone wrong. Months or years have been spent in establishing unit esprit de corps, identity with the unit, pride in the unit. Now the unit has failed and the individual feels part of that failure; he may feel guilt, even if he himself fought the good fight to the end. Except for the reaction of an officer who really *is* responsible to a large extent for the defeat, Jones felt that this assumption of unit guilt probably brought the strongest guilt feelings.[13] In this sense, "the greatest guilt occurs when you know the least about it" (that is, when you know the least about what happened and had the least control over it). But this is all within the context of a prisoner-of-war experience. In general, the experience of defeat is only for the soldier who knows or believes that he himself could have prevented the failure.

In summary, then, if we can base any conclusions on discussions with thirty-nine veterans of operations that were in some sense failures, they are:

Tactical considerations are probably the most important factors leading to failure of a mission.

Sometimes failure is foreshadowed by confusion or obvious lack of the means to fight, but often it comes as a complete surprise to the soldier in the field.

Failure to accomplish a mission is one thing; defeat is another. Failure is objective; defeat is subjective—basically a feeling, not a fact.

Defeat is not what you feel when your unit has been mauled by the enemy, or forced to withdraw, or when you yourself have been wounded. It is what you feel if you believe that you have in some way been responsible for a failure, whether you are a commander of an army or a sergeant who surrendered six men. And you are more likely to feel this way if you are captured and held prisoner than if you are able to go on immediately to new action.

Part II

THE REASONS FOR DEFEAT

Chapter 4

Uncontrollable Unfavorable Circumstances

CAUSES OF DEFEAT

Defeat is the other side of the coin of victory. In other words, it is possible to say that the reason a military force was defeated in a historical battle is that the other side won. This is not necessarily a tautology. In some battles a side that has fought well is defeated only because the winning side either fought harder or better or was more numerous and thus truly "won" the battle. One such battle was Napoleon's famous victory at Marengo in 1800 in his Second Italian Campaign. In the early stages of that battle Napoleon had practically been defeated by Melas, his Austrian opponent. In part this was because of his own errors and in part because the Austrians fought well. However, calling upon inner reserves of will and skill, and marshaling scattered forces that had not yet been committed, Napoleon reversed the tide of defeat. Truly it can be said that he won the battle more than that the Austrians lost it.

In some battles, however, the losing side might well have won had it not been for some blunder or untoward circumstance. Antietam was such a battle. Not that Lee and his outnumbered Army of Northern Virginia didn't deserve to win; of course they did! But if McClellan had provided vigorous leadership to his equally deserving, hard-fighting (and much more numerous) Army of the Potomac and if he had committed his reserves to the battle, it would have been almost impossible for him to have avoided victory. But he didn't provide the needed leadership and he didn't commit his reserves, so he lost the battle more than Lee won it.

It is not usually possible to make such a clear distinction between losing a battle (as McClellan did at Antietam) and having victory denied because the other side won it (as happened to the Austrian general Melas at Marengo). On the other hand, it is always possible to analyze a defeat and to determine its causes—even if the only reason was that a Napoleon or a Lee commanded the victors. This chapter provides the basis for such analysis.

A very useful way to analyze a battle is to examine it in terms of the nine Principles of War as they have been recognized by the U.S. Army for more than half a century. However, these principles (listed and described in Appendix A) are essentially guidelines a commander should bear in mind in order to gain victory or avoid defeat. While useful for overall analysis and to provide insights as to the cause of victory, they are not so clearly focused as is desirable for the analysis of a defeat. With some reluctance, therefore, I have discarded the idea of analyzing defeats by means of the Principles of War and have formulated a set of causes of defeat as the basis for analysis of defeat in this book.

The causes of defeat fall into three general categories. First, a commander and his troops may find themselves engaged in a battle in which the circumstances are so unfavorable that they have no hope of success, no matter how well they may fight. Second, unfavorable circumstances may not necessarily be the fault of the commander, but he may have contributed to or influenced them. Finally, battles are most often lost because of failures on the part of the defeated commander. Each of these categories includes several specific subsidiary causes, as this outline suggests:

THE CAUSES OF DEFEAT

    A. *Unfavorable Circumstances Beyond the Control of the Commander*
        1. Overwhelming odds
           a. Superior numbers
           b. Superior armor

   c. Superior fire support
      (1) Artillery
      (2) Air support
   d. Superior skill
2. Unfavorable environment
   a. Weather
   b. Terrain
   c. Roads/line of communications (LOC)
3. Hostile fortifications
4. Inferior technology
5. Chance or luck

B. *Unfavorable Circumstances the Commander May Influence*
   1. Lack of preparation for battle
   2. Inferior-quality forces
      a. Quality of manpower
      b. Training/experience
      c. Doctrine
   3. Poor morale
   4. Troop and/or commander fatigue
   5. Casualties
   6. Subordinate error/failure

C. *Failure of Command*
   1. Surprise
   2. Inferior leadership
      a. Self-delusion (perception)
      b. Confused mission
      c. Weakness of will
   3. Inadequate control
      a. Poor reconnaissance/intelligence
      b. Poor planning
      c. Faulty tactics
      d. Inadequate logistics
      e. Breakdown in communications

We will examine each of these categories and causes of defeat in more detail, elucidating each in terms of actual historical experience.

UNFAVORABLE CIRCUMSTANCES BEYOND THE CONTROL OF THE COMMANDER

Marshal Ferdinand Foch, the victorious Allied generalissimo of World War I, had many opportunities on the battlefield to demonstrate his conviction that battle outcomes were directly dependent upon the will and determination of the commander. He was fond of saying that "a battle won is a battle in which one will not confess oneself beaten." British Maj. Gen. J. F. C. Fuller, a strong believer in the importance of the will of the commander, nonetheless derided this Foch statement by observing that "morale does not render [soldiers] bullet-proof."[1]

As we shall see in a later chapter, at Waterloo Napoleon never lost his will to victory until he was swept off the field by his fleeing army. He lost, as Fuller once observed, because his enemies brought to the battlefield nine Englishmen and Germans for every five Frenchmen. Not that Waterloo was inevitably an Anglo-Prussian victory. If it had not rained the night before, Napoleon could undoubtedly have attacked early enough on the morning of 18 June 1815 to have driven Wellington off the field and could then have turned to defeat Blücher's arriving troops in detail. But French defeat became inevitable when the Prussians entered the battle behind Napoleon's right flank, while Wellington's line was still intact.

In other words, no matter how skillful the commander, no matter how indomitable his will, there are some circumstances he cannot overcome.

OVERWHELMING ODDS

Superior numbers. Possibly the most intractible of unfavorable circumstances is overwhelming hostile numerical strength. Leipzig in 1813 is another example of odds too great even for Napoleon to overcome. But one of the best examples is Gettysburg in 1863, in the American Civil War.

Civil War enthusiasts, particularly those with Southern sympathies, are fond of trying to relive Gettysburg as a possible Confederate victory. They point out that two months earlier Lee had overcome even greater odds at Chancellorsville. They suggest that things could easily have gone a bit differently at the Peach Orchard, at Little Round Top, or at Devil's Den, in which case Meade's left flank would have been compromised. Apologists for Lee are particularly critical of Longstreet's "delay" in committing his corps on the second day, and only slightly less critical of Early's lack of aggressiveness on the third day or of Jeb Stuart's absence on a cavalry raid. They are wasting their breaths.

So long as Meade did not make a serious blunder in fighting his purely defensive battle, Lee did not have a chance of success at Gettysburg. In order to overwhelm the 93,000 men of the Army of the Potomac deployed defensively on the heights south of Gettysburg during the first three days of July (and allowing for Lee's tactical skill superiority over Meade) the Confederate general would have needed at least 150,000 men. He had only 79,000. That is the essential reason for his defeat.

Superior armor. Armored tanks were first introduced on the battlefield by the British in the first Battle of the Somme in July 1916. There were too few of them, and those few were too prone to mechanical breakdown to have any significant effect in that battle. However, in October 1917, British tanks broke through German lines at the Battle of Cambrai, the first clean rupture of the trench lines in three years. But the effect was fleeting. The Germans did not have tanks themselves, but they were ready because they had been forewarned by the premature introduction of tanks at the Somme the year before. This readiness, combined with the continuing tendency of the British tanks to break down, enabled the German infantry to slow the tank advance the first day and then counterattack successfully on succeeding days, throwing the British back to their starting line. The British were probably more surprised by the prompt and aggressive German response to the armored assault than the Germans had been by the large numbers of tanks the British threw into the battle.

Beginning with the German invasion of Poland in September 1939, tanks dominated the European battlefields of World War II. When the Germans invaded Western Europe eight months later they had fewer tanks than the Western Allies (the French and the British), and the average quality of the Allied tanks was superior. But the Allies—particularly the French—scattered their tanks throughout their forces, while the Germans concentrated theirs in armored units and then concentrated those units in a few areas, which thereby became decisive areas. As a result, wherever the German tanks were committed they greatly outnumbered the opposing Allied armored vehicles. The resulting overwhelming German victory was in large part due to the great preponderance of German tanks in those decisive areas.

Superior Artillery Support. In a number of battles in modern history superior artillery fire support gave one side an advantage the opposition could not overcome. One such instance was the Battle of New Orleans, in 1815. The attacking British infantry, veterans of Wellington's victorious campaign in the Iberian Peninsula, were probably the finest troops in the world at that time, far superior in quality to the largely militia ragtag army assembled by Gen. Andrew Jackson. But they had to advance against Jackson's fortified defensive line through a swamp, which precluded them from using artillery, and their warships were too far away to provide naval gunfire support. The fortifications alone might have been enough to enable Jackson's militiamen to repulse the British veterans. But numerous and well-served cannon, unanswered by British artillery, assured the American victory.

Another example shows the other side of the coin: the inability of defenders to defend successfully because of the overwhelming strength of the attackers' artillery. At the beginning of the second Battle of the Somme, on 21 March 1918, the attacking German armies were supported by 6473 artillery tubes, coordinated by a master-artillerist, Georg Bruchmüller, with a stockpile of millions of rounds of ammunition. The defending British armies were supported only by about 2500 artillery pieces and had no such accumulation of ammunition reserves as did the Germans. This overwhelming superiority of artillery was the principal cause of the initial stunning German victory in this offensive. However, the German artillery was unable to keep up with the advancing infantry (due to the nature of the churned-up, trench-stitched, muddy terrain) and as a result the Germans were unable to exploit the initial victory and thus failed to accomplish their objective of winning the war before American manpower could make itself felt.

Between the wars the Germans carefully studied the lesson of their initial victory and eventual defeat at the second Battle of the Somme. The result of that study led to *blitzkrieg* and to the use of track-laying tanks and close air support to provide firepower that could substitute for slower-moving artillery in the exploitation phase of a breakthrough.

Superior air support. We have already noted the part that the concentration of armor played in the victorious German thrust through the Ardennes in 1940. Also contributing substantially to the victory was the German commitment of great masses of close-support aircraft, in accordance with their study of World War I experience. This assured the Germans of a substantial firepower superiority in the areas where they committed both armor and air support. This firepower superiority, enhanced by the surprise the Germans achieved by making their main effort in an area the Allies thought unsuitable for tanks, gave the Germans an overwhelming combat-power superiority in that area and enabled them to continue the momentum of their initial breakthrough.

Superior skill. The concept of overwhelming odds is generally one of quantification, involving greatly superior numbers of troops, or of tanks, or of artillery pieces, or of combat aircraft, or some combination of all of these numerical superiorities. There can also be overwhelming qualitative odds.

Both Marshal Gebhard von Blücher and Arthur Wellesley, Duke of Wellington, have been credited with equating Napoleon's presence on the battlefield with 40,000 additional French soldiers. Some years ago an analytical test suggested that this was not an unreasonable comparison, although a comparative leadership factor appeared to be a more suitable way of quantifying qualitative differences in the leadership capabilities of two generals.[2] Either way, it was demonstrated that a quantitative measurement could be applied to skill on the battlefield, and that the superiority of one general over another could be overwhelming.

Examples of the existence of such overwhelming odds in skill can be found not only among the battles of Napoleon, but also those of other great generals. For instance, in his two battlefield encounters with Alexander the Great, Persian Emperor Darius III had the benefit of seemingly overwhelming numerical odds, but these odds in numbers of soldiers were more than offset by Alexander's superiority in skill. Similarly, the skill of Frederick the Great outweighed the numerical superiority enjoyed by Austrian Marshal Daun at the Battle of Leuthen. It is clear from the historical record that superior skill can be as overwhelming on the battlefield as superior numbers.

Unfavorable Environment

Sometimes a military force is committed to battle under environmental circumstances that virtually assure defeat, no matter what the commander and his troops may do to try to cope with the unfavorable environment.

Weather. Possibly the most common environmental factor contributing to defeat has been bad weather. It may seem strange that weather, which seemingly would have a comparable impact on both opponents exposed to it, should favor one side over the other. Why this is so is readily demonstrable by the Battle of Waterloo, where a violent rainstorm may have had a greater effect on world history than any other fleeting instance of bad weather.

Wellington placed his troops in defensive positions on a low ridgeline near Waterloo during the afternoon of 17 June 1815 as Napoleon's French army approached from the south. A heavy downpour during the night made the ground so soggy that the French artillery could not move cross-country until the ground dried, late the following morning. There can be little doubt that if Napoleon could have attacked early in the morning of the eighteenth a combination of a slightly more numerous army, troops of better quality, a substantial artillery superiority, and his own formidable battlefield skill would have assured him of a victory by noon on the eighteenth. As it was, the French were unable to attack until shortly before noon, and the Prussian army began to approach their right rear shortly after 1:00 P.M. From that time onward Napoleon's defeat was inevitable.

Another example of bad weather affecting one side far more unfavorably than the other is to be found in Napoleon's invasion of Russia, two and a half years before Waterloo. The French were unprepared for winter operations; the Russians were fighting under circumstances to which they were well acclimated and for which they were well prepared.

This example was, of course, almost identical to what happened in the same region of Russia in late 1941, when German invaders were no better prepared for winter than the French had been 129 years earlier. In both cases the invaders were defeated by the weather as much as by the Russians.

Terrain. Two modern great powers have suffered ignominious defeat in Afghanistan. In both cases this was due more to the forbidding nature of the terrain than to the undoubted ferocity of the defending Afghans. In 1839 a British army, invading from the south, occupied Kabul, capital of Afghanistan. Three years later the remnants of their defeated army evacuated the country. One hundred forty years later a Russian army, invading from the north, also occupied Kabul. The Russians stayed a little longer than the British (nine years instead of three), but this was probably because they were more stubborn and less realistic. Eventually, frustrated by the difficulties of fighting a determined enemy in the most formidable terrain in the world, they also withdrew.

We have already noted how unfavorable terrain prevented the British from employing artillery at the Battle of New Orleans, thus contributing directly to the American victory in that battle. Similar swampy terrain prevented the United States army from ever achieving a clear-cut victory over the Seminole Indians of Florida in two prolonged nineteenth-century wars against that tribe.

For two years during World War I the British army was frustrated by desert terrain in its efforts against the Turks in the Sinai–Palestine area and in Mesopotamia. Why weren't the Turks equally affected? Because they were on the defensive, with established lines of communications behind them. Not only were they not adversely affected by the desert; in fact the desert, by impeding the British, contributed to the effectiveness of their defense.

Inadequate Roads and Lines of Communications. There are many instances in history in which an army has been defeated because of inadequate lines of communications (LOCs), usually because of insufficient and inadequate roads or railroads.

One of the most striking examples of this was in Mesopotamia in World War I. In late 1915 a small British army was repulsed by the Turks south of Baghdad, at Ctesiphon. Outnumbered, and running out of supplies, the British commander, Maj. Gen. Charles Townshend, withdrew to Kut al Amara to await supplies and reinforcements. Here he and his troops were surrounded and invested by the Turks. Because the LOC would not support large forces, the Turks easily repulsed all British relief attempts and Townshend was forced by starvation to surrender in April 1916.

Another striking example, also involving the British, can be found in World War II. In 1943 the Japanese attempted to invade eastern India from Burma, through the cities of Imphal and Kohima. The Japanese invading army, halted by the British defense of the two cities, literally starved to death because of the inadequacy of their jungle supply routes. Only a handful of survivors eventually trickled back into Burma through the mountainous jungle trails.

As we shall see in Chapter 9, this Japanese defeat took place soon after an Allied army had been similarly repulsed in Tunisia because of an inadequate LOC.

HOSTILE FORTIFICATIONS

Over the course of history many armies, and smaller military forces, have been defeated because of the sturdy defense of fortifications by a less powerful foe. Only a few examples need be cited.

One, of course, was the Turkish defense of Baghdad, at Ctesiphon, in World War I, noted above. Also in World War I was the German repulse at Verdun by hard-pressed French armies. In fact, most of the defeats of both sides in World War I were due to the defensive strength of field fortifications.

In the American Civil War field fortifications, combined with effective use of rifled small arms, foretold the importance of entrenchments in the First World War and played a major role in many successful defensive battles. Lee's defeats at Malvern Hill and Gettysburg were due in large part to hastily prepared Union entrenchments. So too were the repulses suffered by Grant at Cold Harbor and, for nine dreary months, at Petersburg and Richmond in 1864–1865.

Paradoxically, one of the most dramatic defeats in history took place early in World War II because the defenders did not trust the effectiveness of their fortifications. The French had put a tremendous effort (and vast sums of money) into construction of the Maginot Line of fortifications along the Franco-German border in the 1930s. The Germans were convinced that attacks on the Maginot Line would be suicidal and never seriously considered the possibility. Instead, they devised a strategy that would take them around those formidable defenses. The French, on the other hand, remembering five major German invasions across that frontier in the previous 150 years, placed half of their mobile field armies in reserve behind the Maginot Line. Thus, when the Germans went around that line to the north, the French did not have enough troops deployed in that region to stop the German advance. Before they could redeploy their badly positioned reserves the Germans had broken through and had destroyed the Belgian army, the Dutch army, the British expeditionary force, and a quarter of the French army.

INFERIOR TECHNOLOGY

Inferior technology has only occasionally been important in wars between major powers. On the other hand, lack of technologically sophisticated weapons and equipment was frequently—indeed, usually—a major factor in the almost uninterrupted victories of major powers against less-developed countries in the colonial wars of the sixteenth through the nineteenth centuries. This era can be said to have begun with Cortez' use of firearms in the Spanish triumph over the Aztecs at Otumba in 1520 and ended with Kitchener's use of machine guns in the British victory over the Dervishes at Omdurman in 1898.

Interestingly, several of the relatively few instances in which technology has been important in wars between major powers occurred in sea battles.

The English victory over the Spanish Armada in the Battle of the English Channel in 1588 was due mostly to superior guns and better ships. Four years later, in a battle that had something in common with the defeat of the Spanish, the Koreans with superior armored warships defeated the Japanese in the Battle of the Yellow Sea. In both instances the winning side had superior leadership that made the best possible use of its superior technology.

Not far from where Korean Admiral Yee Sun Sin won the Battle of the Yellow Sea, 313 years later another great and decisive sea battle took place between two technologically disparate naval forces. This time, however, it was the Japanese who had the superior technology, which they used to smash an obsolescent Russian fleet at the Battle of Tsushima in 1905.

The use of submarines by the Germans in World War I almost brought Great Britain to its knees. The Allies barely avoided defeat at sea by the massive employment of overwhelmingly superior surface seapower.

The Germans posed an almost equally severe threat to the Allies at sea in World War II by the use of technologically improved submarines. This time the Allies staved off the threat not only by use of massive surface seapower; they also introduced substantial airpower into the Battle of the Atlantic, as well as highly sophisticated new search and detection technologies.

CHANCE

One final circumstance is beyond the control of a defeated commander: chance or luck.

We shall never know whether the death of King Harold, caused by a Norman arrow in Duke William's last desperate attack at Hastings in 1066, was the real cause of the Saxon defeat. The Norman accounts of the battle (and we have only theirs) suggest that the Saxon army was beginning to disintegrate when Harold was killed. Maybe yes, maybe no. But if, as some scholars believe, the Saxon line was still firm up to that time, there can be no doubt that the Saxon collapse was due to the chance death of the defending commander.

Had Montcalm not been killed on the Plains of Abraham in 1759, it is not at all certain that the British would have taken Quebec. If they had not, French might today be the official language of the United States of America. (There are other reasons to believe that this would not have happened, but in the hypothetical situation postulated it could have.)

We have already seen how the outcome of the Battle of Waterloo was determined by a rainstorm. Was this chance? So it would seem.

A review of the record of the Battle of Midway suggests that the Americans were luckier than the Japanese on 4 June 1942. It can be argued that the Americans made their luck. But, as the Duke of Wellington said of the Battle of Waterloo, "it was a damned close-run thing."

We find in the 1973 Arab–Israeli War an incident that is more than a little reminiscent of the Battle of Hastings. On the northern wing of the Israeli Golan Heights position the excellent Israeli 7th Armored Brigade was hammered for two days by the numerically superior but qualitatively inferior Syrian 7th Infantry Division. But the 7th Division was one of the better Syrian units and its commander, Col. Hassan Tourkmani, had a reputation as one of the best officers in the Syrian army. He was also a graduate of the U.S. Army Command and General Staff College. After two days of bitter battle, Tourkmani was reinforced with an armored brigade and ordered to make one more assault against the depleted and weakening 7th Armored Brigade. Late on the afternoon of the eighth, Col. Tourkmani was with the leading elements of his division and ready to direct the attack when he was killed by Israeli artillery fire. The attack was postponed, and when it was mounted under a new division commander later that night, its command seemed to lack the vigor that would have been expected from Tourkmani. On the verge of exhaustion, the Israeli 7th Brigade nonetheless repelled the 7th Division early the next morning, then drove it back in a counterattack.

On balance, war and battle are quite deterministic, with chance and luck rather equitably distributed among opposing generals and forces. Yet the examples mentioned do show that circumstances, apparently totally random, unforeseeable and unpredictable, and totally beyond the control of the commander, can cause defeat in battle.

Chapter 5

Sometimes-controllable
Unfavorable Circumstances

We have just examined how armies and commanders can be defeated by unfavorable circumstances beyond their control. There can be other unfavorable circumstances that are equally intractable but to which the commander might have contributed in some way or whose effects he might have been able to influence. This chapter examines such circumstances and the several differing ways in which they contribute to defeat.

LACK OF PREPARATIION FOR BATTLE

Sometimes military forces are committed to battle without adequate preparation. A distinction needs to be made between two different kinds of background circumstances that can lead to such a situation. Sometimes the forces and resources available to a commander are theoretically adequate to meet a hostile threat, but through his own failures or inadequacy the commander has not properly prepared himself to use those resources and forces. This kind of background circumstance is unreadiness because of a failure in command and is discussed in the next chapter.

The background circumstances that concern us here are those in which, through no fault of the commander, an unready force is unexpectedly thrust into battle against a better-prepared enemy. Such a set of circumstances is most usually found at the beginning of a war or when a subordinate commander finds himself engaged in an unexpected battle because of a command failure by a superior commander.

Yet even when a commander is thrust into battle unexpectedly by circumstances beyond his control, some have been professionally foresighted enough to take measures mitigating the unforeseen circumstances and potential consequences. The 1973 Arab–Israeli War provides some excellent examples of such circumstances and varying approaches to them by different commanders.

In 1973 the Israel Defense Force (IDF) had three major components. The army had over 80,000 men on active duty, to include about 60,000 conscripts undergoing their initial three-year training and service obligation, expandable by well-trained reserves to about 275,000 within forty-eight hours of mobilization. There was a small navy, with about twenty small combat vessels and 6000 personnel on active duty, expandable to a strength of about 8000 upon mobilization. The air force of more than 450 combat aircraft was manned by about 13,000 men, mostly professionals, expandable to about 20,000 men and women in time of war. The active-duty personnel of all three services were well-trained, high-quality troops, comparable to the best professionals of any of the world's military forces.

Deployed in the Sinai Desert area was an Israeli armored division of about 20,000 men, with three armored brigades, plus some 7000 infantrymen in a line of fortified observation posts (the so-called Bar Lev Line) along the Suez Canal. Another, smaller armored division of about 15,000 men was deployed on the Golan Heights. This Golan Defense Force consisted of two armored brigades (one under-strength) and an infantry brigade, with about half the infantrymen (some 2500) garrisoning a line of fortified observation posts along the eastern rim of the occupied region.

In early October 1973, the Egyptian army of about 275,000 men had been quietly augmented by reservists, brought to active duty during a period of intensive training field exercises west of the Suez Canal to a strength of more than 300,000 men. At the same time most of the Syrian army, its full strength of 130,000 men augmented by about 20,000 reservists, was also engaged in maneuvers in southwestern Syria, southwest of Damascus and just east of the Israeli-occupied Golan Heights.

The Israelis were keeping a close eye on the Arab maneuvers in both areas. During similar maneuvers earlier in the year Israel had initiated a partial mobilization, but the Arab exercises had ended without incident. Because mobilization brought the nation's industry nearly to a standstill, Israel did not want to mobilize again unless the government could clearly identify an Arab intention to use the exercises as a springboard for a surprise attack.

Thus Israel, unmobilized, and the nation at prayer during the holy day of Yom Kippur, was almost completely surprised by the Arab offensive of 6 October. Early that day Israeli intelligence had provided a few hours of warning, but had estimated that the Arab attack would be four hours later than it actually was.

On the Golan Heights, nearly 100,000 Syrians attacked the 15,000 men of the Golan Defense Force. Along the Suez Canal the 7000 men in the Bar Lev garrisons were assaulted across the canal by more than 30,000 well-prepared, carefully rehearsed Egyptian troops, closely followed by about 50,000 more Egyptians.

In two major battles along the Suez Canal—north and south of the Great Bitter Lake—the Israelis were defeated. Not only were they outnumbered and surprised, they were also unready. It may be debatable whether the Israeli army should have been surprised. But there was nothing that the unready, outnumbered troops along the Canal and in the desert just behind the Bar Lev Line could have done to avoid defeat. It is to their credit that they fought well enough, and with sufficient determination, to permit the full, prompt, and efficient mobilization of the Israeli army behind them.

The story was similar on the Golan Heights, but with one exception. One Israeli armored brigade was overwhelmed and virtually destroyed as a fighting force. However, the other armored brigade, holding the north and center of the line, repulsed the Syrian attacks. This was the 7th Armored Brigade, which had a reputation as the best unit in the Israeli army. But also its commander, Col. Avigdor Ben Gal, had been more concerned about the threatening nature of the Syrian maneuvers than most other Israeli officers had been. There can be no question that, although caught up in the general Israeli unpreparedness for war, Ben Gal's brigade was as alert and as ready as was humanly possible under the circumstances.

INFERIOR-QUALITY FORCES

The 1973 Arab–Israeli War also provides a number of excellent examples of the importance of troop quality, as well as a striking corroboration of a Clausewitz observation 150 years earlier that troop quality is "a given quantity." When both sides were fully mobilized there were more than 160,000 Arabs (mostly Syrians, but also some Iraqis, Jordanians, and Moroccans) deployed in a virtual stalemate west of Damascus against about 60,000 Israelis. A simple arithmetical ratio shows that the quality of the Israelis with respect to the Arabs must have been about 2.67 to 1.00.

There was a similar stalemate along the Suez–Sinai front, where more than 200,000 Egyptians were opposed by about 100,000 Israelis. Again, a simple arithmetical ratio suggests an Israeli combat-effectiveness superiority of about 2.00 to 1.00.

These strength-to-effectiveness ratios are very consistent with calculations of relative combat effectiveness based on assessments of performance in sixteen battles along the Suez–Sinai front and seventeen battles in the Golan region during three weeks of hostilities. Those calculations show an Israeli combat-effectiveness superiority over the Egyptians of 1.98 to 1.00 and over the Syrians of 2.54 to 1.00. Given the approximations involved in the data and in the calculations, the two sets of figures—one a battle calculation, the other a numerical ratio—are virtually identical: 2.6 to 1.0 in the north, 2.0 to 1.0 along the Suez Canal.[1]

Military science is not yet sufficiently sophisticated to tell us for certain what the components of combat-effectiveness superiority—troop quality—are. Presumably these include such things as training, experience, morale and (probably) doctrine. It certainly includes manpower quality, presumably measured in terms of levels and scope of education, and it certainly includes leadership, a subject that deserves closer scrutiny, which it will receive in the next chapter.

For purposes of the analysis of the causes of defeat, however, it is evident that once war began individual Egyptian or Syrian commanders could do no more to offset the qualitative superiority of the Israeli troops than the Israelis could do to offset the numerical superiority of the Arabs. The two sides were quite evenly matched, the qualitative superiority of the Israelis being almost exactly offset by the numerical superiority of the Arabs.

POOR MORALE

Morale is an ephemeral quality of military forces and is certainly intangible. Yet even though it may not be easily defined and can probably never be quantified, troop morale is very real and can be very important as a contributor to victory or defeat. The significance of morale is probably inversely proportional to the quality of troops. A well-trained, well-led, cohesive force of veterans will fight well and effectively even if morale is low. This was demonstrated by the performance of the German army in 1944 and early 1945. There could be little doubt among officers and men that Germany was losing—and had probably already lost—the war. Yet the skill and efficiency with which the Wehrmacht fought, despite the lowest possible morale, declined little during those months of almost incessant defeat.

Yet for ordinary armies, poor morale can contribute to defeat. One of the most striking examples of this was the collapse of General Bragg's Confederate army at Missionary Ridge during the Battle of Chattanooga in late November 1863.

Even the German Army could be adversely affected by poor morale. In late July 1918, after the failure of Ludendorff's five major offensives earlier that year, Marshal Foch ordered a general Allied counteroffensive. Having done their very best, having come close to winning but then having failed, the German army's morale plummeted. On 8 August the British army mounted a surprise offensive near Amiens. Thousands of Germans fled, more thousands surrendered, and only with great difficulty did the German leadership reestablish a new defensive line. General Ludendorff bitterly called this "the black day of the German Army." He said flatly: "The war must be ended."

TROOP AND/OR COMMANDER FATIGUE

In at least two very famous historical battles fatigue was a major contributor to the defeat of the loser.

Late on 29 September, 331 B.C., in eastern Mesopotamia, the Macedonian army of Alexander the Great approached the Persian army of Emperor Darius III. The Persians, more than 200,000 men, were drawn up in line of battle on the Plain of Gaugamela, near the site of ancient Nineveh, about seventy miles west of Arbela (Erbil). Alexander halted his army of some 47,000 men and bivouacked about seven miles west of the Persian host. He spent the next day reconnoitering the enemy dispositions while his army rested. The Persians, who had slept in their battle positions the previous night, were alert throughout the day, and there were occasional clashes of cavalry patrols as both sides tried to determine the intentions and dispositions of the other. The Persians, observing some activity in the Macedonian camp late in the afternoon, expected a night attack, and the troops were kept in ranks throughout the hours of darkness. But Alexander had merely been shifting units to be ready to assume the unorthodox formations he had planned for the next day, and—save for security guards—his soldiers slept through the night.

Thus, as Alexander's rested troops moved quickly into their positions early on the morning of 1 October 331, the Persian soldiers were already weary. In the ensuing hours some of the Persians fought badly, some fought well, and their Greek mercenaries fought very well; but all were tired, and none performed at their best. Probably the morale of the troops was also adversely affected by lack of rest, as well as by the state of mind that pervaded an army that had stood at alert all night fearing a surprise attack. Early in the battle Alexander led a cavalry charge against the left center of the Persian line, shattering the units in front of him and approaching the Persian Great King's command post. In panic, Darius fled the field, and much of the Persian left wing followed him in flight. The battle lasted several more hours, but those Persians who continued the fight were already tired. They became even more exhausted, and eventually the whole army collapsed into a mass of fleeing men, butchered by pursuing Macedonians.

We have already seen how a chance arrow seems to have been the deciding factor in the Battle of Hastings, but exhaustion undoubtedly also contributed to that Saxon defeat.

Early in September 1066, before the Normans landed on the southern coast of England, a Norwegian invading army landed in Northumbria, in northeast England. On 16 September newly crowned King Harold marched north from London with a small army augmented by local levies as he approached York, which was occupied by the Norwegian invaders. The two armies met each other at Stamford Bridge on 25 September, and Harold and his Saxons won an extremely hard-fought battle. Particularly hurt by casualties were Harold's housecarls, who constituted the only regular standing force in England.

While recovering from the battle, burying the dead, and restoring royal authority in the north, on 1 October Harold learned that William and the Norman army had landed at Pevensey in Sussex on 28 September. Early the next day Harold and his remaining housecarls began the long march back to southern England. He arrived at London on 6 October after an exceptionally rapid march of 200 miles. He remained four days in London, to give his housecarls some rest and to gather militia. On the eleventh he left London for the Sussex coast and reached Senlac the afternoon of the thirteenth—about fifty-six miles in forty-eight hours. Expecting a Norman attack, he took position on a ridge about eight miles northeast of Hastings. As Harold anticipated, William attacked the next day, giving the Saxons no time to rest. Yet they fought well—particularly the housecarls, who stood firm throughout the long day. However, their thin-stretched morale snapped when Harold was killed.

CASUALTIES

The physical and psychological impact of casualties incurred is commonly assumed to be a major—if not the principal—reason that a military force and/or its commander realizes that it is defeated, and we examine the validity of this assumption in some detail in later chapters. Valid or not as a general proposition, there can be no question that awareness of casualties suffered has led some armies and some commanders to acknowledge defeat.

The most disastrous defeat suffered by Frederick the Great was at Kunersdorf, 12 August 1759. Frederick had become accustomed to winning battles against more numerous foes by fighting ferociously against odds and despite losses until his iron will and the grim determination and professional skill of his grenadiers drove the enemy off the field. So he ignored the evidence of defeat as he failed, through faulty coordination, to accomplish an attempted double envelopment of an Austro-Russian army nearly twice the strength of his own. He simply rallied his troops and continued vain attacks. Not until he realized that he had lost nearly half of his 50,000 men as casualties did he recognize that further efforts would be hopeless.

It is likely that a major influence on Wallenstein to withdraw from the field at Lutzen on 16 November 1632 was his awareness of the casualties he had suffered: 12,000 men out of an army of 28,000, or 43 percent. Yet the

Swedes, who held the field, had suffered approximately 10,000 losses (including their beloved general-king, Gustavus Adolphus) out of 20,000, an even greater loss rate of 50 percent.

As we shall examine in a later chapter, awareness of casualties suffered, and recognition that a further assault would be fruitless and equally bloody, led Ulysses S. Grant to acknowledge defeat and to call off his attack at Cold Harbor, 3 June 1864.

SUBORDINATE ERROR OR FAILURE

In Chapter 2 we saw some examples of great captains losing battles because they were poorly served by subordinates. Errors or failures by subordinates were either the primary causes or contributory factors in the defeats of Turenne at Valenciennes, Prince Eugene at Cremona, and Frederick at Kolin. As will be seen in Chapter 7, two of Napoleon's marshals—Michel Ney and Emmanuel de Grouchy—contributed to his defeat at Waterloo.

In several of these, and other similar cases, the ultimate responsibility for the subordinate's failure is often that of the senior commander. For instance, at the outset of the Waterloo Campaign, Napoleon had deliberately left his most able subordinate, Marshal Louis Davout, in command of the garrison of Paris because he remembered that his final defeat in 1814 had been due to the surrender of Paris to the Allies by two less strong-willed marshals. Had Davout been present in the field (as he should have been) to carry out the missions Napoleon assigned to either Ney or Grouchy, the Emperor's chances of victory at Waterloo would have been greatly increased.

Thus a subordinate error or failure may sometimes be avoidable by the commander. But in other instances of subordinate failure—as that of the duc de La Ferte-Senneterre which resulted in Turenne's defeat at Valenciennes—there may be nothing the commander can do to prevent it.

SUMMARY

Grant's example at Cold Harbor is worth pondering. The unfavorable circumstance that defeated him was: He had ordered an assault against well-led, entrenched troops armed with rifled muskets firing conoidal bullets. It may be argued that this circumstance was in part his doing and his responsibility. (A counterargument is that Lee had ordered even less promising assaults at Malvern Hill and Gettysburg and that a little more than six months earlier Grant had seen his assaulting troops successful at Chattanooga under apparently less favorable circumstances.) Regardless of whether Grant or Lee was more responsible for the circumstance leading to Grant's failure at Cold Harbor, his immediate recognition that this circumstance was now beyond his control, and his prompt action to call off the battle, were demonstrations of objective, competent generalship under such circumstances.

Through this example we can see clearly that defeat in the face of unfavorable circumstances may or may not result from command failure. On the other hand, defeat under such circumstances should not, in itself, be attributed to bad leadership.

Failure of Command

The two previous chapters have examined the reasons for defeat that are due either to circumstances beyond the control of the losing commander or to circumstances that he may or may not be able to influence. This chapter examines the causes of defeat for which the defeated commander is wholly responsible.

SURPRISE

In the first paragraph of this book there is a quotation from Frederick the Great, who won most of his battles despite circumstances that would have defeated most generals, stating that it was no disgrace for a commander to be defeated, but that it *was* a disgrace for him to be surprised. Nevertheless, as we have seen, Frederick—himself a master of surprise—was a victim of surprise in each of his three defeats.

Over the course of history surprise has probably been the principal cause of military defeat. It was the major contributor to defeat in close to half of the 100-odd examples of defeat listed in Appendix B.

Let's look briefly at twelve of those battles, which might be called classics of surprise:

Cannae, 216 B.C.
Sajo River, 1241
Trafalgar, 1805
Austerlitz, 1805
Chancellorsville, 1863
Tannenberg, 1914
Megiddo, 1918
Flanders/Ardennes, 1940
Pearl Harbor, 1941
Midway, 1942
Hollandia, 1943
Suez Canal, 1973

Cannae. Hannibal was one of the great masters of surprise, and obviously an equally great student of human nature. At Cannae he enticed an over-eager Roman general to attack into a trap, which Hannibal then sprang with a massive defensive-offensive double envelopment. As von Schlieffen perceptively observed in his classic book, *Cannae*, Terrentius Varro cooperated (quite unintentionally) to assure that possibly the most famous victory of history was also its most famous defeat.[1]

Sajo River. The Battle of the Sajo River was a triple-staged surprise, planned and executed by the Mongol general Subotai, who was virtually the alter ego of the great Genghis Khan. Following his invasion of Hungary, he pretended to retreat eastward in some confusion from the Danube River, enticing Hungarian King Bela to pursue. After retreating for two days he struck with a surprise dawn attack on the Hungarian camp. This, however, was only a holding attack, soon followed by a wide envelopment which fell like a thunderbolt upon the rear of the already surprised Hungarians. Badly defeated, some Hungarians detected a gap in the Mongol encirclement and infiltrated out. Others followed, until the whole Hungarian army was streaming westward in flight. Then, with all organization and cohesion gone, the fugitives were pounced upon by a *touman* (division) of waiting Mongols mounted on fresh horses. Only a handful of Hungarians got back to the Danube.

Trafalgar. As in the examples already cited, Nelson used enticement to set the stage for his greatest, and last, victory. When Villeneuve's Franco-Spanish fleet—somewhat larger than Nelson's—sailed from the safety of port, the British admiral was waiting with a totally unexpected, brand-new (but carefully thought-out) battle concept. This was to use the fundamental force of wind on sails to enable him, with fewer ships, to concentrate overwhelming superiority of force upon a portion of the enemy fleet before the remainder of that fleet could possibly turn around and enter the battle. Thanks to a brilliant concept, to a system of command that ensured that all of his subordinates understood and worked within his plan, and to a leadership flair that made him one of a handful of the greatest military commanders in all history, Nelson did exactly what he planned to do. Completely surprised, Villeneuve never had a chance. Nelson died in the moment of his greatest glory.

Austerlitz. At Austerlitz, six weeks after Trafalgar, Napoleon used surprise to establish on land French military supremacy comparable to that Nelson had given Britain at sea (although a less enduring supremacy). Again deception and enticement set the stage for surprise. The French Emperor dangled as an attractive lure an apparently weak right flank, inadequately protecting his long, exposed line of communications from Central Europe to France. The Russo-Austrian allies, confident in their numerical superiority, could not resist the baited trap. As half the Allied army moved to envelop and crush the inviting flank, Napoleon's precisely timed counterblow cut the enemy army in two, enveloped the putative envelopers and won one of the most decisive victories of all history. Although he was outnumbered, he never even had to use his reserves.

Chancellorsville. Unlike the previous examples, Lee did not use enticement as the basis for the surprise he achieved at Chancellorsville. The stage was set by his opponent, Hooker, who offered Lee an opportunity that would not have been perceived by a lesser general. Taking advantage of a numerical superiority of approximately two to one, Hooker moved—too slowly and too ponderously—to crush Lee's army by a wide strategic envelopment. Boldly dividing his army not once but twice, Lee held off the two converging wings of the Union army with vigorous defensive tactics, then sent Jackson's corps on a wide envelopment of the right flank of the Union envelopers. Jackson's dusk counterattack, coming from a direction 180 degrees away from that in which Hooker expected Confederate defensive resistance, was a total surprise. The Union main effort—the right wing—was thrown into irretrievable confusion, and Lee won his greatest victory.

Tannenberg. A two-pronged Russian invasion of East Prussia at the outset of World War I threatened to destroy the German Eighth Army, approximately half the strength of two converging Russian armies. Hastily placed in command of the Eighth Army after it had suffered a slight setback at the hands of one of the advancing Russian armies, the newly created team of von Hindenburg and Ludendorff used roads and railroads boldly to concentrate almost the entire Eighth Army against the other Russian army—Samsonov's Second Army—advancing north from Poland into the heart of East Prussia. Before Samsonov even realized that battle was imminent, the Germans struck in a double envelopment consistent in concept and in results with von Schlieffen's paradigm of a modern Cannae.

Megiddo. The most successful British general of World War I was Sir Edmond Allenby, another master of surprise, and a student of the Bible. In mid-September 1918, Allenby's army in Palestine was facing a strongly entrenched Turkish army with its right flank anchored on the Mediterranean just north of Jaffa and its left flank on the Jordan River, where it was protected by the Dead Sea and the Jordan Valley escarpment. Thanks to a brilliant deception plan, the British attack of 19 September was totally unexpected, breaking through the defenders' line near the coast, while the Turks thought the British were concentrating near the Jordan. Allenby's cavalry corps dashed through the breach and raced north. Their principal route through central Palestine was by way of the Mus Mus Pass, which Allenby knew from the Bible had been used by Egyptian Pharaoh Thutmose III in his surprise offensive that won the first Battle of Megiddo in 1469 B.C. This rapid drive through the unprotected pass enabled the British to cut off the right wing of the Turkish army, which collapsed completely, leading Turkey to sue for peace. (Incidentally, no modern tank army has been able to exceed, against opposition, the advance rate of Allenby's horse cavalry.)

Flanders/Ardennes. The most dramatic military campaign of the twentieth century was undoubtedly the German victory over the French, British, Dutch, and Belgian armies in May–June 1940. The Germans were outnumbered by the Allies, and their tanks were not only inferior to those of the British and French, they were also fewer in number. The factor of surprise was again important, but probably slightly less so as a contributor to the Allied defeat than were French failures in planning and in battlefield command. Nevertheless, the Germans could not have won without surprise. This was accomplished by leading the Allies to believe that the Germans would repeat the Schlieffen Plan strategy of World War I, with a main effort in the north, on their right flank, against the Dutch and Belgian armies. Instead, the Germans made their main effort in the center, through the Ardennes Forest, which the French thought was too wooded and too rugged for successful armored operations. The unexpected location of the German main effort and the vigor with which it was launched enabled the attackers to make a clear breakthrough before the Allies could shift their badly located reserves, even though these were ample, to deal with the thrust.

Pearl Harbor. The Japanese attack on Pearl Harbor on 7 December 1941 was brilliantly planned and executed. As had been the case in the Ardennes-Flanders campaign, American command errors facilitated the attackers' victory. But the operation could never have succeeded had the Japanese failed to achieve surprise. Even though the Americans (who had broken the Japanese radio codes) knew that war was likely to break out that weekend, they were certain that the Japanese would be attacking the Dutch East Indies, and probably Malaya and the Philippines. Nevertheless, the U.S. Navy was conducting routine patrolling to the west and southwest of Hawaii, the directions from which it was assumed a Japanese threat to Hawaii would come. Instead, preserving complete radio silence while dummy radios in Japan were keeping up normal fleet radio traffic being monitored by the Americans, the Japanese fleet struck from the north and virtually wiped out the American Pacific Fleet.

Midway. Surprise turned the tables on the Japanese a scant six months after Pearl Harbor. Confident in their overwhelming naval superiority in the Pacific resulting from the Pearl Harbor victory, in May 1942 the Japanese put to sea the largest naval armada ever assembled up to that time. The objective was the seizure of Midway Island. As a result of earlier combat operations, they knew that the only major naval opposition the United States could mount was a one-carrier task force. But the Japanese did not know that we were reading their coded radio messages. Nor did they know that, through almost superhuman efforts, the United States had assembled a three-carrier task force. While the Americans could not match the strength of the remainder of the Japanese fleet, these three carriers were almost a match for the strongest element of the Japanese fleet, a four-carrier task force. Furthermore, because we could read the Japanese messages, we were able to get our carriers west of the planned Japanese submarine scouting line one day before those submarines took their positions. Thus they not only did not know that there were three American carriers opposing them, they thought that there was not even a single American carrier available to help protect Midway. Thus the Japanese were totally surprised, and in the fierce carrier-air battle that took place on 4 June west of Midway they lost all four carriers in their main task force, while the Americans lost only one of theirs.

Hollandia. By early 1944 the tide of the war in the Pacific was clearly running against Japan. However, they were benefitting from their original strategy of establishing a line of outposts thousands of miles from Japan in the central and southwest Pacific. It seemed that it would take years for the Americans to approach the inner chain of islands that was the heart of the East Asia Co-Prosperity Sphere, stretching from Japan south through the Philippines to the Dutch East Indies.

Forces of Gen. Douglas MacArthur's Southwest Pacific Theater were slowly making their way westward along the coast of New Guinea, limited by the 350-mile radius of action of land-based fighter planes. These aircraft were essential for the support of any major landing operation along the coast, and overland advance through the jungles was impossible. The Japanese had built a major supply and aerial base at Hollandia on the north coast of New Guinea, more than 500 miles west of the closest American positions at Saidor, in eastern New Guinea. Knowing it would be impossible for MacArthur to attack Hollandia without fighter support, the Japanese concentrated most of their defensive strength west of Saidor. However, MacArthur was able to obtain support for four days from the Navy's Fast Carrier Task Force of the Central Pacific area. Though fighter air support would be needed for far longer than four days, he nevertheless planned an amphibious strike directly at Hollandia with his ground forces. While the main force was going ashore at Hollandia with naval carrier support, a simultaneous landing would be made near Japanese airfields at Aitape— midway between Saidor and Hollandia—with fighter support from Saidor. The captured Japanese airfields at Aitape would have to be secured, and American planes moved on to them within four days so that, when the carriers left, air support to the troops at Hollandia could be continued from Aitape. Expecting an American attack near Saidor, the Japanese were completely surprised by the simultaneous landings farther east at Aitape and Hollandia. And when the carriers left, on schedule, air support at Hollandia was uninterrupted, provided by land-based aircraft from the newly captured fields at Aitape.

Suez Canal. On 6 October 1973 the Egyptian army initiated an assault against Israeli forces across the Suez Canal that will go down in history as a classic of surprise, deception, and overwater assault. The basic components of that operation have been described in a previous chapter, and surprise was obviously only one of several elements in the Egyptian success. But without surprise the assault could never have been successful. This was accomplished by a brilliant cover and deception plan that totally misled the extremely competent Israeli intelligence service. One example of the meticulous nature of the plan can be seen in the means used to get an Egyptian submarine to the southern waters of the Red Sea, to establish a blockade, without arousing Israeli suspicions. Several months before the planned attack, Egypt arranged to have one of its submarines repaired at the nearest suitable shipyard, at Bombay, India. Thus, when the submarine steamed south into the Red Sea at the beginning of October, ostensibly it was keeping its appointment at Bombay. As the Egyptians expected, Israeli intelligence knew all about the planned repairs and saw nothing unusual in the voyage of the Egyptian boat. Arriving at the Strait of Bab el Mandeb on 6 October, the sub remained there, on its blockade station, and never went to Bombay. (After the cease-fire the Egyptian government apologized to India.)

Aware of the efficiency of Israeli intelligence, the Egyptian high command did not issue plans for the attack to division commanders until forty-eight hours before H-hour. The plans did not go to brigade headquarters until twenty-four hours before H-hour; they went to battalion commanders twelve hours before H-hour. The Israelis learned of the plan about ten hours in advance—although they thought it was fourteen hours before H-hour. This was too late to interfere seriously with the planned attack, which was even more successful than the Egyptians had anticipated.

INFERIOR LEADERSHIP: SELF-DELUSION

One of the most serious failures of leadership is the tendency of poor commanders to delude themselves about the capabilities and intentions of their enemies. Obviously, every example of successful surprise by one military force is to some degree also an example of self-delusion on the part of the commander of the force that is surprised. In these cases, of course, the self-delusion is engendered, or at least abetted, by the deception activities of the force achieving surprise.

There can be no better example of self-delusion than the French high command's faulty perception of the likely course of hostilities on the Western Front in World War II. In the late 1920s and early 1930s the French government had invested tremendous sums of money in the construction of the most modern and most extensive fortification system in the world. This Maginot Line (named for the minister of defense who initiated the work) extended eastward from Montmedy along the Franco-German border to the Rhine River, then south along the Rhine to Switzerland. Since 1792 there had been five major invasions of France from Germany across this border, and the purpose of the Maginot Line was to discourage any repetitions.

When in 1939 war broke out again between Germany, on the one hand, and Britain and France on the other, the Allies mobilized nine field armies—eight French and one British—to defend northern and eastern France. These forces operated under the French high command, with Gen. Maurice G. Gamelin as the Allied commander in chief. The average strength of these armies was about 240,000 men. In addition to the armies, approximately 200,000 additional French fortress troops manned the Maginot Line.

Five of the Allied field armies were deployed along the Franco-Belgian frontier, to be ready to deal with any German invasion attempt through the Low Countries, as had occurred in 1914. Prior to the invasion, both Belgium and the Netherlands had retained strict neutrality and refused to enter into any formal discussions about cooperation in the event of German invasion. However, the Belgians and Dutch had both made clear their determination to defend themselves and informally indicated their desire for Allied assistance should this occur. Two of the Allied field armies (the British and one French) had the mission of marching north to support the Belgians and the Dutch in such an event. The other three French armies along that frontier would form a hinge, linking the forces advancing into the Low Countries with the Maginot Line. Four French armies, almost half the field forces of the French army, were in reserve behind the Maginot Line.

General Gamelin and his staff, obsessed with the history of German invasions of France, did not see any anomaly in this disposition of forces. They failed to recognize that, having devoted a major national effort to the creation of the Maginot Line, they were deploying their forces as though the line were not there. Had two or three of those reserve armies in Alsace and eastern Lorraine been more centrally located—west of Sedan and Mezières, and east of Amiens—the German thrust through the Ardennes would unquestionably have been halted at the Meuse River and the course of World War II would have been totally altered. Self-delusion by General Gamelin and his staff assured the defeat of France.

INFERIOR LEADERSHIP: CONFUSED MISSION

The lack of a clear-cut mission, fully understood at all levels of command, is a manifestation of a failure of top leadership. As Napoleon expressed it, "A poor general sees too much." This not-uncommon failing contributed to serious German defeats in two world wars, each of which had disastrous consequences.

In the years before World War I the Chief of the General Staff—Gen. Helmuth von Moltke, nephew of the great Prussian-German Chief of Staff of mid-nineteenth-century fame—had inherited and elaborated an operational concept designed by his predecessor, Gen. Count Alfred von Schlieffen. The purpose of this plan was to enable Germany to deal with the dangers of a war simultaneously in east and west against the Triple Entente of Russia, France, and Britain. Schlieffen considered France, with its high-quality army and rapid mobilization capability, a much more serious immediate threat than the much larger but less efficient armies of Russia, with its slow, ponderous mobilization system. Thus a very small force was to stand on the defensive against Russia in the east, while 95 percent of the German army was to be assembled against France. And of this force in the west, 90 percent was to be concentrated into five field armies on the extreme right flank. These armies were to march in a great wheel through the Netherlands, Belgium, and northern France to sweep the French army back and crush it against the Rhine and the Swiss frontier. Schlieffen visualized this as a modern Cannae, and the concept was developed as a result of the studies that had led to his famous book. Schlieffen's dying words, in 1911, are reputed to have been "Keep the right flank strong!"

However, by 1914 Moltke had somewhat modified the plan. Of the German mobilized forces of 2,400,000 about 400,000 (nearly 17 percent) were to protect Germany's eastern frontiers. Of the remaining 2,000,000 men—all mobilized against France—1,500,000 were to be in the five right-wing field armies. But Dutch neutrality was to be respected, which meant that the two armies on the extreme right would be terribly crowded, and slowed down, in their movements across the frontiers through Belgium and into northern France. (Yet speed on the periphery of the wheel was a key element of the Schlieffen Plan.) Another 500,000 were to be in Alsace and Lorraine. Thus only 75 percent of the available forces in the west would be in the right wing, instead of the 90 percent specified by Schlieffen, and that wing would not move with the celerity he had envisaged. The five right-wing armies made up 63 percent of the entire German army instead of 86 percent as planned by Schlieffen.

Rather than the clear-cut, overriding envelopment mission against France that had been the heart of the Schlieffen Plan, Moltke was diverting forces to protect German territory in the east and in the west. Had Schlieffen been alive and commanding in 1914, it is hard to see how his plan, carried out as he had envisaged it, could have failed.

As a matter of fact, in light of the way in which the early battles went, it is hard to see how even this watered-down Schlieffen Plan could have failed if Moltke had not allowed his confusion of missions in the planning phase to continue into the period of execution. First, when it looked as though the Eighth Army might be defeated in East Prussia, he pulled two army corps out of the two right-wing armies and sent them east. Thus 200,000 men who could have changed the result of the Battle of the Marne were out of operations, arriving in the east too late to take part in the Battle of Tannenberg—where they were not needed.

Then Moltke failed to keep close enough control over his right-wing armies, now reduced in strength. And when these armies shortened their sweep to pass east of Paris (instead of swinging to the west as originally planned) he did not interfere. As a result, the French Sixth Army was able to assemble north and east of Paris and to lead a counteroffensive against the exposed right flank of the German First Army. That ended the entire Schlieffen concept and led directly to the German defeat at the Battle of the Marne.

In World War II the personal intervention of Hitler on the Eastern Front twice resulted in confusion of missions and to two great German defeats.

First, in the late summer of 1941 Hitler thought he saw an opportunity for an encirclement of large Russian forces in the Ukraine. Usually the proper objective for a military force is the enemy forces rather than geographic objectives. However, the German Army General Staff had modified that concept for this campaign, for good reason. Because of the nature of the road and—particularly—railroad networks of Russia, it was important to capture Moscow as early as possible. With this hub of the Russian transportation network in German hands, the Russians would be terribly handicapped in moving supplies and reserves to various parts of the front. Hitler, however, assumed from early victories that Moscow would fall easily into the hands of his troops. He diverted a panzer army from Army Group Center, on the Moscow axis, to cooperate with a panzer army from Army Group South to encircle Soviet forces near Kiev in the Ukraine. The encirclement was successful, and nearly a million Soviet troops were captured.

But six weeks had been lost in the drive to Moscow. The German tanks had been worn down by their rapid movements over great distances, and the good weather of midsummer had turned—predictably—to the rains of early fall, further slowing the advance on Moscow. The Russians had lost nearly a million men, but they had been given close to two months of precious time to bring in at least as many reserves from Siberia to bolster the defense of Moscow. The Germans were repulsed in front of the Soviet capital in early December. Instead of an almost-certain German victory, the specter of a long, stalemated, two-front war loomed in front of the Germans.

However, the qualitative superiority of the German army over the Soviet army was still so great that the Germans had another opportunity to retrieve the situation in the summer of 1942. But again Hitler intervened, and again his intervention was disastrous.

German planners believed they could break through the long Russian lines south of Moscow, and a thrust across the Volga River at Stalingrad had the potential of cutting off all of southern Russia, with its grain and its oil wells, from the rest of the Soviet Union. In such a case it was difficult to see how the isolated forces in the south could long continue resistance. Such a breakthrough also could have opened the possibility of a German thrust northward, east of Moscow, through the Volga Valley, once German control of south Russia was consolidated. Hitler, however, meddled with this plan. Although his army was far weaker than it had been the previous summer, he wanted it to conduct two divergent offensives in the south. While Army Group South drove eastward toward the Volga River at Stalingrad, a new Caucasus Army Group would thrust south into the Caucasus to seize a vast agricultural region and in particular occupy the rich oil fields near Baku. Neither of these divergent thrusts was strong enough to be sure of success, and as long as they continued their advances, the lengthening line between them was increasingly vulnerable to a Soviet counteroffensive. The Russians did counterattack, and the offensives ended in disaster. The consequent loss of the Sixth Army at Stalingrad virtually assured eventual German defeat in Russia.

INFERIOR LEADERSHIP: WEAKNESS OF WILL

Many a commander with the intellectual and other professional capabilities required for competent battlefield leadership has failed because of indecision, excessive caution, or general lack of bold aggressiveness. The line between boldness and rashness is sometimes thin, but it is almost always clear. A good general "knows it when he sees it."

We have already seen how in 1914 the younger Moltke reacted to political and other pressures to protect all of Germany. While trying to carry out a decisive offensive against France, he weakened—and eventually emasculated—that offensive because he allowed himself to be diverted from the main objective by less important considerations.

Several instances of defeat in the American Civil War, on both sides, resulted directly from weakness of will on the part of a commander.

Few men have had such opportunities for greatness thrust upon them so insistently, and with such little effort on their own part, as was the good fortune of intelligent, efficient, handsome George B. McClellan. Unfortunately, however, McClellan was weak-willed. Every day in the Seven Days Battles near Richmond, 25 June to 1 July 1862, McClellan's subordinates, with no guidance from him, repulsed Confederate attacks, and every day McClellan ordered a retreat.

Few men, having once failed, are given a second chance to retrieve the failure. McClellan was one of those few. Despite his earlier failure in front of Richmond, he was restored to top command of the Army of the Potomac later that year. With a captured copy of Lee's campaign directive in his possession, on 17 September 1862 McClellan confronted Lee near Sharpsburg, Maryland, at Antietam Creek. He had 90,000 men; Lee at the start of the battle had less than 40,000. In the bloodiest battle day of the Civil War the Confederates, constantly on the brink of defeat, desperately repulsed a series of uncoordinated Union attacks. Finally, when a Confederate division of about 10,000 men arrived late in the afternoon, Lee was able to reestablish a solid, if exhausted, defensive line, and retain undisputed possession of the battlefield. McClellan never ordered his reserves, 20,000 strong, into the battle. Nor, once repulsed, did he try again the next day.

INADEQUATE CONTROL

The principal manifestation of McClellan's weakness of will at Antietam, as in the Seven Days, was his failure to control or direct the operations of his subordinates. Providing his corps commanders with only the vaguest of prebattle instructions, McClellan allowed them to fight as best they could, with no guidance, no coordination, and no supervision.

Inadequate control is displayed in several ways. Important among these are poor reconnaissance (which generally leads to faulty intelligence), poor planning, faulty tactics, inadequate logistics, and breakdown in communications. Each warrants examination.

POOR RECONNAISSANCE

For reasons that are not readily explicable, possibly the most pervasive failure of poor commanders is lack of effort to reconnoiter. One would expect that even if a commander were unaware of the multitude of historical examples of battles lost through inadequate reconnaissance, he would be so anxious to learn something about the whereabouts and dispositions of the enemy that he would not need to be reminded to send out reconnaissance patrols. Yet, strangely, reconnaissance is all too often neglected.

One of the most recent examples of this failure is to be found in the Argentinian performance in the Falkland Islands in May and June 1982. After the British landings on 21 May, the Argentinians should have patrolled vigorously to find out where the British troops were going, so as to be prepared for British attacks, even if not to try to seize the initiative. Not at all. The British had a free hand, unobserved by the Argentinians, and with no opposition other than the actual uncoordinated defense of previously prepared Argentinian positions.

Probably the principal reason for the Russian defeat at the Yalu River, in 1904 in the first battle of the Russo-Japanese War, was the failure of Gen. Mikhail Zasulich to try to obtain information about the approaching Japanese so that he could deploy his forces for the most effective possible defense.

Ten years later at Tannenberg another Russian general, Aleksander Samsonov, showed that the consequences of lack of reconnaissance are at least as great for a force with an offensive mission. Reconnaissance would have revealed to Samsonov that battle near Tannenberg was imminent and would have obviated the possibility of surprise. It might even have provided him an opportunity to maneuver effectively to envelop the dangerously exposed German left flank. But the mere absence of surprise would have been enough to change Tannenberg from a Russian disaster to an inconclusive battle. And, with the Russian First Army approaching (albeit slowly) from the northeast, an inconclusive battle, or even a hard-fought defeat, could have set the stage for a German disaster.

POOR PLANNING

It is easy, in retrospect, to be critical of battle plans that fail. However, failed battle plans are usually plans that are nonexistent or that have been inadequately prepared. Thus the weakness of such plans is usually evident before they fail. The elder Moltke (the "good" Moltke) was fond of saying that previously prepared plans become irrelevant as soon as two forces meet in battle. Yet Moltke did not really mean that, and he never failed to prepare (or have his staff prepare) detailed plans. The point of his remark was that no matter how well prepared plans might be, they could not envisage all possible enemy reactions. Thus, once forces entered battle, it was almost certain that plans would have to be adjusted to circumstances and sometimes completely changed. But if good plans exist, adjustment and adaptation are easy. If there are no plans, or if the plans are poor, a whole new planning process is necessary, and in the heat of battle there is rarely time to do that systematically or well.

The better the plans and the stronger the commander, the less adjustment is likely to be necessary. In some instances, as for Nelson at Trafalgar, Napoleon at Austerlitz, and MacArthur at Hollandia, the plans were so good, and the execution so good, that almost no adjustment was necessary. Gen. Heinz Guderian, in his memoirs, tells the story of how, in the approach of his corps to the Meuse River in May 1940, the plans and preparations had been so good that his corps headquarters issued orders for the assault across the river simply by changing the date on an order they had prepared in an earlier war game and issuing it without further change.[2]

FAULTY TACTICS

As with plans, it is easy in retrospect to criticize the battlefield tactics and tactical decisions of commanders. However, simply because it is difficult to apply tactics properly or judiciously in the heat of battle, and easy to criticize after the battle, does not invalidate the criticism.

"Fortune favors the brave."[3] The ancient Romans understood that the cautious, unimaginative approach is less likely to be successful than creative boldness. This is unquestionably true of battlefield tactics.

Had Pompey made imaginative use of his substantial numerical superiority at the Battle of Pharsalus, 48 B.C., he probably could have won the Roman Civil War that day, with incalculable effects upon the course of world history. Simply to say that his cautious use of the standard Roman tactical formation was the proper way to use his advantage against a Julius Caesar is to ignore the fact that a Caesar was likely to (and did) deviate substantially from that standard formation. The very fact that Caesar was his opponent was in itself reason to eschew an ordinary, cautious approach. Pompey's troops may not have been quite as good as Caesar's, but there could not have been much difference. And his own experience as a successful general should have given Pompey confidence in creativity. But he opted for caution and Caesar established an empire.

Most of the battles won by Napoleon could probably have been victories for his opponents had they been willing to use imaginative tactics. Austerlitz is a prime example. The best way for Emperor Alexander (or General Kutusov, who was advising Alexander) to take advantage of Napoleon's weak strategic right flank would have been to carry out a wide envelopment of that flank, not to try to crush it in an unimaginative frontal attack. Presumably, of course, Napoleon would have responded in a way that would have offset such an Allied move, since neither Alexander nor Kutusov could match tactical wits with Napoleon. But such an envelopment might have cut Napoleon off from Vienna and forced him to withdraw through Bohemia. In any event, the Allied army could not have been so readily smashed by Napoleon.

INADEQUATE LOGISTICS

Even good generals often allow logistics to determine strategic and tactical decisions. Great generals adapt logistics to their operational concepts, not vice versa (though, of course, those operational concepts cannot ignore logistics). Poor generals usually do not pay enough attention to logistics.

Logistics, and everything having to do with supply, maintenance, and administration, are not very glamorous and are all too often ignored by historians, who simply take it for granted that food, ammunition, and fuel will be available to the fighting troops as they need these things. Failures in logistics are more likely to prevent battles from being fought than they are to have a significant effect on the outcome of a battle of one, two, or a few days.

It is perhaps instructive to look at the effect of logistics on two campaigns of World War II and to look briefly at a fallacious criticism of the effects of logistics upon a World War I campaign.

In the Rome Campaign of May–June 1944, the German logistical situation was adversely affected by a very effective Allied air interdiction campaign. Although the remarkably flexible German logistical system never broke down, endemic shortages of fuel and ammunition undoubtedly contributed to an overwhelming Allied victory.

In the 1944 Battle for France following the Allied breakout from Normandy, Germany was saved from complete defeat by Allied logistical problems, and the Allied operational decisions that had to be made because of that situation. This led to one of the great, still-unresolved controversies of World War II.

There were constraints on the amount of supplies that the Allies could put ashore in France after the breakout from Normandy. This was due to the limits on the artificial and permanent (but damaged) port facilities in Normandy and to the fact that the foresighted Germans were occupying other ports that the Allies might otherwise have used for logistical purposes. Within those constraints, the Allied logistical performance was very efficient.

What could or should be done about the effects these constraints had on Allied operations? Generals Montgomery, Bradley, and Patton gave their advice (without being asked) to General Eisenhower. Conceptually this advice was the same; specifically it was quite different. Ike was urged to concentrate allocations of scarce fuel and ammunition to a relatively small section of the front—probably one field army—to enable that army to strike as rapidly and as deeply as possible through France into Germany. The Germans were close to collapse, these generals told Eisenhower; don't give them a chance to recover. Exploit if possible, they said, to the heart of Germany and the incipient collapse would become an actual collapse, and the war could be won before the end of 1944. Montgomery, of course, thought that the supplies should go to one of his British armies; Bradley thought they should go to one of his American armies; Patton thought they should go to his Third Army.

Eisenhower, properly respectful of the Germans, was fearful that if such a deep and narrow penetration of Germany were to be attempted, the penetration would be cut off and would lead to an Allied disaster. Also, for political reasons he was reluctant to favor the British over the Americans, or vice versa. So he decided on a "broad front" strategy. Supplies were allocated relatively equitably to all armies along the front and, when fuel ran out early in September, all armies came to a halt. The pause was only for two or three weeks, but in that time the Germans made a remarkable recovery. The subsequent Allied advance was slowed greatly. The Germans were able to mount their great Ardennes offensive, resulting in the Battle of the Bulge. The war dragged on for eight more months.

No one can be certain either that Eisenhower made the right decision or, on the other hand, that he should have adopted the strategy suggested by Montgomery–Bradley–Patton. It is not accurate to say that the Allies were defeated by logistics and the operational decision which the logistical situation imposed upon them. Certainly, however, they were not victorious as a result of the decision Ike made. Furthermore, this historian believes, the war probably would have been shortened by four to six months had he made the other decision.

Returning to World War I, some critics have suggested that the Schlieffen Plan was inherently flawed because Schlieffen and his successor ignored the logistical problems it created. The two principal critics were the German Gerhard Ritter and the British Basil Liddell Hart. They claim that the German defeat at the Battle of the Marne was a direct result of Schlieffen's logistical naievete. However, Liddell Hart and Ritter were the ones who were naive. In their assessment they completely ignored the performance of the German First Army in the battles of the Frontiers and the Marne campaign. If any one German army was more subject to logistical problems than any other, it was that one, on the extreme rim of the great German wheel. In fact, that army fought superbly. It had enough ammunition and other supplies to outfight the French Sixth Army in the Battle of the Ourcq and was forced to retreat during the Battle of the Marne only because of the tactical defeat of the Second Army, on its left. The Marne campaign was one military operation in which defeat was *not* due to logistical inadequacy.[4]

BREAKDOWN IN COMMUNICATIONS

A number of battles have been lost due to breakdowns in communications. We have already noted three: the Seven Days Battle, when McClellan remained out of communications with his corps commanders; Antietam, when McClellan again made no effort to coordinate the operations of his corps commanders; the Marne, where Moltke failed to coordinate the operations of his subordinate army commanders.

Many years ago (shortly after the Boer War) the British staff college wrote a scenario of a battle in which the commander made every possible mistake the British instructors could imagine. It was called *The Defence of Duffer's Drift*,[5] and any British officer who studied it should have been able to avoid any possible command failure in war. A few years later (shortly after World War I) a similar tongue-in-cheek narrative of failures was written for American students at the U.S. Army Command and Staff School; this one was called *The Battle of Booby's Bluff*.[6] The British and American instructors needn't have bothered. All they had to do was to write a truthful narrative scenario of Russian performance at the Battle of Tannenberg.

It is difficult to say which of many causes was more responsible for the Russian debacle at Tannenberg. In addition to inadequate reconnaissance, to the surprise that largely resulted from that failure, and to the general unreadiness of the Russian armies, there was a near-total breakdown in communications. In the first place, the First and Second Russian army headquarters were not in communication. (This probably would have been the case even if the two generals—Rennenkampf and Samsonov, personal enemies who hated each other—had been on speaking terms.) Had they been in communication, Samsonov might have had some inkling of what the Germans were doing. He was also out of communication with his corps commanders except by messenger, and once the battle began there were no messengers. In despair Samsonov left his command post to visit his corps commanders. He was never seen again. His body was never found. Did he get lost? Was he killed by infiltrating Germans? Did he commit suicide? No one will ever know. We only know why he was defeated.

Part III

DEFEAT IN HISTORY

Chapter 7

Napoleon in Victory and Defeat

B Y V I N C E N T H A W K I N S

A N D T . N . D U P U Y

Napoleon Bonaparte commanded in more battles than any other general in history. By one count he exercised command in fifty-five major or significant battles, to say nothing of perhaps another hundred engagements or skirmishes or sieges. Of those battles he won forty-eight, drew three, and lost four.[1] Over a period of twenty years, he directed twelve campaigns, winning the first eight and losing the last four.

Without a doubt modern military theory begins with Napoleon and is based on his victories. There is much also to be learned from his defeats.

In attempting to learn from Napoleon's defeats we focus on two of his campaigns. One of these—his third—was a one-battle campaign in which victory brought him the imperial throne, yet he had virtually lost the battle before he was victorious. In the other, his penultimate campaign, he lost the first battle, had one draw, won seven brilliant victories over great odds, yet he lost the campaign and (for the first of two times) his throne.

Throughout his life, Napoleon kept up an amazing volume of correspondence with his family, friends, and a wide variety of the political and military leaders of his day. In many of his letters he propounded maxims, explaining his views on the art of war. These maxims were as much the result of his study of the campaigns of other great commanders as they were lessons learned from his own experiences in war, and formed the basis for the tactical and strategic concepts that comprised Napoleon's method of warfare.

In one of these maxims Napoleon stated that "In war the chief alone understands the importance of certain things; and he alone by his will and superior knowledge can conquer and overcome all difficulties." Napoleon adhered more strongly to this maxim than others during the course of his political and military career. It was this unshakable belief in the supremacy of his will that led him initially to triumph and ultimately to ruin.

This chapter will focus on the significance of this maxim, so far as Napoleon was concerned, not only for its relevance to his victories and to his ability to transform defeat into victory but particularly as it may have contributed to his defeats.

DEFEAT TO VICTORY: MARENGO, 1800

RETROSPECT

The campaign of 1800 was perhaps the most important of a series of events that brought Napoleon to the imperial throne. He referred to the Battle of Marengo for the rest of his life as an example of the power of his will to triumph over adversity in fulfilling his destiny.

The significance Napoleon placed on the outcome of this campaign was appropriate considering the uncertainties surrounding him at this time. The successful coup d'état of 9–10 November 1799 had left Gen. Napoleon Bonaparte first consul and virtual ruler of France, but it was a France beset internally by civil and economic strife and externally by hostile powers committed to destroying the country's revolutionary spirit.

FIRST CONSUL

The internal problems facing First Consul Bonaparte were the lack of a cohesive central administration, the poor condition of the economy, and a people worn out by nearly a decade of war. Externally, Napoleon faced the active opposition of England and the Holy Roman Empire—or at least the Austrian Hapsburg regime dominating that Empire—as well as the latent hostility of most of the rest of Europe.

For Bonaparte to consolidate his position of power and to increase his control he needed an extended period of peace in which to devote his energies to the internal stabilization and recovery of the country. His peace overtures to England and Austria did not bring the results he desired. The Austrians, in particular, took advantage of France's difficulties and her resulting military weakness to reconquer nearly all the territory they had lost as a result of Napoleon's first Italian campaign of 1796–1797. Unable to acquire the general peace he needed to resolve the civil problems of France, Bonaparte had no choice but to appeal to his war-weary nation to support yet another series of campaigns.

The First Consul had to levy, equip, and organize the forces needed to deal with the Austrians in Italy while maintaining tight control over the armies, and especially their commanders, already in the field against the forces of Austria and her allies in Germany. He took readily to these tasks, showing by his handling of affairs the touch of the future Emperor. He had demonstrated his tactical and operational virtuosity in his earlier campaigns, but there was still widespread uncertainty among his countrymen about his strategic ability as commander in chief. Failure in the ensuing campaign would probably mean the end of a brief, meteoric, career.

In order to secure and extend his base of power, to acquire the time needed to resolve the internal difficulties ruining France, and to retain the faith placed in him by the people, the campaign of 1800 had to result in victory. Bourrienne, Napoleon's private secretary, wrote: "Bonaparte's fortune was now to depend on the winning or losing of a battle. A battle lost would have dispelled all the dreams of his imagination, and with them would have vanished all his immense schemes for the future of France. He saw the danger, but was not intimidated by it; and trusting to his accustomed good fortune said, 'I have, it is true, many conscripts in my army, but they are Frenchmen. . . . The sun which now shines on us is the same that shone at Arcola and Lodi.' "[2]

THE ARMY OF RESERVE

On 6 May 1800 Napoleon left Paris to take command of a newly formed Army of the Reserve, initially numbering nearly 60,000 men. This newly raised army was deployed in east central France and western Switzerland in the Dijon–Lyon–Geneva area. Although primarily composed of recently conscripted troops and old reservists, Napoleon had built the units around veteran cadres and had seen to it that they were properly outfitted and well equipped. Their morale was basically good. The army was organized by corps, each having elements of all three arms: infantry, cavalry, and artillery. This system was intended to enable each corps to operate independently and to fight a sustained engagement against a superior enemy.

The Army of Reserve had been assembled to make the Austrians believe that it was intended to reinforce the French army already in southern Germany. While Bonaparte considered this option, he was inclined to lead it through Switzerland and—in June, after the snow melted—across five Alpine passes into northern Italy. There he believed more decisive results could be achieved by falling upon the rear of the Austrian Army in Italy, which was poised in the Po River Valley for an offensive against the French Army of Italy. The Austrian army, nearly 100,000 strong, was commanded by Gen. Michael Melas. The French Army of Italy, roughly 36,000 men, commanded by Gen. André Masséna, held a thin strip of land along the coast of the Gulf of Genoa from Genoa in the east to the French frontier near Nice.

Bonaparte's intention to use the Army of Reserve in Italy had been solidified in early April when he learned that on the sixth General Melas had launched a surprise offensive against Masséna. By the time he reached Geneva a month later, Napoleon knew that the Austrian offensive had been very successful. Masséna's army had been split in two; with fewer than 15,000 men Masséna had been driven back into Genoa, where he was beseiged by the Austrians. The remainder of the Army of Italy, commanded by Gen. Luis Suchet, had been driven back almost to Nice, just inside the French frontier. This left Masséna completely isolated, invested by Austrian troops on land and blockaded by a British fleet in the Gulf of Genoa.

ACROSS THE ALPS

This turn of events forced Bonaparte to hasten preparations for the invasion of Italy. He would have to move before his army was completely prepared, cross the Alps before the snows had melted, and debouch from the passes without time for adequate reconnaissance into hostile territory.

Melas' attention, however, was focused on Masséna in Genoa and Suchet in Nice. Advancing through the closest pass, the Great Saint Bernard, Bonaparte led his army across the Alps with almost suspicious ease. The stubborn resistance of the Austrian garrison in Fort Bard delayed the passage of his artillery, but by 24 May elements of two French corps held

Ivrea in the valley of the Po River. Pushing aside scattered resistance by surprised Austrian troops, Bonaparte quickly moved to sever Melas' communications at Milan.

LOMBARDY

When he reached Milan on 5 June, Bonaparte learned through captured Austrian dispatches that Masséna had surrendered Genoa the previous day—a serious setback since this released over 20,000 Austrians to rejoin Melas' main body, now in the Turin–Alessandria area.

Bonaparte feared that the Austrians might fall back on Genoa instead of trying to reopen their lines of communication to Austria through Lombardy, thus thwarting his anticipation of a quick and decisive victory. Therefore he decided to advance and seek an engagement as soon as possible.

Leaving one corps to hold northern Lombardy and his line of communications back to France, Bonaparte marched rapidly south from Milan with three corps—Lannes, Victor, and Desaix—totaling about 30,000 men. His objective was to reach and to block the road between Alessandria and Genoa before Melas could use that road to make good his escape. Scraps of information seemed to confirm his estimate that the Austrians would try to escape to the south.

In fact, Melas had very different intentions. He knew that General Suchet, with the remnants of the Army of Italy, had begun a rapid advance eastward from Nice, with the apparent intention of joining Bonaparte's Army of Reserve somewhere north of Genoa. Melas, having much superior cavalry, had been able to obtain better information about the French than they had about his army. He very commendably decided that he would attack Bonaparte, defeat him, and then turn to drive Suchet back to Nice. By 12 June he was assembling about 34,000 troops in Alessandria, in anticipation of advancing eastward to meet Bonaparte. Meanwhile, Lannes' corps, leading the French advance, had advanced beyond Tortona and had become aware of the Austrian concentration in Alessandria. He at once reported this to Bonaparte.

On the thirteenth Bonaparte pushed Victor's corps through Lannes to spearhead an advance westward on Alessandria. Lannes followed close behind. Bonaparte, still expecting Melas to try to escape southward from Alessandria, ordered Desaix's corps, somewhat scattered by the rapidity of the advance, to march south and west through Tortona and Rivalta to block the Alessandria–Genoa road further south. He sent one of Lannes' divisions to block the road leading north from Alessandria in the event Melas tried to escape toward the Po River. At dusk the leading elements of Victor's corps skirmished with elements of Melas' army east of the Bormida River, which flowed north just east of Alessandria and west of the town of Marengo.

MARENGO: PHASE ONE

Although Melas was surprised by the unexpectedly rapid arrival of the French in the vicinity of Alessandria, he was well aware that his 34,000 troops were numerically superior to the forces Bonaparte had available. He ordered an attack against Bonaparte for the following morning.

At 6:00 A.M. on the morning of 14 June, the Austrian army, now totaling nearly 31,000 men and 100 guns, crossed the Bormida and "awakened [the French] by a reveille of gunfire."[3] (Melas had mistakenly left a garrison of 3000 men in Alessandria.) Confined by the narrow bridgehead on the opposite bank the Austrian attack developed slowly, but by nine o'clock it had gained momentum and crashed down upon the two forward French divisions in Victor's corps in front of the village of Marengo.

Bonaparte, still convinced that Melas was trying to run for Genoa or toward the Po River, considered the attack on Marengo merely an aggressive feint designed to cover the Austrians' real movements. However, as reports on the size and intensity of the Austrian attack came in, Bonaparte finally realized that his assessment of Melas' intentions had been totally incorrect and he quickly realized the seriousness of the situation he was facing. He hurriedly ordered up Lannes' corps to support Victor's line. Victor had about 10,000 men, but detachments had reduced Lannes' strength to about 5000.

Bonaparte sent urgent recall orders to Desaix and to the division he had sent north. That division, however, was too far away to arrive before the fifteenth. Desaix, on the other hand, had heard the sound of the guns and on his own initiative had delayed his march south. Upon receiving the recall, he turned around and marched with all haste back toward Marengo.

Bonaparte arrived on the field around 11:00 A.M. and began to direct the placement of his troops personally. He was particularly concerned about his right flank; a breakthrough there would give the superior Austrian cavalry an opportunity for a deep strike against his line of communications. Fortunately for Bonaparte, however, Melas had received a false report that

General Suchet was advancing on his rear; he detached 2340 cavalry from his attack force, and sent them toward Cantalupo. This reduced Melas' total strength to about 28,500 men.

By 1:00 P.M. one of Desaix's divisions had arrived and Bonaparte placed it on the right of his line. He now had nearly 20,000 men on the field, all committed to the battle. He now anxiously awaited the arrival of the remainder of Desaix's corps, about 5000 men.

By around 2:00 P.M., just as the French right moved to attack Castel Ceriolo, the Austrians took Marengo. Victor's two divisions, low on ammunition and exhausted from having borne the brunt of the enemy offensive, gave way and the Austrians began to surge forward. Soon the whole French line began to waver and by 3:00 P.M. was streaming back toward the village of San Guiliano. With the army falling back in disorder and the Scrivia River at their back, Victor and Lannes concluded that the battle was lost and that retreat was their only option. Bonaparte, however, would not hear of retreat and ordered the army to reform in front of San Guiliano.

MARENGO: PHASE TWO

About this time Desaix rode up and reported to Bonaparte that General Baudet's division was close behind him. When Bonaparte told him the situation, Desaix is reported to have said: "The battle is completely lost; but it is only two o'clock, we have time to gain another today."[4]

By this time Melas also concluded that the battle was won. Tired and lightly wounded, he decided to return to Alessandria for treatment and turned over the pursuit of the French to his chief of staff, General Zach. That officer then began to form up the Austrian units into march columns for the pursuit.

Taking advantage of this lull in the fighting Bonaparte reformed his army west of San Guiliano. As Baudet's division marched up he placed it on the left of the line and massed his remaining artillery into one battery between Victor's and Desaix's corps. Riding among his troops and exhorting them to one final effort Napoleon said: "Soldiers, you have retreated far enough; you know that it is my habit to bivouac on the field of battle." Inspired by their commander's determination and encouraged by the presence of fresh reinforcements, the army renewed its spirit and began to advance.

The Austrians, now moving slowly forward in several ponderous columns, provided excellent targets as the massed French guns tore large holes in their flanks. Desaix's corps, emerging from the smoke, then attacked in oblique order across the front of the Austrian advance, throwing the leading columns into disorder. At the height of this confusion, French general Kellermann charged with 400 cavalry against the flank of the rightmost Austrian column, effectively cutting it in half. Within a few minutes 6000 victorious Austrians found themselves prisoners of war as the remainder of their columns broke and ran. The entire French line now swept forward. Kellermann reformed his cavalry, charged and routed the main body of Austrian cavalry, then joined in the pursuit of the fleeing infantry.

Kellermann's first charge had clinched the battle, turning defeat into complete victory. "A minute earlier, or three minutes later, and the thing could not have succeeded, but the timing was perfect, and North Italy was recovered in that moment for the French Republic."[5] Not only was North Italy secured but so also was Napoleon's political position. The timely arrival of Desaix's corps and the decisive charge by Kellermann had turned a disaster into the victory he so desperately needed. The personal cost, however, was high: The gallant Desaix was killed at the climax of the French victory.

In the subsequent Convention of Alessandria the Austrians agreed to cease hostilities and abandoned all of northern Italy west of the Mincio to the French. It also gave to Bonaparte the period of peace he needed to resolve the internal affairs of France. The victory at Marengo also assured his reputation as a man of destiny and set him firmly on the path to an imperial crown.

Having virtually regained all of northern Italy in one day, Bonaparte returned to Paris.

RISING AND FALLING STAR: THE YEARS BETWEEN

FROM WAR TO PEACE TO WAR

Bonaparte's victory, combined with that of French general Jean Moreau at Hohenlinden later in the year, forced Austria to make peace. A treaty was signed on 9 February 1801. This meant the virtual collapse of the Second Coalition, and a year later—27 March 1802—Britain also made peace in the Treaty of Amiens. Four months later, on 2 August 1802, Napoleon was proclaimed consul for life, making him virtually the king of France.

Peace between France and Britain lasted for little more than a year. In May 1803 the war was renewed with a British blockade of the Continent. Planning to invade England, Bonaparte began to assemble a large army in northern France, centered around the seaport of Boulogne. While this was going on, Bonaparte was crowned Napoleon, Emperor of the French, on 2 December 1804.

British diplomacy soon established the basis for a Third Coalition. The secret alliance of Britain, Austria, Russia, and Sweden began to plan for a massive offensive against France in the fall of 1805. Napoleon, learning of these plans, decided to seize the initiative. On 31 August his Grand Army secretly began to march east and southeast into Germany from its encampments near Boulogne.

ULM

Two days later, unaware of Napoleon's move, the allies began to carry out their own plan. An Austrian army under Field Marshal Karl Mack von Lieberich marched up the Danube Valley from Austria into Bavaria, heading for Ulm. Another Austrian army, commanded by the Archduke Charles, was concentrating at Innsbruck, prepared to move south into Italy. Two Russian armies, some 120,000 men, started to march westward toward Germany. The total allied strength was nearly 300,000, considerably more numerous than the 200,000 in Napoleon's Grand Army. But Napoleon's army was concentrated; the Allies were not.

The French began to cross the Rhine River on 28 September. They reached the Danube on 6 October, behind Mack's army, cutting him and his 50,000 men off completely from Vienna and from the other allied armies. After one weak effort to break out of the encirclement, Mack surrendered on 17 October.

Without delay, Napoleon marched eastward down the Danube Valley, leaving detachments to hold open a secure line of communications to France. He brushed aside Austrian and Russian efforts to stop or delay him and occupied Vienna on 14 November. Then, with about 65,000 men, Napoleon marched north to Brunn, in Moravia. He had deliberately placed himself in the path of a Russian army approaching from the east, with Austrian armies to the northwest and southeast. As he hoped, the allies quickly tried to take advantage of his exposed position.

AUSTERLITZ

On 1 December an Austro-Russian army of 89,000 men was concentrated at Austerlitz, just east of Napoleon's army. The nominal allied commander was Tsar Alexander of Russia; the actual field commander, however, was Russian General Mikhail Kutuzov. Deliberately Napoleon placed his army on low ground and overextended his right flank in plain view of allied scouts on high ground just west of Austerlitz.

As Napoleon expected, shortly after dawn on 2 December 1805, the allies threw about one-third of their army against his right wing, expecting to cut him off from his line of communications with Vienna. However, during the night, the right wing had been reinforced by 8000 additional troops, who had arrived from Vienna under Marshal Davout. Thus, because of effective defense on the French right, the advance of the allied left wing was much slower than they had anticipated. At about 9:00 A.M., as the allies were throwing more men into the attack on his right wing, Napoleon ordered the main body of his army to advance against the allied center, which was soon thrown back and cut off from its left wing. With the allied line thus ruptured, the French quickly encircled the allied left wing, which was soon destroyed as an effective fighting force. Meanwhile, Napoleon's left had slowly driven back the allied right wing. By 4:00 P.M., as the sun began to set, Napoleon had won one of the most decisive victories of history; Austerlitz was a tactical masterpiece worthy of comparison with Arbela, Cannae, and Leuthen.

As a result of this battle Austria capitulated. Alexander of Russia, however, refused to make peace, and his armies sullenly withdrew into Russia. The next year Russia gained an ally. Prussia had previously resisted British diplomatic pressure to join the coalition but now decided to enter the war. In October 1806 Napoleon led his Grand Army north into Prussia. On 14 October, at the twin battles of Jena and Auerstaedt, the Grand Army inflicted crushing defeats on the Prussians. Although the Russians moved quickly to the assistance of their new ally it was too late. On 8 February 1807 the Russians and Prussians fought a drawn battle with Napoleon in a blizzard at Eylau, in East Prussia. But the following spring Napoleon outmaneuvered them, then decisively defeated them at the Battle of Friedland, on 14 June 1807. Less than a month later Alexander of Russia and Frederick William III of Prussia concluded a humiliating peace with Napoleon at the Treaty of Tilsit. Napoleon was now the virtual ruler of Western and Central Europe.

WAR IN THE PENINSULA

Although Britain stubbornly remained at war, most of Europe was at peace under the domination of the French Empire. But the peace did not last long. Napoleon's Continental System—an economic counterblockade against England—was resisted by neutral Portugal, a traditional British ally, which continued to trade with Britain. In November 1807 a French army invaded Portugal. Although the French were initially successful, this action aroused resentment in both Portugal and Spain and was the beginning of seven years of almost constant warfare—the Peninsular War—in the Iberian Peninsula.

Napoleon himself took part in operations in Spain late in 1808 and won several resounding successes. However, events elsewhere forced him to return to Paris and to Central Europe in January 1809. His subordinates in Spain, performing (as he expressed it) like "post-office inspectors," were unable to duplicate his successes. This was in large part due to the fact that they were opposed by one of Britain's greatest generals, Sir Arthur Wellesley, known to history as the Duke of Wellington.

1809 CAMPAIGN

Napoleon had returned to Paris because he had learned that Austria was again about to join England against France. In April the Archduke Charles led an Austrian army into Bavaria. He was initially successful, but Napoleon reached the Danube area on 17 April, took command, and seized the initiative. In a series of lightning blows he defeated the Austrians at Abensberg (19–20 April), Landshut (21 April), Eggmühl (22 April), and Ratisbon (23 April). He then marched east and captured Vienna on 13 May.

On 21–22 May, however, Napoleon suffered his first defeat, when Charles repulsed his attempted crossing of the Danube River at Aspern-Essling. Realizing that he had underestimated his opponents, Napoleon now collected more troops and bridging materials. During the night of 4–5 July he made a successful night crossing of the Danube, then on 5–6 July inflicted a crushing defeat on Charles at the Battle of Wagram. Austria sued for peace once more.

There followed nearly three years of peace in Europe—except for the "Spanish Ulcer." But Napoleon's relations with Tsar Alexander of Russia were deteriorating, and in the spring of 1812 England was able to persuade both Russia and Sweden to leave the Continental System.

1812: INVASION OF RUSSIA

Anticipating this, Napoleon had already begun to collect a large army in Poland, just west of the Nieman River. By late June he had assembled 450,000 men, probably the largest army the world had seen up to that time. Of these, 200,000 were Frenchmen; the remainder were Poles, Prussians, Austrians, other Germans, and Italians. Opposing them in central and western Russia were about 415,000 Russian troops, in three principal armies and a number of scattered detachments.

On 24 June Napoleon's vast host began to cross the Nieman River into Russia, heading toward Moscow. The Russian armies of Prince Barclay de Tolly and Prince Peter Bagration attempted to stop the French at Smolensk on 17 August but were badly defeated and barely escaped destruction. As the Russian armies retreated toward Moscow, Tsar Alexander (probably mistakenly) appointed General Kutuzov to replace Barclay de Tolly as commander in chief. At Borodino, on the Moscova River, on 7 September Kutuzov attempted to stop Napoleon, and again the Russians were defeated in a close, bitterly contested battle. A week later Napoleon entered Moscow, which had been set on fire by the retreating Russians.

Napoleon now expected that Alexander would make peace, but the Russian emperor refused his offers. With little food or other provisions in burnt-out Moscow and with winter approaching, Napoleon now knew that he would have to withdraw. He left Moscow on 19 October.

The retreat was a disaster. It began with a drawn battle against Kutuzov at Maloyaroslavets on 24 October. He was unable to trap Kutuzov into fighting a decisive battle, and then one of the coldest winters in history closed in on central Russia. The march was impeded by a combination of snow and bitter cold. Surrounded by swarms of regular and irregular Russian forces, the freezing, starving Grand Army, all of its commissariat broken down, marched through snow to disintegration. Nevertheless, a semblance of order was maintained by Napoleon and his best corps commanders. With only a handful of effective troops, he broke through when Kutuzov tried to cut him off at Krasnoi on 16–17 November. A few days later Napoleon, with only 37,000 men still in fighting condition (accompanied by perhaps 100,000 demoralized refugees), was cornered on the east bank of the unfordable Berezina River by two of Kutuzov's contingents totaling 144,000 men. Again the Emperor showed his undiminished battlefield genius. For three days—26–28 November—he held off the Russians while his engineers built bridges across the half-frozen river, then made a successful fighting withdrawal. As the sad remnants of his army approached the Polish frontier, Napoleon left and traveled rapidly back to France to raise a new army.

1813 CAMPAIGN

Early the following year first Prussia, then Austria, deserted Napoleon's cause and joined his enemies. Nevertheless, with a newly raised army, he marched back into central Germany and won a number of victories over the much more numerous allied armies of Russia, Prussia, and Sweden. But none of his victories was decisive. This was due not only to the superior strength of his enemies but also to the fact that they had learned from him the new methods of war he had introduced in 1796. None could match his genius, but their soldiers and their officers were now as good as his—and there were many more of them. Finally, outnumbered two to one and facing enemies to whom he had taught his system of war (including former French Marshal Bernadotte, now Crown Prince of Sweden), Napoleon was defeated at Leipzig in the three-day "Battle of the Nations," 16–19 October. Despite heavy losses, Napoleon withdrew in good order from the battlefield and marched back to France to prepare for the inevitable allied invasion.

VICTORY TO DEFEAT: 1814

THE EMPEROR AT BAY

When Napoleon reached Paris early in November 1813, he realized that the allies would certainly continue their offensive west of the Rhine and invade France. He hoped, however, that they would first go into winter quarters and give him time to rebuild the French army. He also counted on differences of opinion between the allied monarchs and disagreements among their military commanders to delay their advance and to prevent effective cooperation.

There were, as Napoleon expected, prolonged and heated arguments among the allied leaders. Prussian Field Marshal Blücher, Russian Tsar Alexander, and the English insisted that France should be invaded immediately. Austrian General Schwarzenberg, however, demanded a halt to give rest to his worn-out army. Finally the Austrian general agreed to an

all-out offensive without further delay. The objective would be the defeat
and overthrow of Napoleon and reduction of France to her 1789 frontiers.

The situation facing Napoleon was bleaker than any he had ever known.
The last two campaigns had seriously drained France's available manpower. The defection of the German Allies and the continuing campaigns
in the Peninsula also contributed to the lack of experienced combat troops
in the French army. Napoleon was forced to call up levies of conscripts
before they reached the minimum age for service. These young troops
(named Marie Louises by the older veterans, after Napoleon's second wife),
had no experience and were given little training other than what they
learned on the march or in battle. In one famous incident, Marshal Marmont came upon a Marie Louise who, though in the midst of a battle and
being heavily fired upon, was standing at attention instead of returning fire.
When Marmont asked him "Why don't you fire back?" the conscript
replied "I would do so gladly if someone would show me how to load my
musket." Marmont quietly loaded it for him.

For a variety of reasons, in his two previous campaigns Napoleon had
been plagued by the problem of a weak cavalry arm. This was still true in
1814. The lack of cavalry meant that he would have to fight the campaign
not only without the capability for efficient reconnaissance and screening
but also without the rapid strike and pursuit capability upon which he had
relied heavily in earlier campaigns.

In addition to the dubious quality of his enlisted men, Napoleon also had
to deal with the quality and morale of his officers. Most of his line officers
were veterans recently promoted from the ranks. Although experienced
and fiercely devoted to the Emperor, they lacked education and leadership
experience. While the ability of his senior commanders was not in question, their dedication was. Most of the marshals had been serving Napoleon
for almost twenty years. They were tired of war and desired nothing more
than to retire and live the remainder of their lives in well-earned peace and
quiet. They would of course fight for Napoleon and to defend their country,
but for the most part they were uninspired and had little hope of winning.
Further, some of his better marshals (and some of his best troops) were not
available for the campaign. Davout was blockaded in Hamburg, Oudinot
and Soult were defending the southwestern borders of France against
Wellington.

The French people were also at their breaking point. The disastrous
campaigns of 1812 and 1813 had drained the country of finances as well as

manpower, and with the armies of all Europe now approaching their borders, the French were eager for peace.

Last, there was Napoleon himself. After ten years of Empire his will was more resolute and determined than ever and he could not admit his fallibility. The campaigns of 1812 and 1813 had taught him nothing in that he still obsessively clung to his faith in his "star" and the belief that he would be victorious in the end. He was not as physically fit as he had been in earlier years, but health did not seriously interfere with his command performance. He had lost, however, some of the driving, tireless energy that had contributed so much to earlier victories.

In November 1813 the Allies had offered generous terms of peace that would allow France to retain her "natural" frontiers of the Rhine River, the Alps, and the Pyrenees. Napoleon, trying to buy time, waited until December to reject the offer. In writing to his plenipotentiary, General Caulaincourt, Napoleon stated: "I myself desire [peace] but only on honorable and lasting terms. France without its natural boundaries, without Ostend, without Antwerp could no longer take its place among the other powers of Europe. . . . Do they wish to confine France to its ancient borders? They are mistaken if they think the miseries of war can make the nation desire such a peace. . . . The deprivations of the Cossacks will drive the people to arms and double our numbers. If the nation supports me the enemy marches to his doom. If fortune betrays me my resolution is taken; I will degrade neither the nation nor myself by accepting dishonorable terms."[6] Napoleon would later try to make peace on these same terms but by then it was too late.

INVASION OF FRANCE

The allied armies—Prussians, Austrians, Bavarians, Russians, and Swedes—began crossing the Rhine on 1 January 1814. Opposed to Napoleon's 118,000 men, they had approximately 350,000, divided into three main forces converging on Paris: 210,000 under Schwarzenberg advancing through northern Switzerland; 75,000 under Blücher, crossing the Rhine near Mainz; and about 65,000 under Bernadotte advancing through Belgium. There were about 90,000 additional French troops opposing Wellington in Spain and another 50,000 under Eugene holding northern Italy.

Blücher's advance toward the Meuse River and Schwarzenberg's march through Switzerland toward Langres revealed the allied war plan to Napoleon. He remained in Paris but directed Marmont and Macdonald to operate against Blücher, while Victor, Ney, and Mortier were to oppose Schwarzenberg. Meanwhile Augereau was to organize a new army at Lyons, to be used later against Schwarzenberg's line of communications.

The first operations were disappointing to Napoleon. The French marshals retreated too quickly before Blücher; the open cities in eastern France surrendered without resistance. The population had obviously been affected by clever allied propaganda that promised the French people liberation from Napoleon and assured them of the friendliness and strict discipline of allied troops. The effect of this propaganda, however, was very soon dispelled by the brutality of the Prussian and Bavarian soldiers. The French populace responded by ambushing stragglers and isolated allied detachments and by organizing partisan bands to harass the invaders.

LA ROTHIERE

On 25 January 1814 Napoleon left Paris for the front and on 30 January he attacked Blücher at La Rothiere. The Prussian was marching from the east toward Paris, ahead of Schwarzenberg. Napoleon forced the Prussians out of Brienne and La Rothiere. However, Blücher was reinforced by Bavarian and Russian troops and counterattacked on 1 February. With more than a two-to-one superiority, Blücher forced Napoleon to retreat. Each side lost about 6000 men, and Napoleon had to abandon fifty guns. He withdrew to Troyes to reorganize his army. The allies were too battered to pursue.

The allies now decided to march straight on Paris. Blücher with 57,000 men would move along the south bank of the Marne River, while Schwarzenberg with 150,000 advanced along both banks of the upper Seine. But Napoleon, noting that Blücher's army was spread out, concentrated for a quick blow.

NAPOLEON AT HIS BEST

On 10 February Napoleon struck Blücher's left flank at Champaubert, about sixty miles from Paris. He destroyed one of Blücher's corps, then boldly placed himself in the center of Blücher's army, leaving the Prussian main body actually closer to Paris than he was. On the eleventh he struck westward against Blücher's main body at Montmirail, inflicting a sharp defeat. The Prussians hastily withdrew northeastward across the Marne

River in order to regain contact with the Allied line of communications. They had lost 7000 men and 20 guns against 2500 French casualties.

Napoleon was about to turn against Schwarzenberg when he learned from Marmont that Blücher had halted his retreat and was again moving west. The Emperor decided to finish with Blücher first and instructed Marmont to lure him back toward Montmirail. On 14 February Napoleon struck and destroyed the Prussian advance guard at Vauchamps. Blücher tried to retreat. But while Napoleon attacked him from the front, blasting him with artillery and enveloping his right flank, Marshal Emmanuel Grouchy's cavalry swung behind the Prussians and blocked their retreat.

Blücher was saved from complete destruction only because Grouchy's artillery had not been able to keep up, on account of deep mud. But the Prussian breakthrough to the rear was difficult and costly. During the whole operation Blücher lost 7000 men, 16 guns, and most of his supply trains, against 600 French casualties.

Napoleon left the pursuit of the Prussians to his subordinates and turned south against Schwarzenberg, who had been steadily marching west toward Paris. During 17–18 February, Napoleon drove the Austrian army south across the Seine in a number of separate engagements. The most serious of these took place on 18 February at Montereau, where two stone bridges crossed the Seine and Yonne rivers. Napoleon personally directed the action, which resulted in the capture of the bridges undamaged. The allies lost 5000 men and 15 guns against 2500 French casualties.

Schwarzenberg promptly retreated to Troyes. Napoleon pursued vigorously and "in this situation," as Yorck von Wartenburg (son of the Prussian general who fought in the Napoleonic wars) dryly reports in his brilliant analysis of Napoleon's genius, "Schwarzenberg decided upon a retreat behind the Aube, since he only had a superiority of two to one, with which to face the Emperor in person."[7]

In the meantime, with Napoleon gone, Blücher had resumed his westward advance. The Prussians had reached Mery on the Seine when Blücher learned of the Austrian retreat. Boldly he marched due west, reaching La Ferte, only twenty-five miles from Paris, on 27 February. Napoleon, concerned about the safety of the capital, hastened northward with about 30,000 men, leaving about the same number opposite Schwarzenberg's 120,000. Napoleon reached the Marne opposite the Prussians on 1 March, joining the two corps of Mortier and Marmont, which gave him a force of about 60,000 men. After a brief engagement, Blücher, who had almost

100,000, decided to retreat northward to Soissons. It was at about this time that Blücher is reputed to have said that the mere presence of Napoleon on the battlefield was worth at least 40,000 men.

Napoleon's pursuit was delayed some sixteen hours because the Prussians had destroyed the bridges over the Marne and the Aisne. This gave Blücher time to retreat through Soissons. Napoleon found an undamaged bridge at Berry and crossed the Aisne in pursuit of Blücher. On 7 March he appeared unexpectedly at Craonne, where he defeated an isolated Russian corps. However, the Russians fought with typical tenacity, and the French suffered 5400 casualties compared to an allied loss of 5000.

POSTPONING THE INEVITABLE

Blücher now concentrated his remaining 85,000 men around Laon. Unaware of Blücher's actual strength, Napoleon rushed toward Laon only to find the enemy strongly entrenched. All French probing attacks were repulsed. Blücher, realizing that he had a great numerical superiority, was about to attack, then thought better of it. It was a stalemate, but Napoleon could afford nothing less than victory. He withdrew in the evening of 10 March toward Soissons, where he reorganized his force.

In the meantime, Schwarzenberg, pressed by Emperor Alexander and King Frederick William, reluctantly resumed his advance toward Paris with 90,000 men. He defeated Oudinot and Macdonald near Fere-Champenoise, pushing them back toward the capital.

Though concerned about the failure of his troops north of the Seine to stop Schwarzenberg's advance, Napoleon remained at Soissons to watch Blücher, whom he considered much more dangerous than the Austrian. When one of Blücher's corps captured Reims, Napoleon marched there with lightning speed. He surprised and overwhelmed the Prussians, inflicting 7000 casualties while losing only 700.

The news of Napoleon's victory at Reims temporarily stunned his enemies. Schwarzenberg halted his advance. Blücher, who had moved west to Compiègne on the Aisne, hastily retreated to Laon and went on the defensive.

From Reims, Napoleon was in position to threaten both Blücher's left flank and Schwarzenberg's right. He decided to move south against Schwarzenberg. He planned to get behind the Austrian and to strike a decisive blow against his line of communications. But at the news of

Napoleon's approach on 17 March Schwarzenberg began a retreat toward Troyes. Since Napoleon probably had no more than 30,000 men and Schwarzenberg had about 100,000, this was an amazing situation.

After nearly two months of campaigning, the allies had been unable to make any progress toward Paris. Tsar Alexander called an allied council of war to seek ways of making their nearly four-to-one superiority prevail over Napoleon. At the meeting the allied monarchs and generals read some intercepted dispatches from Paris. These reported that the French capital was indefensible and that allied propaganda had completely demoralized the war-weary Parisians.

THE END OF THE LINE

Meanwhile Napoleon had reached Schwarzenberg's line of communications at St.-Dizier, where he was preparing his decisive blow. But both Blücher and Schwarzenberg, recognizing the weakness of Paris, suddenly advanced westward on the French capital.

Joseph Bonaparte, who had been left by Napoleon in charge of the defense of Paris, fled as the allies approached. Marshals Mortier and Marmont attempted to defend the city. On 29 March the allies began disconnected attacks on the northern suburbs. After a gallant fight Mortier and Marmont, badly outnumbered, surrendered Paris and withdrew south.

Napoleon rushed to Fontainebleau, where he concentrated 60,000 troops. But while he was planning an attack on the allies in Paris, his marshals mutinied. They refused to fight further and demanded his abdication. Napoleon met this last blow with calm and resignation; on 6 April he agreed to abdicate. When the allies refused to accept his abdication in favor of his three-year-old son, he abdicated unconditionally on 11 April 1814.

THE HUNDRED DAYS

TO ELBA AND RETURN

Under the peace terms, Louis XVIII (younger brother of Louis XVI) became king of France and Napoleon went into exile on the island of Elba. But a little more than ten months later, on 1 March 1815, Napoleon and a handful of supporters landed at Cannes on the Mediterranean coast of

France. He marched to Paris, gathering adherents as he went. Several contingents of French troops were sent to oppose and capture him, but they could not resist the magic of his personality and joined him. On 20 March he arrived in Paris (whence Louis XVIII had fled) and resumed his imperial throne.

While Napoleon mobilized France, four allied armies were put in motion against him. By early June an Anglo-Dutch army of 95,000 men, under the Duke of Wellington, and a Prussian army of 150,000, under Marshal Gebhard Blücher, were assembled in southern Belgium, awaiting the arrival of Austrian and Russian armies.

TO LIGNY AND QUATRE BRAS

On 14 June—the fifteenth anniversary of Marengo—Napoleon joined his Army of the North, 124,000 men secretly assembled just south of the Belgian frontier. The next morning he marched north into Belgium with a campaign plan strikingly similar to that which had brought him his first victories in Italy in 1796. He thrust his army between the dispersed armies of the Duke of Wellington and Blücher, intending to concentrate first against the Prussians and then against the English and Dutch.

It came very close to success. The allies were completely surprised. With two-thirds of his army Napoleon defeated Blücher at Ligny on 16 June. But Marshal Ney, commanding the French left wing, was dilatory. He failed to smash Wellington, who had a portion of his army exposed at Quatre Bras, before the arrival of British reinforcements halted the French attack.

Wellington retreated north during the night and received a message from Blücher. Although the Prussian had been defeated and had himself been seriously injured, elderly Marshal "Vorwarts" assured his colleague that he would collect his troops and join forces with Wellington.

WATERLOO

Napoleon, with the main part of his army, pursued Wellington and sent Marshal Grouchy with his right wing to pursue the Prussians. But Grouchy was even more dilatory than Ney had been the previous day. As a result, Blücher was able to assemble most of his army by late on 17 June. Leaving one corps to hold off Grouchy, early on the eighteenth Blücher marched northwest with more than 60,000 men to join Wellington, as he had promised.

Meanwhile, Napoleon had prepared to attack Wellington's army, in defensive position south of Waterloo. Napoleon had 72,000 men; Wellington had 68,000. A violent rainstorm during the night made it difficult for cavalry and horse-drawn artillery to move across the soggy ground. So Napoleon did not attack until noon, when the ground had partially dried. About 1:00 P.M. the leading elements of the Prussian army began to appear on the right flank of the French army.

By 4:00 P.M. the Anglo-Dutch army had been pushed back all along the line, and the time was ripe for Napoleon to throw in his reserves to complete the victory. But he had no reserves. He had been forced to divert them to cover his right flank as the Prussian army began to attack from the east. The battle continued for four more hours, as Napoleon endeavored to defeat Wellington while holding off Blücher. But the task was impossible, as more and more Prussians arrived on the field. At dusk (about 9:00 P.M.) Wellington counterattacked, while Blücher threw in his last reserves. The French army collapsed into a mob of refugees, harassed through the night in their flight by the Prussians.

Napoleon abdicated again on 21 June and surrendered to the British. He was taken by British warship to his second and last island exile on St. Helena. There he died 5 May 1821.

ASSESSMENT

Why was Napoleon defeated in the battles he lost? Why did he lose his last four campaigns? Could he have won any or all of these battles or campaigns? If he was the military and intellectual genius he is reputed to have been, how and why did he lose his empire not just once, but twice?

There are no easy or unequivocal answers to any of these questions. We shall return to them after having analyzed, in some detail, the two campaigns to which primary attention has been devoted in the earlier portion of this chapter.

MARENGO

General Desaix—who might have been the greatest of all of Napoleon's subordinates had he survived Marengo—was correct in his assessment of the first six hours of that battle, before he arrived. Bonaparte had been defeated, but there was time to fight another battle.

The French defeat in the first phase of the Battle of Marengo was due primarily to Bonaparte's faulty assessment of the intentions of his opponent. The secondary reason was that, due to this misperception, he allowed himself to enter combat against a force with substantial numerical superiority and as a consequence was surprised by both his enemy's intentions and strength.

However, Bonaparte's genius was never more in evidence after he finally realized that he was facing the entire Austrian army. He refused to acknowledge defeat by retreating as his generals advised. Rather, he chose to break contact and fall back to a new position, trading space for time, until his reserves could reach the field. His dispositions had been such that he had available most of the rest of his army as a reserve to redress the numerical odds against him. Making the best possible use of this reserve, he quickly mounted a counterattack that caught the Austrians unprepared, surprising them far more than they had surprised him in the morning. Inspired by the presence of their commander and heartened by his infectious confidence and determination, the French army rallied and surged forward. The courage and initiative of Desaix and Kellermann were instrumental in exploiting this confusion and turning a victorious Austrian pursuit into a headlong rout. It was primarily to these two officers that Bonaparte owed the victory at Marengo. But they, of course, were inspired by him.

Marengo became an omen of good fortune to Napoleon; he referred almost mystically to its significance during the remainder of his life. Friedland, another climactic victory, was fought seven years later on the anniversary of Marengo and reassured Napoleon, in his own mind, that he would inevitably be successful on the fourteenth of June.

Napoleon's fixation with Marengo reached its peak while he was dictating his memoirs to Las Cases while in exile on St. Helena. In recounting the battle, he made it appear that Desaix's role was part of his overall strategy and that he had ordered Kellermann's charge. Marengo was to be his victory and not that of anyone else. Yet, in justice to Napoleon, the exaggeration was not great. He had disposed his forces so that Desaix could converge on the battlefield, wherever the battle might occur. And he had placed Kellermann on the battlefield in such a position that the cavalryman would have been derelict had he failed to charge.

1814

The reasons for Napoleon's defeat in 1814 can be divided almost equally among circumstances beyond his control, those he could influence, and some failures of command.

Overpowered by Superior Numbers The odds against Napoleon in 1814 were, quite simply, too great for even a general of his genius to overcome. The allies outnumbered him in men and guns by more than three to one. By the end of the campaign it was more than four to one. While the allies could replace their losses, notably the regeneration of Blücher's army after Napoleon's stunning victories in early February, the French could not. On top of this was the fact that Napoleon got precious little help from the French populace even though the war was being fought on their home soil. He had counted too much on a "popular uprising" to repel the invaders when he laid his plans for the campaign. Even if the French had risen up, however, their effectiveness would have been of dubious quality against the allied armies.

Then there was the problem of finances. The treasury was barely able to provide even the most basic equipment for the army. For the want of a simple bridging train Napoleon missed three major opportunities to inflict decisive defeats on his enemies, thereby nullifying his prior successes.

Unfavorable environment Weather also played a significant role in Napoleon's defeat. Snow and fog prevented effective reconnaissance at both La Rothiere and Laon with almost disastrous consequences. Snow and rain consistently turned into quagmires the roads essential for Napoleon's strategy of quick maneuver, causing serious delays and resulting in the exhaustion of his troops.

Inferior-Quality Forces Napoleon's army in 1814 was not what it once had been or what he needed it to be to win. The quality of his troops—including some senior commanders—was poor overall. Although the Marie Louises learned quickly and fought bravely, their lack of training and experience was a major drawback. They did not have the stamina for the long marches on empty stomachs that Napoleon demanded of them and their morale was easily shaken. Desertion added to the attrition of casualties, resulting in a steady decline of vital fighting strength.

The most serious problem was the lack of good cavalry. Napoleon was often without necessary intelligence vital to his plans and more often than not relied on his own instincts to tell him what the enemy might attempt.

Troop and Commander Fatigue Lack of replacements forced Napoleon to use every soldier to the limit of endurance. Constant marching and fighting with little food steadily wore down the combat effectiveness of his men. It was due to Napoleon's presence, his victories, and the soldiers' love for him that the army kept moving. His commanders, on the other hand, were becoming less and less capable of carrying out their duties because of the constant strain and exhaustion produced by the rigors of the campaign.

Failure of Command Napoleon's failure of command resulted directly from his overbearing force of will; his will distorted his perception of the situation and clouded his reason. He was surprised and came close to being decisively defeated on two occasions because he underrated the capability of his enemies and overrated his own abilities.

He rejected more than reasonable terms for peace in November because he had deluded himself into believing that France would not accept such a "dishonorable settlement" and that he could snatch victory from impending disaster, as he had so many times before. His faith in himself was such that twice more during the campaign he rejected peace settlements that would have left him the ruler of the largest nation in Europe west of Russia.

His will, apparently confirmed by brilliant victories against tremendous odds, caused him to ignore the inevitable. Even when Paris surrendered and his marshals rebelled against him Napoleon could not face the truth and acknowledge that he had been defeated by his political and military mistakes rather than some unquestionable weakness and disloyalty among his generals.

Napoleon, though heavily outnumbered and with little support from his government and people, fought what was perhaps the most brilliant campaign of his career. He demonstrated that his military genius had not dimmed and was in fact as strong as ever. His boast to Fouché after the victory at Reims, "I am still the man I was at Wagram and Austerlitz," was essentially correct. Unfortunately, his humility and reason were not equally good.

THE QUESTIONS

Why was Napoleon defeated in the battles he lost? There is no single answer to this question. Each of the four battles lost—Aspern-Essling, Leipzig, La Rothiere, and Waterloo—was *sui generis*. However, it is probably fair to state that in each case the several reasons, widely varying though they were, included three that were common: (1) He overreached; (2) He underrated his opponents; and (3) His perception of reality was to some extent distorted by self-delusion. Or, in other words, a combination of self-confidence, belief in his "star," and stubbornness led him to attempt to do more than was reasonably possible under the circumstances.

Why did he lose his last four campaigns? Again, in addition to reasons unique to each of these campaigns, common to all four were the same three military reasons common to the lost battles. But political reasons were more important than military reasons in the loss of these four campaigns. One political reason was common to three of them, and another political reason was the principal determinant of the outcome of the fourth. His enemies still so feared and respected him that, by relatively modest political compromise, he could have avoided embarking on the campaigns of 1812, 1813, and 1814, or could have negotiated favorable peace terms while they were in progress, at almost any time before these campaigns were irretrievably lost militarily. As to the Waterloo Campaign, political compromise was probably impossible. And had he won militarily in June 1815 (which might have been possible) the array of enemies was such that he almost certainly would eventually have been overwhelmed.

Could he have won any or all of these battles or campaigns? Militarily he probably could not have won the campaigns of 1812, 1813, or 1814. His enemies were too strong, and though none of them were in his class as generals, they had learned enough from him to use those odds to assure eventual victory. Paradoxically the Waterloo campaign, where political compromise was probably impossible, might have been won militarily. But had it been won, he would inevitably have been overwhelmed later when the Russians and Austrians arrived.

Could not a man of true genius have avoided these defeats? Of Napoleon's genius there can be no doubt. However, one of his greatest strengths was, again paradoxically, his greatest weakness. A man of iron will and determination who had combined intellect and skill with this determination to achieve successes probably beyond the reach of any other man of his times, he had come to believe that it was always possible to repeat Marengo. No matter how desperate the situation, even if he had actually been defeated, he felt confident that skill, intellect, and—above all—determination, could overcome the greatest odds. He believed himself to be superhuman. He was not.

Chapter 8

Grant and Lee in Defeat and Victory

At midnight 3 May 1864, the Union Army of the Potomac, concentrated in the Culpeper triangle between the Rappahannock and Rapidan rivers, moved southeastward toward Germanna and Ely's Fords over the Rapidan. That army consisted of a cavalry corps under Maj. Gen. Philip H. Sheridan and four infantry corps: Maj. Gen. Winfield S. Hancock's II Corps, Maj. Gen. Gouverneur K. Warren's V Corps, Maj. Gen. John Sedgwick's VI Corps, and Maj. Gen. Ambrose G. Burnside's IX Corps. The army's total strength was slightly less than 105,000 officers and men.

Some of these veterans had previously followed five generals south of the Rappahannock and Rapidan only to meet defeat each time.[1] This new man, Grant, had made quite a reputation for himself out West. Yet Pope had had the same recommendation. Was there any reason to think that Grant would do any better than the others when he found himself up against the first team—Lee and the Army of Northern Virginia?

The veterans realized, of course, that the commander of the Army of the Potomac was still Maj. Gen. George Gordon Meade, who had been in command for ten months, since the eve of Gettysburg. But they knew that the new General-in-Chief, Ulysses S. Grant, was accompanying the army, and they correctly sensed that Grant would be making all the fundamental decisions about where, when, and how the army would operate and be committed to battle.

Of course they did not know (nor was there any need for them to know) why Grant was accompanying the Army of the Potomac instead of staying in Washington as his predecessor, Maj. Gen. Henry W. Halleck, had done. Nor did they know how their operations fitted into the big picture of the war as envisaged by Grant.

Grant's overall plan was for a coordinated offensive around the entire periphery of the Confederacy. Taking advantage of the numerical superiority of the Union armies, pressure was to be maintained all along the line. This would prevent the Confederates from shifting reserves to oppose the two principal operations. These were the pincers of a vast strategic double envelopment to be undertaken by Meade's Army of the Potomac in the north, east of the Appalachians, and by the small group of armies around Chattanooga under Maj. Gen. William Tecumseh Sherman farther south and west of the mountains.

Grant viewed the Army of the Potomac as the pivot of maneuver around which Sherman and the various smaller Union forces were to operate. Meade's army was to engage Lee's Army of Northern Virginia, fighting it relentlessly until it was destroyed in battle, dispersed, or forced to surrender. But Grant knew from Meade's performance at Gettysburg and afterward that he could not oppose Lee in offensive operations on equal terms. Meade was a competent but unimaginative commander. He was still too respectful of Lee's reputation and unquestioned prowess to press the battle with the ruthless vigor Grant knew would be required if Lee were ever to be defeated. Grant had decided, therefore, to place his command post with the Army of the Potomac and directly supervise that army's operations. He knew that he could keep in communication by telegraph with the other armies just as well from the field as he could in Washington. Issuing orders directly to Meade and meticulously respecting the chain of command within the Army of the Potomac, Grant could make the on-the-spot decisions necessary to carry the fight to Lee and the Army of Northern Virginia in the way Grant wanted it done.

His scheme of maneuver was simple. He and the Army of the Potomac would go around Lee's right flank and attempt to cut his communications with Richmond. Whether or not he accomplished this, Grant felt that by continuously turning Lee's right he would eventually force the Southerner either to fight a battle against superior numbers under unfavorable circumstances or be driven into the mountains, where destruction of his army would be inevitable.

Another reason for turning Lee's right would be to ease the Federal supply situation. It would be impossible for the Union troops to live off the wartorn country of central Virginia; Grant intended to obtain logistical support, with the assistance of the navy, from various ports or landings in tidewater Virginia. He abandoned his overland line of communications along the Orange & Alexandria R.R.; the army would carry with it, over the Rapidan, ten days' supply of food and ammunition in a train of about 5000 wagons. Though slowing the advance, this would permit complete freedom of maneuver. He expected that his wagon train would first be replenished from supplies moved by ship to Belle Plain on the Potomac, near Fredericksburg.

When Grant began his advance, Lee's army was still generally in the positions of the Mine Run campaign of late 1863. Lt. Gen. Richard S. Ewell's corps, with its right flank on Mine Run, held the Confederate right; the corps of Lt. Gen. A. P. Hill was on the left, near Orange Courthouse. The corps of Lt. Gen. James Longstreet, recently returned from east Tennessee, was in reserve south of Gordonsville. Lt. Gen. J. E. B. Stuart's cavalry was in the vicinity of Fredericksburg, where forage for the horses was relatively plentiful. A thin screen of pickets observed the Rappahannock and Rapidan fords between Mine Run and Fredericksburg. Lee's effective combat strength was probably about 61,000; Confederate records for the 1864 campaign are most sketchy and unreliable.

Lee, anticipating the direction and route of march of the Union army, made no effort to interfere with the Federal river crossing. Uninterested in partial success or in merely discouraging the Union forces, he realized that he and his men were much more familiar with the area into which the Union army was entering than was Grant or any of his subordinates. This was the Wilderness of Virginia, an area of dense forest and almost impenetrable thicket about ten miles deep extending along the southern bank of the Rapidan roughly from Chancellorsville and Spotsylvania on the east to beyond Mine Run on the west. In this region, where movement off the few miserable roads was difficult in the extreme, a few determined men could easily stop much greater numbers. Lee had conclusively demonstrated that at Chancellorsville.

Lee chose the Wilderness as a battleground deliberately, as always seeking complete victory. If he was surprised by the speed of the Federal advance—the II, V, and VI Corps and much of the train were across the river by evening of 4 May—he was unconcerned by it. His intention was to beat all of Grant's army, not just part of it. In fact, since Longstreet could not arrive until late on the fifth or early on the sixth, Lee had instructed Ewell and Hill, the leading corps commanders, to feel out the Federal advance but to avoid bringing on a general engagement "if practicable."

Shortly after dawn of the fifth, Warren and Hancock (whose corps led the two-pronged Union advance) moved southward from their respective bivouacs in the vicinity of Wilderness Tavern and Chancellorsville. Simultaneously, Ewell's corps resumed its eastward march from Locust Grove up the Orange–Fredericksburg Turnpike. By 7:00 A.M. the Confederate advance guard halted about two miles west of Wilderness Tavern, having sighted columns of Federal troops marching southward across the main road. Ewell immediately formed a line of battle across the road but, mindful of his orders to avoid a general engagement, he reported the situation to Lee and awaited instructions.

The Federals soon simplified Ewell's problem. When scouts reported the Confederate location, Meade ordered Warren to attack in the belief that this was merely a Southern diversion to delay the Union army's advance. Warren's attack was initially successful; Ewell's leading division was put to flight. But the Northerners, unprepared for a counterattack now delivered by the full weight of Ewell's two remaining divisions, were soon thrown back. The Confederates regained their initial positions and both sides entrenched. Sedgwick's corps came up on Warren's right about noon and established a line north of the Turnpike. However, there was no further major action on Ewell's front during the fifth.

Meanwhile, to the south, A. P. Hill had been advancing up the Orange Plank Road. At Parker's Store his scouts ran into part of Wilson's cavalry division, which had been covering the advance of Warren's corps. Hill, also mindful of Lee's instructions, halted, deployed, and reported the situation.

Almost simultaneously the leaders on both sides realized the significance of the action developing along the Plank Road. The Army of the Potomac, astride the Rapidan (Burnside's corps was still on the north bank), was being snubbed in its southerly advance along the axis of the Brock Road. Its right flank was open to attack, and its overwhelming superiority in numbers was unavailing in that tangle of brush where maneuver was practically impossible.

The junction of the Brock and Plank roads had become a key point. Lee ordered Hill to press forward to seize it if this could be done without bringing on a general engagement. Grant watched while Meade ordered

Sedgwick, who had been following Warren, to rush his leading division (Getty's) south past Wilderness Tavern to the same objective. Hancock, farther south, who had already advanced from Chancellorsville to Todd's Tavern, was ordered north up the Brock Road to assist Getty.

Hill's scouting had convinced him that the crossroads was held in strength. He reported that an advance would probably bring on the engagement Lee was anxious to postpone. But the Northerners had no qualms about precipitating a full-scale battle. About midafternoon Hancock, on orders from Grant—through Meade—moved forward from the crossroads, with Parker's Store his objective. But, while waiting for instructions, Hill's men had entrenched. A desperate fight took place in the tangled underbrush on both sides of the Plank Road. It continued until dark, with heavy casualties on both sides but with no advantage gained by either.

Up to this time the Battle of the Wilderness had consisted of two entirely separate engagements within one mile of each other. The dense, junglelike thicket had prevented any effective coordination between the separate elements: Ewell and Warren on the Turnpike in the morning; Hill and Hancock on the Brock Road in the afternoon.

It was a battle between bewildered brigades and regiments and companies, where officers could not see the whole length of their commands; where no one was sure if the men on his right and left were advancing or retreating. Brushfires, ignited by the musketry, smoldered and smoked, still further befogging the contestants. Worse yet, the little, licking flames were roasting helpless wounded men whose thin screams punctuated lulls in the battle din. In one small clearing between two firing lines, a cluster of wounded lying in the matted vines and creepers was swept by a gush of flame that began exploding the paper cartridges in the men's belts, and Yank and Reb alike flung down their arms to rush out and try to drag the unfortunates to safety.

In late afternoon Grant had ordered Warren to send his reserve division (Wadsworth's) to assist Hancock. But Wadsworth's men, hacking their way slowly through the underbrush, guided by compass and the sound of firing, did not reach Hancock's right flank until after dark, when both sides had stopped fighting to try to get some sleep in their shallow trenches and rifle pits.

Grant ordered a general attack to commence at 5:00 A.M. on the sixth. Burnside had crossed the Rapidan with three of his divisions before dark on the fifth and was ordered to fill the gap between Hancock and Warren in time to take part in a coordinated operation. Recognizing that there had been a similar gap in the Confederate line, Grant ordered Burnside to press forward to envelop Hill's left flank and thus split the Confederate army.

Lee had been reasonably satisfied with the results of the battle on the fifth. Longstreet and Anderson's division of Hill's corps were expected to arrive around dawn. Lee planned to pass these fresh troops through Hill's two exhausted divisions on the Plank Road and to envelop the Union left flank.

Sedgwick, Warren, and Hancock attacked promptly at 5:00 A.M., as ordered. But Burnside was not in position and would not reach his assigned starting point until early afternoon. Grant excused the extreme slowness of the IX Corps advance as being due to the denseness of the underbrush through which it had to advance. This dense thicket was to affect all operations during the day, and the fighting consisted of a series of confused and desperate struggles between small groups of men all along the line.

In the north, Ewell's corps had little difficulty in holding its positions astride the Turnpike against the attacks of Sedgwick and Warren. Hancock, however, had better luck in his initial assault, and Hill's troops were thrown back in confusion. Hancock's units pushed slowly after them through the underbrush. As Lee was trying personally to rally his defeated troops, Longstreet's corps swung up the Plank Road, having completed a forty-two-mile march in thirty-six hours.

Lee, who was apparently more perturbed than at any other time in his career, made ready to lead Longstreet's men in counterattack. But the soldiers would have none of it. One of them grabbed his horse's bridle and led the fuming general back down the road while his comrades shouted: "General Lee to the rear! General Lee to the rear!" Others made it clear to the general that they would refuse to move forward while he was there.

Reluctantly acceding to their demand, Lee rode off to find Longstreet, and the leading division deployed to attack the unsuspecting Federals, less than one hundred yards to eastward. Lee found Longstreet just as the attack got started. In the hail of bullets Longstreet pointedly suggested to his commander that if Lee was planning to remain there to direct I Corps, he, Longstreet, would be happy to go to the rear to a safer spot. Lee apparently was touched, amused, and frustrated by the firm solicitude for his safety he had encountered from all ranks of I Corps. But, realizing that no one could conduct a hard-fought tactical battle better than Longstreet, he rode off, confident of success.

Nor was the confidence misplaced. Before noon Hancock's men had been pushed back to their original position and were in danger of being driven through the crossroad. Grant threw one of Burnside's divisions into the fight and ordered Sedgwick and Warren to stop their attacks in order to send assistance if necessary. (All of these orders, of course, were issued through Meade's army headquarters.)

Longstreet, meanwhile, had sent four brigades along an abandoned and unfinished railroad line to strike Hancock's left flank. The attack, a complete surprise, was very successful. As Hancock's left collapsed, Longstreet ordered an advance all along the front. The Federals were pushed back to the crossroads itself. Thoughts of Chancellorsville, and Jackson's flank attack, flashed through the minds of Northerners and Southerners alike. The parallel was to become even closer.

Following his advancing troops toward the crossroads, Longstreet and several other senior officers were suddenly cut down by heavy fire from their right. It was the enveloping force from his own corps, not realizing how the line had advanced and unable to see clearly through the thicket. The situation was soon straightened out, but Longstreet was seriously (some thought fatally) wounded, about two miles from the spot where Stonewall Jackson had been wounded by his own men almost exactly one year earlier.

Longstreet, in dreadful pain, ordered the attack to continue before he was taken to the rear. Lee rode up, and Longstreet insisted upon explaining the situation to his shocked commander. Lee now personally assumed command of the right wing, but the momentum had gone from the attack. The Union troops, still holding grimly to the crossroads, repulsed the renewed Confederate assault, and the fighting ended on the Plank Road around 5:00 P.M.

But Lee thought there might be an opportunity for one more blow against the Union right. Riding north to Ewell's headquarters, he discovered to his great annoyance that early that morning Ewell had received a report from one of his brigadiers, John B. Gordon, that the Federal right extended only half a mile north of the Turnpike and that it was completely unprotected. Ewell and his senior division commander, Jubal Early, did not believe Gordon. So he had not been permitted to attack.

Though it was now nearly sunset, Lee ordered the attack to take place at once. Gordon, supported by another brigade, complied promptly and proved his point, throwing back Sedgwick's right flank in considerable confusion. Sedgwick promptly established a new line, refusing his right flank, but it is impossible to say how far the Southern advance might have gone had it not been halted by darkness.

The terrible Battle of the Wilderness had come to a close. Grant saw no reason to continue the battle on the seventh and prepared for his next move. Lee's army, physically and morally exhausted by the two-day conflict, was thankful for the opportunity to rest and to bury the dead. Both armies' respites were interrupted, however, by efforts to put out the forest fires and to rescue the wounded caught in the flaming underbrush. The Union army had lost 2246 killed, 12,037 wounded, and 3383 missing; there is no record of Confederate casualties, but these could not have totaled less than 12,000 to 14,000.

The question in the minds of officers and men on both sides, as the armies held their lines on the seventh, was what would Grant do now?

Under similar circumstances McClellan, Hooker, and Meade had acknowledged failure or defeat when fought to a standstill by Lee, had withdrawn to lick their wounds, and waited for Lee to assume the initiative. Most Southerners, and not a few Northerners, expected that the same thing would happen this time. There had not yet been an instance of a Northern advance following a great battle on Virginia soil.

But Lee made a different estimate of the situation. An aggressive Union commander would push southeast down the Brock Road, trying to turn the Confederate right flank, and get to more open country where the Northern numerical superiority could be brought to bear. Obviously, this man Grant was aggressive.

Lee therefore ordered his engineers to cut a road through the thicket, parallel to the Brock Road, that would enable his right-flank corps to reach the Shady Grove Church Road to Spotsylvania without having to make a long detour. This would permit Maj. Gen. Richard H. Anderson (who now commanded Longstreet's corps) to march quickly to the vicinity of Spotsylvania Courthouse and block any Union advance down the Brock Road.

On the seventh various reports reached Lee, corroborating his estimate that the Union army would march southeastward. He ordered Anderson to leave his entrenchments after dark, to give his men some rest in the rear, and then to start for Spotsylvania before 3:00 A.M. Lee also alerted Stuart, who had units of Fitzhugh Lee's cavalry division prepare road blocks by felling trees along the Brock Road.

In his Western campaigns, Grant perhaps had had a bit more than his share of good luck. Now was to come the first of three instances of bad luck that would materially affect the 1864 campaign.

Grant had ordered his own army to start moving down the Brock Road, and parallel roads further east, shortly before midnight. Had Anderson waited until three o'clock to move, Warren's V Corps would have been in Spotsylvania three or four hours before the Confederate I Corps could have arrived, and Lee's communications with Richmond would have been cut, perhaps irretrievably. But as Anderson pulled back after dark, he discovered that his proposed rest area was being consumed by a forest fire. So he decided to march directly to Spotsylvania and rest there.

As it turned out, the men would get no rest, but thanks to Lee's foresight, combined with a lucky forest fire and effective delaying tactics by Stuart's cavalry, Anderson reached the Brock Road, two miles west of Spotsylvania, less than five minutes before Warren's advance guard arrived in musket range of the same spot. The Northern infantry were driving Fitzhugh Lee's cavalry screen down the road when they were suddenly taken under fire by Anderson's skirmishers, hastily thrown across the road. The Battle of Spotsylvania had begun.

As the main bodies of their respective corps came up, Anderson and Warren deployed them on both sides of the Brock Road. Both sides promptly entrenched; digging-in had now become an automatic tactical practice in both Northern and Southern armies. Whenever possible the trenches were strengthened by chopping down trees, then earth was thrown on and packed down. If necessary, the trenches were quickly widened and deepened during lulls in the fighting.

Anderson was able to send some reinforcements to Fitzhugh Lee, who was trying to eject Wilson's cavalry division from the village of Spotsylvania. Wilson was driven off toward Fredericksburg as Sedgwick came up from the other direction on Warren's left, extending the Union front. Shortly after noon the two Union corps attacked Anderson, and as additional units of VI Corps came on the field, extending the Federal left, the Confederate position became precarious. But late in the afternoon Ewell arrived to take up position on Anderson's right. This ended the first day's battle, and both sides fell to work in improving and extending their trenches.

Due to the illness of A. P. Hill, Jubal Early had taken temporary command of the Confederate II Corps. Early had hoped to move via the Brock Road to Spotsylvania, not realizing that this had become the principal artery of Union advance. As he approached Todd's Tavern, shortly after noon on the eighth, he ran into Hancock's corps, which had stopped and entrenched there while the Brock Road was blocked by Warren's and Sedgwick's men. After some skirmishing Early withdrew, bivouacking his corps near Shady Grove Church. On the ninth, he moved eastward to

Spotsylvania along the Shady Grove Church Road while Hancock continued down the Brock Road.

On the ninth, Burnside moved southeastward to the Fredericksburg–Spotsylvania road, where he turned right to approach Spotsylvania from the northeast. To meet this threat to his right rear, Lee sent Early to take a position at right angles to Anderson's and Ewell's line. Early, therefore, was facing generally east, from Ewell's right flank to Spotsylvania.

The Confederate line, about four miles long, now took the shape of an inverted V, with Ewell's corps holding the apex. The left flank was on the Po River, here an insignificant stream, and the right was on a minor tributary of the Ny. The battlefield was situated at the eastern extremity of the Wilderness, and though the country was heavily wooded, there were a number of farms and open fields, and the underbrush lacked the junglelike density of the region the armies had just left.

There was no major action on the ninth. During the morning Sedgwick was killed by a Southern sharpshooter and Maj. Gen. H. G. Wright assumed command of the VI Corps. Hancock's corps, moving from Todd's Tavern, probed the Confederate left flank late in the day. Early on the tenth Hancock withdrew north of the Po, behind Warren, the Confederate left following in a brief flurry of activity.

Grant had ordered a coordinated attack of Hancock's, Warren's, and Wright's corps to be mounted at 5:00 P.M. between the Po and the apex of the Confederate vee. But Warren thought he detected a weakness in Anderson's lines and was given permission to attack at four o'clock, before either Hancock or Wright was ready. This attack was repulsed and the idea of a general assault that day given up. Col. Emory Upton, shortly after six o'clock, with two brigades of the VI Corps supported by Mott's division of Hancock's corps, made a carefully prepared assault against the left side of the apex of the vee.

This attack, delivered in a column of short, heavy lines, had great initial success. A considerable stretch of Ewell's line was seized and about 2000 prisoners captured. But Mott, his division halted by heavy artillery fire from the apex of the Confederate position, never came up. Gordon's (formerly Early's) division of Ewell's corps, in reserve just below the apex, counterattacked Upton. A fierce hand-to-hand struggle took place. To try to relieve the pressure on Upton, Grant ordered Hancock, Warren, and Wright to make the general attack previously planned. Launched hastily, this was repulsed at dusk after heavy losses. Upton had to withdraw from his hard-won position under the cover of darkness. The young colonel, seriously wounded, was rewarded by Grant with an immediate promotion to brigadier general. It was after this fierce struggle that the Confederate soldiers, and later the Northerners, began to call Ewell's salient, at the apex, the "Bloody Angle."

There was little action on the eleventh. Burnside, who had been relatively inactive opposite Early, was moved north, to eliminate the gap between his corps and Hancock's and to engage in a major assault on the Bloody Angle, ordered by Grant to take place early on the twelfth. Hancock would make the main effort against the tip of the apex, supported by Burnside and Wright. Hancock's troops were formed in several heavy lines, to attack in mass on a very narrow front: a formation similar to that used so successfully in Upton's much smaller attack of the tenth.

The attack was launched just after 4:30 A.M. and smashed through the apex, virtually destroying one of Ewell's divisions and capturing about 4000 men. Much of the Confederate artillery had been withdrawn during the night in anticipation of another turning movement by Grant, so there must be some doubt whether this violent charge could have been as successful if Confederate infantry had been adequately supported by cannon.

In the excitement and confusion of the struggle, the second and third lines of the attackers became intermingled with the first. They pressed forward, however, to be met by a well-organized and gallantly led counterattack by Gordon's division, again in reserve behind the apex. Though greatly outnumbered, Gordon and his men, observed by General Lee himself, stopped the advance, then threw it back. Assisted by units rushed up from Anderson's and Early's lines, Gordon actually pushed the Northerners right back to the original entrenchments at the apex.

As he was organizing his counterattack, Gordon saw Lee ride up and requested the older general to withdraw from danger. When Lee refused, the men took up the cry shouted by Longstreet's men on the sixth: "General Lee to the rear! General Lee to the rear!" Escorted by a volunteer bodyguard, Lee was hustled from immediate danger.

For the remainder of that foggy, rainy day the Bloody Angle more than earned its name in the most sustained and most desperate hand-to-hand fighting of the war. The Confederates held their original line of entrenchments, with its high parapet of logs and earth. But the Northerners refused to withdraw and stayed on the opposite side of the parapet. Bayonets, pistols, clubbed muskets, and even rocks were the principal weapons. Every time a man tried to fire his piece over the parapet he risked the danger of having his arm grabbed from the other side and of being pulled over bodily.

Grant ordered Warren to attack Anderson's entrenchments to relieve the pressure, but this effort was repulsed. He then planned to move Warren up to join in the attack on the Bloody Angle, but rejected that idea since there were already more Union troops in that small area than could maneuver or properly protect themselves.

Lee, meanwhile, had decided to abandon the Bloody Angle salient; it was now obvious that it could be held only at a fearful cost in Lee's scarcest commodity: manpower. So, during the struggle at the apex, Confederate engineers had labored all day to construct a new line of entrenchments across the base of the salient, just east of the Brock Road.

After dark, as though by mutual agreement, both sides withdrew from the scene of slaughter.

There was no important action on the thirteenth, but Grant was preparing for another assault on the fourteenth. During the night Warren and Wright were to slip quietly out of their entrenchments on the west side of the line, march around behind Hancock and Burnside, and envelop the Southern right flank south of Spotsylvania. Plans were carefully made to permit a surprise attack at 4:00 A.M. on Early's exposed right flank.

Grant now had his second stroke of bad luck. A torrential night-long rain so mired the dark and muddy trails that the head of Warren's corps did not reach its planned position until 5:00 A.M.; Wright's corps arrived several hours later. It was evening before the units were in place and ready to attack, so the assault was called off. By late afternoon the Confederates realized what was happening, and during the night Anderson's corps was rushed over to cover Early's right, south of Spotsylvania.

There was little fighting on the fifteenth, sixteenth, and seventeenth. On the eighteenth, Grant attempted one more effort against the new Confederate entrenchments below the Bloody Angle. This was now the left flank of the Southern line, the armies having almost completely reversed their initial positions. When the attack was repulsed, Grant determined to start south again, around Lee's right.

Grant had intended to continue the battle on the Spotsylvania line. Confederate casualties, he believed, must be as great as his own. He could afford the loss; Lee could not. So, by the grim arithmetic of attrition an unreinforced Lee must finally give up or make a dangerous withdrawal. On the eleventh Grant had written Halleck to the effect, concluding: "I propose to fight it out on this line, if it takes all summer."

But Lee *was* receiving reinforcements. This was because two other, smaller Union armies, which should have kept the Confederates tied down elsewhere, had completely failed in their missions. So Lee might be able to maintain the bloody struggle indefinitely, and Grant had no intention of spending Union lives unless Union objectives could be gained. Consequently he decided to continue southward, in accordance with his original plan, hoping to catch Lee at a disadvantage in the more open terrain nearer Richmond.

Grant's movement was delayed for one day because of a reconnaissance in force carried out by Ewell on the nineteenth, to find out if the Union right flank had been withdrawn, since Lee now expected another of Grant's leap-frog movements around his right. Ewell was repulsed with considerable loss. This was the last action of the Battle of Spotsylvania.

During the twelve days of intermittent combat the Union army had had 14,267 casualties. There is no record of Southern losses, but they lost more than 6000 captured and probably suffered at least another 6000 in killed and wounded.

While the Battle of Spotsylvania had been going on, Sheridan's cavalry corps had been busy elsewhere. Four days after crossing the Rapidan, Sheridan proposed to Grant that his cavalry corps raid south toward Richmond, draw off Stuart, and if possible bring on a cavalry engagement.

Grant agreed, so Sheridan started on 8 May, with slightly more than 10,000 men organized in three divisions: Merritt's, Gregg's, and Wilson's. This operation has been criticized by some military analysts as merely one more useless cavalry raid that deprived both armies of their needed eyes and ears at a time of critical operations. But Sheridan accomplished all of his objectives. As he had predicted, Stuart followed, and three days later, at Yellow Tavern on the outskirts of Richmond, a fierce battle took place between the two cavalry commands. Stuart, outnumbered by about 10,000 to 4500, was defeated, his force was thrown back into the fortifications of Richmond, and he was mortally wounded. This in itself was a fearful blow to Lee and to the South.

Sheridan, realizing that it would be useless to try to storm the now-alerted fortifications of the Southern capital, turned eastward, fought his way across the Chickahominy, and reached Butler's supply base at Haxall's Landing opposite Bermuda Hundred on the thirteenth. Resting men and horses for three days, Sheridan moved out on the seventeenth and rejoined Grant's army in his positions above the North Anna River on the twenty-fourth.

As to whether or not the raid was useless, Grant (a critic of earlier cavalry raids) was satisfied. "Sheridan . . . ," Grant wrote later, "passed entirely around Lee's army; encountered his cavalry in four engagements and defeated them in all; recaptured 400 Union prisoners and killed and captured many of the enemy; destroyed and used many supplies and munitions of war; destroyed miles of railroad and telegraph, and freed us from annoyance by the cavalry of the enemy for more than two weeks."[2]

Meanwhile, Grant began moving south again from the Spotsylvania battlefield after dark on the twentieth. An alert Lee took advantage of more direct roads to the south and reached the railroad at Hanover Junction, just below the North Anna River, early on the twenty-second. The Southerners threw up entrenchments on the south bank of the river, covering the main road and railroad, and awaited the arrival of the Northerners. Union troops reached the river on the twenty-third. For two days Grant probed the Southern defenses, but Lee's position had been too well chosen, and was too well fortified for Grant to attempt a major assault. He decided to continue around Lee's right.

On the twenty-seventh, after a rapid night march the leading elements of the Army of the Potomac began to cross the Pamunkey River at Hanover Town. It was necessary to delay here for two days, while the remainder of the army and the trains crossed the river. On the twenty-eighth Sheridan's cavalry pushed westward, engaging entrenched Confederate cavalry near Haw's Shop. Behind this screen Lee was taking new positions south of Totopotomy Creek, a small stream northeast of Mechanicsville, covering the approaches to Richmond.

On the thirtieth and thirty-first the Northern army felt out Lee's new position, but Grant found it too strong to be assaulted. The night of the thirty-first he shifted his lines southeast to Cold Harbor, again in hopes of being able to turn Lee's right. The Southerners, however, moved with equal promptness. Lee's right was now on the Chickahominy, about three miles from the outermost fortifications defending Richmond. Fighting was sporadic on 1 June, and the men entrenched as both commanders built up their new lines. Grant ordered an assault on June second, believing that the Southerners were spread too thin to stop a determined attack. Though he could no longer get between Lee and Richmond, there seemed to be a good chance of splitting Lee's greatly overextended army by a drive to the Chickahominy from Cold Harbor.

General W. F. Smith, with the XVIII Corps from Butler's Army of the James, about 10,000 men, had just joined the Army of the Potomac.

Smith, with Hancock and Warren, would make the attack at 4:30 A.M. But Hancock's men, making a night march of fifteen miles, were slow in arriving; Smith protested that he had inadequate ammunition and was too weak to attack. Reputedly, Meade commented angrily: "Why in hell did he come at all?" Grant, equally annoyed, had to postpone the attack for twenty-four hours.

The situation early on 2 June had probably been as propitious for a Union attack as at any time during the campaign. Lee had fewer than 40,000 men holding a line about six miles long between the Totopotomy and the Chickahominy. Grant had now been reinforced to more than 100,000, with about 50,000 concentrated on a three-mile front just west of Old Cold Harbor. It is difficult to see how Lee's men, spread out as they were in shallow, unimproved trenches, could have stopped a vigorous attack in that relatively open country.

But twenty-four hours later the situation was considerably different. Lee had set his infantry and engineers to greatly strengthening the trenches. More important, 14,000 relatively fresh troops, buoyed up by recent successes over Northerners, arrived during the day and were put into the threatened center of the line. These included two brigades brought by Breckenridge from the Valley and two of divisions that had recently stopped Union General Butler at Drewry's Bluff.

The Northern attack began as scheduled at dawn on the third. But instead of a weak, thinly held line, the Union troops were facing confident, ready defenders, strongly supported by artillery with clear fields of fire along the entire front. In a few places the Union troops reached the Confederate entrenchments, only to be thrown back. But along most of the line the attackers were pinned down by fire within five minutes after leaving their trenches. It was repulse, complete and absolute. Grant, admitting defeat, called off the attacks. The Union attackers lost between 6000 and 7000 men in less than an hour; the Confederate defenders suffered fewer than 1500 casualties.

Though the armies were to remain in their trenches opposite each other for nine more days, the campaign begun in the Wilderness came to its close with Grant's order calling off the attack at Cold Harbor.

What had been the result of those thirty days of practically incessant warfare?

On the map, the Union army had advanced steadily and inexorably sixty miles from the Rapidan River to the outskirts of Richmond. Many Northerners took this to mean that the war was practically over.

Southerners, on the other hand, saw that Lee's army, outnumbered nearly two to one, had repulsed Grant in four major battles, had forced the Northerners to withdraw from every position in order to seek a new route of advance, and had finally brought the invasion to a complete halt farther from Richmond than McClellan had been, two years earlier.

Neither of these extreme viewpoints was correct. Grant had been unable to cut Lee's line of communications or to destroy the Southern army in battle. Lee had been unable either to throw back the invaders (as he had invariably done in previous campaigns) or to inflict on the Northerners losses sufficiently punishing as to discourage their advance.

Grant had failed because he was opposed by a Lee; Lee had failed because he was opposed by a Grant. There is no comparable historical example of two great, evenly matched generals fighting each other to a standstill in operations marked on each side by wary caution, brilliant boldness, and sound estimates of the opponent's capabilities and intentions coupled with sincere respect for the other's ability.

But when the month ended the advantage unquestionably lay with Grant, despite the disappointment and losses suffered at Cold Harbor. This was inevitable, assuming that there was little or nothing to choose between the fighting abilities of opposing commanders and their armies. Superior Northern resources were bound to make themselves felt in a war of attrition. The picture is best viewed in terms of losses and of the effect these had on the opposing sides.[3]

Grant lost 54,929 men from the Wilderness to Cold Harbor. This is approximately 52 percent of an initial combat strength of about 105,000 men. Lee lost at least 39,000 men in this same period, or 59 percent of his original combat strength of 61,000. More significant than the casualty figures, but corroborating their impact on Lee and his army, is the fact that after the Wilderness no major offensive was undertaken by Lee. He knew that he was taking more losses than the South could afford, and from that time on he took all possible efforts to husband the lives of his men.

It is significant, incidentally, of the solicitude for their men shared by the opposing generals in this campaign that for all the desperate fighting that took place, on no single day of the campaign did their losses approach those suffered by both armies at Antietam or on the second and third days of Gettysburg. The largest day's losses for the Army of the Potomac was about 7500 killed, wounded, and captured on 10 May at Spotsylvania. The heaviest Southern loss was also at Spotsylvania, on the twelfth—around 6000 men; there were at least as many as Northern casualties that same day.

Grant's losses had been severe, but they were magnified at the time by both Northern and Southern press, with the result that his conduct of the campaign is often ignorantly presented as the artless hammering of a bludgeon by a man of little skill but possessing overwhelming superiority of force and inexhaustible source of supply. Grant's critics cite his losses at Cold Harbor as evidence that he was a "butcher." In fact, two years earlier Lee's attack at Malvern Hill had been just as disastrous for the Confederates as Cold Harbor had been for the Northerners. In both cases the bold and aggressive attacking general thought he saw an opportunity for decisive victory but was foiled by an unexpectedly strong and resolute defense. Actually, Grant's attack at Cold Harbor had more chance of success than did Lee's desperate gamble the third day at Gettysburg. But, like Lee after Pickett's charge, Grant was man enough to acknowledge a mistake—and a defeat—without trying to justify it.

So it was that in the early days of June 1864 two great generals warily faced one another, each seeking the earliest opportunity to seize the initiative, each recognizing that bold action against his skillful opponent carried with it the risk of another battlefield defeat, but each determined to do everything in his power to build on defeat as well as victory in order to make his cause prevail. It is not surprising, therefore, that the war dragged on for another ten months of thrust, parry, and counterthrust until the weight of Union resources, combined with the indomitable will of his opponent, overwhelmed the equally indomitable Robert E. Lee.

Chapter 9

Defeat in Four Twentieth-Century Battles

BY HUGH M. COLE

What are the factors determining tactical defeat in modern battle? Are these factors different from those of earlier eras of warfare?

Possibly the best way for a historian to determine the answers to these questions is to apply to some historical examples an analytical methodology, developed in Germany more than a century ago, that has the clumsy Teutonic title "the historical critical applicatory method" This simply means that a critical study of military history will provide knowledge that can be applied to the analysis of a given problem. In this case, the problem is to identify and define major factors determining tactical defeat in modern battle.

The examples from military history to be critically studied in this use of the critical applicatory method are battles from major wars of this century:

A. The Battle of the Yalu River, 1 May 1904, early in the Russo-Japanese War
B. The Battle of Gumbinnen, East Prussia, 20 August 1914, at the outset of World War I

C. The first use of gas at the Second Battle of Ypres, 22–25 April 1915, also in World War I

D. The Allied advance in Tunisia, November 1942, in World War II

These are disconnected, episodic events spread across a period of four decades. But the time span permits the identification of factors that *persist* and *reappear*, despite changes in weapons, tactics, and military organization. Common elements were the infantry magazine rifle, rapid-fire artillery, and (perhaps most important) the employment of combined arms.

The cases examined offer sufficient historical detail to permit us to go beyond the how and what to the why of battle. Each of the four operations discussed has long been acknowledged as of special significance in the history of modern war.

The four analyses suggest factors that may be susceptible to *quantitative* treatment in map exercises, staff rides, computer war-gaming, and contingency planning. Conversely, each case isolates common elements of battlefield failure that can neither be precisely displayed in graphic form nor reduced to arithmetic or geometric quantification and formulas.

Among the characteristics applicable in all three wars, the following are particularly important. The rifle was sighted at 800 to 1100 yards. Divisional field pieces had a useful range of around 11,000 yards. The infantry battalion numbered 700 to 900 men and the regiment or brigade had a strength of about 3000.

CASE A: BATTLE OF THE YALU, 1 MAY 1904[1]

BEFORE THE BATTLE

In late April 1904 the Japanese First Army, consisting of three divisions, marched from central Korea up to the Yalu River, where a Russian covering force, the East Detachment, had just deployed with the mission of slowing the Japanese advance and gaining time for Russian mobilization west of the mountains in Manchuria. The geographic objective of the Japanese commander, Gen. Tamesada Kuroki, was on the left bank of the Yalu, downstream from "frozen Chosan," notorious in the Korean War a half-century later, and close to the river mouth. This sector provided the only feasible crossing site for the further deployment of a large force.

Russian mobilization in Manchuria was around Mukden and was based on the arrival of troops from Europe to reinforce the East Siberian divisions and flesh them out with new companies and battalions, a process not yet complete when the Japanese attacked at the Yalu. The Russian East Detachment was deployed along a thirty-mile stretch of the river opposite Wiju. There a mountain stream, the Ai-Ho, flowed from the northwest into the Yalu, forming a series of large alluvial islands. Cossack cavalry patrolled the Yalu for some 120 miles upstream but had been tied to the right bank when the ice broke a few weeks earlier. In any event, they lacked the numbers to maintain tight surveillance of the enemy.

The East Detachment headquarters had been hanging at the end of the telegraph wire from Supreme Headquarters in Mukden, receiving an incessant stream of messages from Gen. Alexei Kuropatkin, the commander of all Russian forces in Manchuria. In mid-April Kuropatkin dismissed the detachment commander because he moved an artillery battery without permission. He sent in as the new commander a high-ranking officer, Lt. Gen. Mikhail Ivanovich Zasulich, who did not even have a chance to see many of his unit commanders before the day of battle. The stated mission to Zasulich had high-flown words but little precision: Halt or delay the Japanese at the Yalu but do not fight a "decisive battle." If outnumbered, fall back through the mountains on the main army; nevertheless, in the face of superior numbers, the Russian troops must demonstrate "their superiority to the Japanese." (In other words, Zasulich was to demonstrate "superiority" but he was not supposed to fight hard enough to prove it.)

Entrenchments giving the Russians good fields of fire over the two rivers had been prepared, but the ground was still frozen and the rifle pits were shallow—barely chest-high and without sandbags or overhead cover. Because of the shortage of cavalry, there was no attempt to observe the Japanese who were deploying under cover of a chain of hills around Wiju.

On the first of May the East Detachment had a ration strength of 29,200 men, but the actual combat strength numbered 16,400 infantry, perhaps 500 cavalry, and 56 field pieces manned by an estimated 5000 artillerymen. Local reconnaissance was carried out by five small regimental mounted platoons, perhaps sixty men apiece. General Kuroki's Japanese First Army had three divisions totaling 31,880 rifles, perhaps 2000 cavalrymen, and 128 field guns, including twenty heavy 120mm howitzers, for a total strength of about 45,000 men.

The Russian force, which had no heavy artillery, was stretched very thin along a 20-mile arc with wide gaps between units and sections of the front manned only in company strength. The Russian right, around An-tring opposite Wiju, comprised half the front. The center, at Antung, looked down on the Yalu islands and the confluence with the river Ai-Ho. The left wing, in the vicinity of Liu-chia-kou, was screened by friendly cavalry in the Ai-Ho Valley. This attenuated line, fragmented by high hills, was manned by about 11,000 infantry supported by 40 field guns. But there was a reserve some eight miles behind the right wing composed of 5400 infantry and 16 guns. Zasulich was told by the high command in Mukden that this reserve was *not* to be used except in "the final battle" to make a retreat possible.

In the last days of April the Japanese made their presence felt by feints and demonstrations, including gunboats coming upriver to shell Antung, and the prominent display of aluminum assault boats on the south bank of the river. There were also rumors spread by Chinese traders and nightly illumination of the Russian bank by searchlights. On the night of 25 April a Japanese patrol ambushed a Russian mounted patrol north of the river, killing nineteen and all the horses. This created such an alarm that the Russian infantry companies were ordered to stand to in their entrenchments. This was repeated every night, while companies, even battalions, were marched back and forth, sometimes without food, in reaction to the latest intelligence report or rumor.

Zasulich began to look over his shoulder to the single road west through the mountains. On the twenty-seventh he asked permission to withdraw under threat of a Japanese attack that turned out to be a twenty-five-man cavalry patrol. Permission was denied. Late in the afternoon of the twenty-eighth he received a report from the Cossack cavalry commander, dated forty-eight hours earlier, saying that the Japanese had crossed the Yalu upriver. Apparently these were only patrols.

On the twenty-ninth the Japanese began their maneuver when the 12th Division crossed the river upstream from the Russian deployment and began a march through mountain defiles—infantry in single file— intended to debouch on the Ai-Ho and turn the Russian left flank. That same night the Japanese threw bridges across to the Yalu islands and placed the heavy howitzers where they could range onto Chiu-lien-cheng, in the Russian center. At dawn on the thirtieth the combined Japanese artillery started a heavy bombardment; one Russian battery replied and was knocked out of action in thirty-six minutes. The Japanese shelling continued all day, pinning the Russian infantry to the ground but inflicting only fifty casualties. The Russian general staff history states: "One cannot call these losses telling, but undoubtedly the continuous massed fire from sixty enemy cannon, compared to the weak efforts of our few guns, exercised a considerable morale impression on our men and their leaders." At midnight the commander at the Russian center reported that his troops might break when the Japanese siege guns started at sunrise. He sought permission to pull back before dawn. Zasulich had been on the ground the previous day and knew that his second-in-command—General Kaschtalinsky—had received a grazing head wound and had lost all energy. He ordered that there be no withdrawal of the center prior to the coming barrage, and then only to the support breastworks 400 meters in the rear.

THE BATTLE

The night of 30 April the Japanese laid bridges from the islands to the right bank. The Russians made no effort to interfere. Despite the rumble of wheels on the planking and the neighing of artillery horses, the Russians apparently did not know until a few hours before dawn that the assault was forming in front of Chiu-lien-cheng. At sunrise on 1 May the Japanese had on the right bank, facing the Russian center and left, twenty-four battalions from two divisions in assault positions or in close reserve. They were opposed by twenty-nine companies distributed loosely along an eight mile front. Fire from a Japanese artillery groupment of thirty-six pieces destroyed the single Russian battery supporting the center in three to four minutes. The Russian infantry, hammered by high explosives and kept down by shrapnel[2] bursts over the shallow breastworks, returned sporadic salvos.

Kuroki, observing with field glasses from the south bank, saw that the defenders were neutralized. Without waiting for the 12th Infantry Division flanking attack, he ordered his other two divisions to attack the Russian center at Chiu-lien-cheng. A Russian machine-gun company and a four-gun artillery battery, released from the right wing, arrived to reinforce the center but were quickly knocked out. The Russian center then broke, first individuals in flight, then in groups of fifteen or twenty. Zasulich and the wounded General Kaschtalinsky, seeing the center collapse, galloped off the field. The commander on the right at Antung wanted to make a fight and requested the two battalions in general reserve, but headquarters refused. He began to pull back in good order, trying to cover the flight from the center. The commander on the extreme left also ordered a retreat but gave no precise command to his separate companies, which thereupon withdrew precipitously, and in considerable disorder, to the high ground.

By midafternoon the Russian infantry was retreating all along the line. A staff officer rode up to the commander of the general reserve, the 11th East Siberian Regiment, and told him that it was "high time" to leave, since his two battalions were being surrounded. The regimental commander deployed one battalion in defense while forming the other in column of attack to break out of the encirclement. The field priest blessed the troops, the regimental band played the national hymn, then the battalion attacked. The column did break through the Japanese; all officers but two were killed, as were the field priest and sixteen of the thirty-two bandsmen. The battalion that was left behind fought on for several hours, but only a few stragglers escaped. Of a rifle strength of 2119 on 1 May, the 11th Siberian lost 847. These losses, of course, were suffered *after* the initial Russian defeat along the river. The total Russian losses were 60 officers and 2130 men killed and wounded, or about 8.8 percent of the entire detachment. The Japanese losses, nearly half of which were experienced in the initial assault on the Russian center, including only those killed and severely wounded, 1036. If we assumed about an equal number lightly wounded, Japanese casualties were about 4.6 percent.

COMMENTS

The mission of the Russian East Detachment was unclear and contradictory. This may have contributed to the faulty dispositions of front-line units and of the general reserve as well as the failure to commit the reserve in timely fashion.

The Russians were defeated before the Japanese attack began. Three times in the hours before the battle Russian commanders at different levels asked permission to withdraw because, they said, the troops would not stand. Major factors in the collapse of troop morale were fatigue, fear induced by fatigue, and the mix of European and East Siberian troops and officers that put strangers together even in the rifle companies.

The distribution of limited Russian forces over a wide area meant that they did not have enough strength anywhere to stop a determined Japanese thrust. The weakness in numbers on such an extended front made maneuver impossible and mutual support out of the question. Even worse, without local and general reserves available for counterattack, they had a cordon defense that invited disaster. The force ratio in a 3000-yard sector on the extreme left was one Russian battalion versus four Japanese battalions; at the Russian center, three widely separated positions on a ten-mile front, five and a half battalions faced ten Japanese. A gap of 5 miles was left between the Russian center and right. The Russian general reserve was eight miles behind the center and was not engaged until the troops on the center and left were in flight.

The overall ratio of forces on the field was somewhat more than two to one in favor of the Japanese. But these overall strength figures are misleading; the Japanese properly massed at the point they determined to be decisive. They did not attack the Russian right and general reserve until the battle was won. In other words, the true force ratio was seven Russian battalions against the twenty-four battalions in the initial assault by the two Japanese divisions; if artillery strength is included in the comparison, the ratio was more than four to one in the decisive area.

An imbalance of fire also contributed to the Russian defeat. The Russian artillery numbered 62 field pieces and light mountain guns, none more than 75mm in caliber. The Japanese had 108 field guns *and* 20 heavy 120mm howitzers. Once again the overall ratio tells little, for at no point did the Russians bring more than eight guns into action at the same time on their disarticulated front.

With no intelligence or reconnaissance capability save a handful of mounted infantry, the Russians prepared for and fought a battle in which they could logically assess neither the Japanese' intentions nor their capabilities. Indeed, until late in the night before the fight the Russian commander quite wrongly guessed that the assault would be made against his right, at Antung. In any case, surprise was invited by dispersion.

Tactical control failed, in part because of the mixture of units, in part because of the dispersal of units. The same can be said for the communications failure. On top of this, the two Russian general officers present exercised no command from the beginning of the battle until the end and left the field with the first fugitives.

CASE B: THE BATTLE OF GUMBINNEN, 20 AUGUST 1914[3] [THE GERMAN XVII CORPS VS THE RUSSIAN III CORPS]

Before the Battle

Hostilities in World War I were initiated in the east by a two-pronged Russian offensive from Lithuania and Poland into East Prussia. The Russian plan was to overwhelm the small German Eighth Army in East Prussia by converging drives of Russian armies from the east and the south. These were the First Army, commanded by Gen. Pavel K. Rennenkampf, completing its mobilization in Lithuania, and the Second Army, under Gen. Aleksandr Samsonov, mobilizing in northern Poland. In response to an appeal from France to place pressure on Germany, the Russian high command ordered the two armies to initiate their offensive before either was really ready. The Russian leadership recognized that this was somewhat risky, but they knew that their two armies invading East Prussia outnumbered the defending Germans by a ratio of nearly three to one.

On 17 August 1914, Rennenkampf's First Army crossed the eastern frontier of East Prussia. He was two days ahead of Samsonov, whose army would not reach the frontier, fifty miles to the southwest, for another two days. In a sharp engagement at the border Rennenkampf was stopped at Stalluponen by an aggressive German corps commander. However, as Russian numerical superiority built up, the Germans fell back to Gumbinnen, a road center where Gen. Max von Prittwitz's Eighth Army was assembling. The Russians followed slowly, their advance constrained by the fact that the roads east of the frontier were few and poor, which meant that there were many delays in getting troops and supplies to the front. However, by late on the nineteenth the Russians were approaching Gumbinnen. Since he had failed to make use of his cavalry either for reconnaissance or as a screen in front of his advance, Rennenkampf had no idea that a large German force was assembling just west of his leading elements.

Rennenkampf had a numerical advantage of nearly two to one; he had more machine guns but less artillery. Prittwitz knew that he could expect no reinforcement from the German armies in the West, which were just beginning the great wheeling offensive toward Paris. He was also aware of the threat to his right rear posed by Samsonov's slow advance from the south. Nevertheless, counting on Samsonov's continuing slowness, Prittwitz ordered up his XVII Corps (two divisions) from the Polish frontier and directed it to concentrate behind the right wing of the defensive line now forming behind the Angerapp River near Gumbinnen. The "dusk patrol" flown by German reconnaissance planes on the nineteenth reported that the Russian columns couldn't attack the Angerapp line until the twenty-first. This assessment was correct. Because of inadequate reconnaissance, Rennenkampf did not realize the Germans were so close, but he had ordered his command to avoid a serious fight in order to rest his infantry and get his supply trains forward. This order was sent by uncoded radio message and was read by the Germans.

Prittwitz therefore decided that, as soon as the XVII Corps arrived, he would attack on the twentieth. The two divisions of the XVII Corps would be put on the German right and would attack by the left oblique against the Russian left. This was to be coordinated with an attack by the German I Corps farther north. The I Reserve Corps, coming up to the south, was to support the XVII Corps attack.

THE BATTLE

In late afternoon of 19 August the XVII Corps detrained and began a march northeastward to assemble south of Gumbinnen. Scouting reports relayed from the I Corps, already in position, said there was only one Russian division in front of the XVII Corps. Just before dawn, after a night march of 15 miles, the two divisions were in position. They were tired but could be given only a short rest before their advance began. By 9:00 A.M. the right-wing division was deep into the Russian outpost positions. The I Corps to the north was also advancing and reported the enemy in retreat. Aerial patrols saw nothing in front of the XVII Corps but some artillery and perhaps a rifle regiment. The corps commander, Gen. August von Mackensen, committed his reserve, a regiment, to roll up the enemy left and rear. To do this he withdrew nearly half his field artillery to form a new reserve.

The turgid prose of the German official history reflects, for a few sentences, the cadence of the attack: The troops were attacking "at white heat," they "knew" that victory was in their grasp. But suddenly the reserve regiment, put in for the coup de grace, "stumbled upon" a new Russian position on the far back of a small creek. Here a newly arrived Russian division was deployed; the two weary German divisions thus unexpectedly found themselves facing two enemy divisions, one of which was dug in on the high embankments and separate hills east of the creek. The attacking infantry, exposed on the flat ground west of the creek, could not see the enemy riflemen, the machine guns, or the hidden Russian field guns. German artillery was rushed forward into the open to aid the infantry but sustained very heavy losses in guns and men. The German infantry renewed the attack, but short rushes forward were quickly checked by fire from enemy positions. The German infantry began to lose officers and noncoms at a rate that destroyed tactical control. The troops had been marching and fighting for nearly twenty-four hours, supporting guns were ineffective, and ammunition was running low.

The German official history soberly records, at about 3:00 P.M., "a backward movement." Officers, even Mackensen and his staff, tried to stem what soon became a panic. They were brushed aside. Eventually the troops slowed down at a small watercourse and the XVII Corps slowly began to reform.

The German Eighth Army had superior numbers committed at Gumbinnen on 20 August: 105 battalions and 508 guns against 86 Russian battalions and 408 guns. But in the XVII Corps attack Mackensen used 26,000 men against a cumulative 34,000; the artillery was roughly equal. Mackensen's losses were over 8500 men and 200 officers, approximately one-third of his strength. But these losses, more than half of them prisoners of war, represented three-fifths of all the casualties sustained on 20 August by the 105 German battalions in the Eighth Army.

Actually, the Russian casualties at Gumbinnen were greater than those of the Germans. And because of the success of the I Corps in the north, Gumbinnen was a drawn battle. But, with Samsonov slowly moving into East Prussia behind him, Prittwitz could not afford a drawn battle. He was defeated and forced to make a precipitous retreat.[4]

COMMENTS

The battle of Gumbinnen was the only occasion in 1914 where German strength on the field surpassed the Russian: 105 battalions versus 86. The German main effort by the XVII Corps saw roughly equivalent forces engaged, two divisions on each side, 160 German field guns versus 100 Russian, and a slight Russian superiority in machine guns. The Russians had the additional advantage of defensive posture in good defensive terrain. The German defeat on 20 August was initiated by the collapse of the XVII Corps; the German I Corps making the attack on the left was successful. The German I Reserve Corps, which came up on the right of the XVII Corps during the battle, was not successful, in large part due to the defeat of XVII Corps.

The official German history ascribes the defeat and flight of the XVII corps to "a chain of unfortunate happenings" and eschews further critique. The panic is described as "a backward movement," but the official account in fact paints a picture of two whole infantry divisions in flight.

The assembly for the German attack was neither quick nor quiet. Mackensen, the corps commander, expected to attack at 4:30 A.M. but could not start the advance until about 8:00 A.M. Meanwhile the German I Corps on the left had begun its attack on schedule, thus alerting the Russians in front of Mackensen and giving them time to withdraw all but a covering shell and to dig in on the more defensible terrain.

The German advance commenced without serious reconnaissance and with little security since a covering force screening the line of departure had been attacked by the Russians during the night and had turned northeast to deal with the attack. And, as described, the failure of battlefield intelligence and security was pervasive even when the attackers seemed to have victory in hand.

The overall German attack was so widely dispersed that brigades in the north could not be turned in time to help the XVII Corps when, at 1:00 P.M., the corps advance abruptly halted.

The sudden reversal in the fortunes of the German attackers is almost a classic example of fatigue engendering fear (twenty-four hours of marching and fighting) and of the psychological trauma induced when troops in the full cry of victory meet a surprise defense that robs most of the exhausted battalions of vigor, momentum, and courage.

This battle also is a classic example of the manner in which the lack of observation when the enemy is well concealed and his positions are in depth negates the strength of the combined arms.

Even though communications and command operated routinely, the troops were effectively out of control as soon as they suffered the initial reverse. Loss of tactical control was accentuated by officer losses, which were at a rate 3.5 times that for noncoms and soldiers.

Loss figures give no real information as to the defeat suffered by the XVII Corps. The total German losses this day were 14,607, of which three-fifths were incurred in the XVII Corps. Of these losses perhaps 6000 were prisoners taken by the Russians during the panic. Casualties in the two divisions of the Russian III Corps at the hands of Mackensen's two divisions are uncertain: The 27th Division is said to have lost over 6600 men; the commander of the 40th Division reported officially only that "many Jews fled and a few Russians." Total Russian casualties were over 16,000.

The German commander defeated at Gumbinnen was fortunate enough to lead his corps in the great victory at Tannenberg, a week later, and to capture the greatest number of Russian prisoners. Mackensen subsequently was named field marshal, and commanded the Bulgarian-German forces in the Romanian Campaign of 1916.

CASE C: SECOND YPRES, 22–25 APRIL 1915[5]

BEFORE THE BATTLE

In the spring of 1915 a homogeneous battle line extended across Western Europe from Switzerland to the North Sea. In this line were two bulges, or salients, held by the Allies—one at Verdun, in France, and one in front of the Belgian city of Ypres. The German high command decided to reduce the Ypres salient; the operation had two objectives: first, to free some divisions for the Eastern front and second, to battle-test a proposed new weapon—chlorine gas.

The Ypres salient, east of Ypres and the Yser Canal that ran north of the city, was ten miles across north to south and five miles deep east to west. The countryside was open, dotted with small villages and woodlots, reaching heights of only 100 to 130 feet in a series of low ridgelines generally running east and west.

The Allied perimeter extended for fifteen miles. Two-thirds of the line, east and south, was manned by two British divisions and the new 1st Canadian Division—only five days in the line—which linked on its left to two small French divisions, the 45th Reserve and the 87th Colonial divisions, deployed on the northern shoulder of the salient.

THE BATTLE

By late afternoon on 22 April, after a day-long intensive bombardment, winds were favorable for the release by the Germans of gas from cylinders installed on a four-mile front facing the French. At 5:00 P.M. on a beautiful spring day, the cylinders were opened and thirty tons of chlorine gas wafted toward the French, forming a cloud 600 yards deep. German field guns, which had been briefly silenced for fear of roiling the low-lying cloud, now commenced fire as four German divisions moved into the attack supported by a furious bombardment from heavy howitzers. The immediate objective: to capture the ridgeline at Pilckem on the northern shoulder that overlooked the Yser Canal and Ypres, whose possession, according to the attack order, would make it impossible for the Allies to remain in the salient.

Observers on the Allied side first saw the greenish-yellow clouds, then troops from the two French divisions running down the roads clutching at their throats; then the stream of soldiers turned into a torrent of fugitives, teams, and wagons. At 6:00 P.M. the French 75s (75mm field cannon) suddenly ceased fire as gas reached the batteries. Says the French official history, the two French divisions "were reduced to complete impotence." The attacking infantry reached the immediate objective in an hour and a quarter, closed at the canal, and on the opposite wing turned to assault the Canadian flank left open by the French flight. At dark the German advance had driven two and one-half miles into the salient on a front of four and one-half miles east to west. The French northern shoulder simply had disappeared, with a loss of ten batteries, 1100 unwounded prisoners, 70 machine guns, and some 4000 dead and wounded—about half gas victims and about half casualties of artillery fire. The map of the salient on the night of the twenty-second looks like an apple from which a huge bite had been taken.

The left Canadian brigade attempted to form a new line facing north. In the confusion, the first reports to the British V Corps headquarters said that the brigade had been driven back and that no troops were left. An hour and a quarter later this was reported as in error. In fact, within thirty minutes of the first report small local reserves were moving to counterattack. The commander of the British 27th Division on the southern shoulder sent his reserves to support the Canadians despite continuing German attacks on the south shoulder. The French had established a new line at the canal, but there was a gap of more than two miles between the Canadian left and the canal. The German advance had halted only four miles from the rear of the British division on the southern shoulder, and the Germans were only two miles from Ypres with nothing in their path.

The German advance had halted at 7:00 P.M., possibly stopped by the gas cloud, more certainly by orders to consolidate the ground gained so quickly and unexpectedly and to bring forward all the heavy artillery in order to bombard the canal and the single large bridge at Ypres. They planned to resume the attack at daylight with the main effort toward St. Julien, a crossroads village behind the Canadian left. The German high command, not anticipating results so dramatic, had ticketed no reserves, but the army commander quickly ordered up the two brigades of his army reserve.

The ensuing forty-eight hours would decide whether or not the salient would be restored as ordered by the British commander, Gen. Sir John French. The fight would be carried by companies, battalions, and single brigades directed by majors, colonels, and a few brigadiers.

The tactical problem had two possible solutions. One, repair as much as possible of the damage at once, using the troops at hand and accepting the German break-in as only a serious local incident. Or, two, "make a really serious effort with large forces to recover all the lost ground." Gen. Ferdinand Foch, commanding Allied forces in the north, refused to send reinforcements because a large Allied offensive was being readied at Arras. The British would have to restore the salient with local reserves; some French troops were supposed to be available on short-term loan, but they never came.

By midnight of the twenty-second Canadian reserves, only two battalions, were in position to counterattack on the open flank. They advanced in the darkness trying to find the enemy line, came under punishing fire, were reduced to a strength of 400 unwounded men, and had to withdraw because no more troops were available. A Canadian brigade in army reserve was rushed forward to extend the Canadian flank. The British 28th and 27th divisions on the southern shoulder voluntarily sent a total of four battalions, their only reserves, but these were not in place to attack until 3:00 A.M. Nonetheless, by daybreak on the twenty-third the British–Canadian troops had developed "a fairly continuous line" reaching west to within 1200 meters of the Canal. But piecemeal attacks to extend the line northwestward failed with very heavy casualties. The Germans had dug in, commanding the slopes, and their guns pounded the British from three sides of the salient. The German field guns outnumbered the British five to one; the superiority in heavy artillery was even greater.

The improvised and always confused British counterattacks used up the infantry at a rapid rate. In the afternoon of 23 April, the First Army reserve, a brigade worn out from earlier battles, reached Ypres by bus and marched into assembly on the open left flank. Orders failed to reach the troops already in place and two uncoordinated attacks were put in, troops advancing in the open, up the slopes, with no artillery preparation and no certainty where the enemy lay. As usual, nearly all officers became casualties and so no reports came back to the higher headquarters. Of the seven and one-half understrength battalions in that afternoon attack, battle casualties were at least 50 percent. This was the story of all British attacks to restore the north flank of the salient: successive uncoordinated attacks by jumbled units often commanded by officers unknown to the men, staffs who seldom knew where their companies or battalions could be found, little artillery preparation because batteries could not survive in the salient, and heavy casualties in advances across open ground in daylight.

Nonetheless, by the early hours of the twenty-fourth the British situation seemed reasonably in hand. On the new northern flank of the salient twenty-two and one-half battalions had been scraped together against forty-two German battalions. (This latter strength did not include two divisions facing the French at the canal.) At daylight on the twenty-fourth the commander of the German XXIII Reserve Corps concentrated twenty-four battalions to break the Canadian line at its eastern hinge. The Germans advanced in close order behind a tremendous artillery assault and, at the center, a gas cloud 1100 yards wide. The German focal point was St. Julien, the village dominating entry to the slopes in the Canadian sector. Outnumbered three to one, the Canadians fell back, supported only by a few guns firing over open sights.

Late in the afternoon General French, the British commander in chief, ordered that St. Julien be retaken, but this was only a gesture. The troops were confused, fought-out, and delayed by conflicting orders from five or six headquarters at a time. The British official history records that this day "ended in hurry and turmoil and the shadow of defeat." The breadth of the salient north and south had dwindled to less than three miles. Enemy artillery fire from three sides was so intense that "one shell crater ran into another." Ammunition, food, and water could hardly be brought forward; the main bridge at Ypres was a death trap; hundreds of wounded lay in the shallow trenches; artillery could not survive in the constricted salient; observation of the enemy had been lost and communications shot out. The battle was the rifle against cannon.

Gen. Horace Smith-Dorrien, commanding the British Second Army, proposed that the British line be brought back to an old trench position two and one-half miles in front of Ypres. He was peremptorily relieved by

General French in deference to Foch's insistence that the British continue counterattacking. Immediately, however, his successor was permitted to carry out the withdrawal.

COMMENTS

The Allied battle to restore the Ypres salient was lost on 24 April, forty-eight hours after the initial German attack. The local British commanders recognized failure but, as is often the case, higher authority far from the front refused to accept a definitive failure. Three days later Foch, apostle of the offensive on all occasions and in all situations, told General French that withdrawal would allow "moral ascendency to pass to the Germans." And, as earlier, Foch ordered the "counteroffensive." The British official history carefully notes that the British battles in the first two days should not even be called "counterattacks."

The initial use of poison gas was a surprise, both psychological and technical. The second use of the gas cloud, only two hundred yards from the Canadians, was no surprise and largely ineffective, but the tactical situation had changed. The first gas cloud at Ypres should be considered an "area weapon"; it removed the defense from the occupation of the ground. The velocity of the gas cloud gave no opportunity for the defenders to mount an effective and time-consuming counterattack to erase the "break-in."

Both the British and German official histories consider that the artillery arm "affected the result [of this battle] far more than any other, including even the use of gas." But the gas cloud not only released the German guns from the task of breaking the defensive position and enforcing the "break-in," it also introduced the decisive psychological element of surprise. On the other hand, the British artillery did not come immediately under gas attack and so shored up the crumbling or nonexistent infantry line.

The artillery force ratio is important. At the end of the first twenty-four hours the German superiority was five to one. The German superiority in heavy artillery had a marked effect on the battle: Each German division was supported by twenty heavy guns on modern gun-recoil carriages; as late as 24 April the British had only a single 9.2-inch howitzer and a battery of old sixty-pounders reinforcing the north flank.

The fluctuating troop ratio and force to space is difficult to calculate or even to estimate. In the initial gas attack of 22 April there were about forty-eight German battalions to eighteen French and Canadian. By dawn of the twenty-third the two German divisions and the French reserves fighting at the canal may be factored out of calculations relating to the salient. By this time the German superiority over the British in battalions was about thirty to twelve. At the end of the day the figure was forty-two German battalions versus twenty-two and one-half British battalions. At no point did the Allies have anything approaching the three-to-one superiority normally assumed to be required to mount a counteroffensive, and hardly the one-to-two defensive ratio decreed normally necessary to hold the drastically deflated salient.

Casualties of the two sides are not strictly comparable. In three days the Canadian 1st Division lost 5469 officers and men, nearly half its complement. The six German brigades in this sector reported losses of 6368, about 13 percent of their total troop strength during that same period.

Smith-Darrien, the British general, was sent to command a small British force in the operations against German East Africa. His post-war reputation, however, was seen in a much better light; largely because of his earlier command during the British stand at Le Calean in August 1914 as well as the patent unfairness of his relief at Ypres.

CASE D: THE ALLIED ADVANCE
IN TUNISIA, NOVEMBER 1942[6]

On 8 November 1942, Operation TORCH brought American and British troops ashore on the Atlantic and Mediterranean coasts of French North-west Africa. Having dodged the German U-boat packs, fought with some of the Vichy French troops, and negotiated with others, the Allies deployed to garrison and defend the major ports, to initiate long-range bomber attacks against the Axis Mediterranean bases, and to concentrate to repel any possible Axis counteroffensive through Spain and Spanish Morocco.

British Lt. Gen. Kenneth A. N. Anderson landed at Algiers (the easternmost landing site) on 9 November and received orders to "occupy" Tunisia and seize the ports of Bizerte and Tunis 500 miles east of Algiers. He would command the British First Army, consisting at that time of roughly two-thirds of the 78th Infantry Division, the light armor of the 6th

Armoured Division, and some commando and parachute units. The missing infantry brigade of the 78th and the bulk of the 6th Armoured would not close at Algiers until 6 December, when a convoy would arrive from the British Isles. Anderson's force, roughly equivalent to a reinforced division, lacked the logistic materiel required even by a division. All troops in the original 8 November landings had been loaded for tactical assault and so were without trucks, service troops, or any of the major logistic requirements for air or supply bases.

Within twenty-four hours Anderson had one infantry brigade en route by sea for Bougie, a small port west of Bone in eastern Algeria. Bone had a reasonably large harbor with an all-weather airport. This brigade had been in floating reserve during the Algiers landings and so was immediately available. It landed at Bougie on the morning of 11 November.

At that time the Mediterranean littoral was still part of the "Axis Lake"; within hours of the next stop eastward, Allied coastal troop carriers in the vicinity of Bougie and Bone were being sunk by Axis U-boats and planes. The 500-mile coastal shipping route from Algiers to Tunis and Bizerte was only minutes away from Axis airfields and sub pens. On land the route was via rough roads across two major mountain chains, plus one decrepit French single-track rail line.

Nonetheless, Anderson expected to attack Tunis and Bizerte within one week. He used the sea, the railway, and the mountain road to move his small command eastward. The tactical problem was simple. Lacking troops and transport, the First Army could not maneuver but had simply to advance straight-on by the mountain and coastal roads. In fact, the operational objective would be to get through the mountain passes west of the Tunisian coastal plain before the Axis could bring its troops into Tunisian harbors and air bases and then move to block the passes.

The Axis reaction to the 8 November landings had been prompt and forceful. That very day a Luftwaffe captain arrived in Tunis to browbeat the French and arrange for the arrival of planes and troops. By 11 November the Germans had a parachute regiment in Tunis and two battalions in Bizerte. Time and distance factors favored the Axis. Air flight from bases on Sicily was only a few minutes and for sea cargo only a few hours. Actually, of the 30,000 Germans and Italians who arrived in Tunis during November, only 2000 came by ship.

The Germans had seventy-two close-support aircraft on forward Tunisian airfields by 15 November. At that time the British had a single squadron of Hurricanes (ground-support aircraft) at Bone; of these only nine were operational at a time. The Allies flew 1500 combat sorties to 1000 German sorties in November, but the Allied bombers and fighters were flying to interdict the Mediterranean air lanes and ports, defend their new ports and bases in Northwest Africa, and protect their shipping on both sides of the Gibraltar Straits. The Luftwaffe not only had more ground-support planes but also flew very short distances to the combat zone and had hard-sand airstrips that gave all-weather capability.

By 17 November the Axis began to push out the perimeter guarding the airstrips. This led to a three-day series of meeting engagements west of Bizerte and east of Bone, as both sides brought forward newly arrived companies and understrength battalions. The road-bound Allied detachments were spread over a twenty-five-mile sector traversed by a few mountain and valley roads. Generally the Germans had the upper hand, supported by a few heavy tanks and by Stukas flying from fields only minutes away.

Anderson had hoped that his coup de main would strike Tunis on the twenty-first or twenty-second but was forced to wait for four days for more troops, heavy tanks, and, hopefully, some close air support. The heavy armor needed was provided by Combat Command B (CCB) of the U.S. 1st Armored Division, which had landed at Oran—some 700 miles away. The senior American commander at Oran bitterly opposed this attachment to the British and delayed the move, with significant effect on Anderson's operation. Anderson had mixed feelings about this reinforcement. He needed the armored firepower, but he feared that his already fragile line of communications could not sustain the demands of an armored combat command.

The logistical problem attendant on bringing close-support aircraft into the forward area was most severe. Only Bone had an all-weather field, and the rains were just beginning. One landing strip required 2000 tons of steel planking and the "poor little railroad," as Eisenhower called it, could carry no more than 1000 tons per day. The tonnage required to build forward air bases and support the aircraft thereon simply could not be transported in time to help the First Army against the Stukas. An enumeration of the major requirements tells the story: aircraft, replacement aircraft and air crews, vehicles, replacement engines, ground crews and antiair defenses, radar both for planes and ground defense, aviation POL, and new, specially equipped reconnaissance aircraft.

Rail movement from Algiers to the railhead east of Bone often took six days. Coasters were scheduled to bring troops into Bone harbor every fourth night, but often under damaging enemy air attack. The single-track railroad run by the French had to supply an entire French division that had joined the Allies and also to sustain itself with coal and extra locomotives. The system often formed a gridlock because there were too few trucks and service troops to clear the sidings.

Nonetheless the First Army attack moved out on the night of the twenty-fourth, the newly arrived U.S. tanks divided among three widely separated assault columns. German forces had increased each day, but they drew back, waiting to see whether Anderson would launch a left jab at Bizerte or a right hook at Tunis. On the twenty-eighth heavy tanks of the 10th Panzer Division, reinforced by four of the new King Tiger jumbo tanks, debarked and headed for battle. The force ratio on a thirty-five-mile front was roughly even, 15,000 to 20,000 troops on each side. The Allied armor outnumbered the Axis tanks by four battalions to three, but the German tanks had heavier armor and superior guns. The German antitank guns, including twenty 88mm antiaircraft guns stripped from the Axis air bases, lurked in the mountain passes and hills where they knocked out Allied tanks almost at will. Overall the Stukas dominated the battle area, flying at every break in the rain squalls and demoralizing the attackers.

On the twenty-ninth, three weeks after the North African landings, the Commander of the 78th British Division concluded that his troops were fought out; Anderson agreed. He told Eisenhower that the advance must halt until more troops and army air-support squadrons could be gathered. British infantry losses at this juncture numbered 580 men, the equivalent of one of the six understrength battalions. By this time the Allies had reached Tebourba, a road center twenty miles west of Tunis.

But the Germans did not let the battle end. Their tanks swept around both flanks of the British advance guard at Tebourba, destroying most of the American supporting tanks, and demoralized the Allies by incessant air attack. In three days of battle (1–3 December) the Allies were driven back twenty miles and lost nearly 1100 prisoners. Casualties in the brigade at Tebourba reduced its three battalions to a total roster of 660 men. In this sector the Allies lost twenty-one guns in the three-day battle, then lost an additional thirty-two field pieces during the withdrawal.

Symptomatic of this battle was the fate of an American battalion of 155mm guns that left the fight without orders because the daily train had not delivered its caliber of ammunition and the gun crews had no shells. The battalion commander saw no sense in staying exposed to the incessant German air attacks without being able to take any part in the battle.

Bizerte and Tunis would not be captured until May 1943.

COMMENTS

This case shows the impact of logistics, and of the presence or absence of close air support, on large ground-force tactical units operating far from a major base and under severe constraints of time. Eisenhower later said of this operation that it would be studied and condemned at the U.S. Army Command and General Staff College at Fort Leavenworth for years to come.

This case also presents a classic problem of command: when to cut off an operation because it has become a definitive failure. Wild panic by fleeing troops, loss of tactical control, artillery pounding that literally blasts defending units off the face of the earth—all these phenomena make the timing of defeat easy to fix. Failure to achieve the objective of an operational mission is harder to pinpoint in time because of the command proclivity to equate the *capability* to advance with the *desirability* of advancing.

The causes for failure in this operation were easily identified and bluntly reported by Eisenhower and Anderson to Churchill and the Combined Chiefs of Staff: (a) lack of close tactical air support and (b) logistical failure, including the movement of combat troops.

Although a number of high-ranking Allied officers were relieved because of the early reverses suffered in this campaign, Anderson (the First Army Commander) was not removed from command during the operations themselves. Subsequently, however, he was relegated to a training command in his native Scotland.

Although Eisenhower predicted that this failure would be studied and condemned at Leavenworth for years to come, this has not been the case. Since this campaign, U.S. Army combat forces have never experienced enemy superiority in attack air. With the possible exception of the Buna campaign in the Southwest Pacific, no major U.S. operation has been aborted because of logistics in the years since this 1942 phase of the Tunisian campaign.

CONCLUSION

There may be no need for historical analysis to help us prepare for war if we envisage the future battle as fought by men behind impenetrable armor with futuristic sighting and firing gear versus a self-sustaining weapons system served mostly by robots. All that may be required for planning and preparation purposes in such circumstances is engineering data from technical manuals.

If, however, one accepts the historical postulate that human behavioral or moral factors will continue to determine the ultimate value of numbers and ratios of force to force and force to space, one must face the quandary as to the quantification of the behavioral factors and of the concomitant combat worth of individual soldiers as well as of the total military force. The solution is not the U.S. combat efficiency reports of World War II, in which a division was rated in terms of number of cases of venereal disease, trench foot, unauthorized absences or desertions (Absent Without Leave or AWOL), and "filler and loss" replacements. What is desirable, if not necessary, is to find ways to interject behavioral factors into planning as well as into combat simulation and quantitative analysis.

Hopefully, the four case studies examined in this chapter may help in approaching this problem. It is instructive to look at the relevance of some of the causes of defeat listed in Chapter 2 to these four examples. (Figure 9.1 is a matrix chart of such relevance.)

The relevance of superiority of hostile fire support to defeat seems obvious. The four case studies of this chapter all stressed the importance of the artillery weapon as an element of the combined-arms team. Every publication of *Soviet Military Power* in recent years shows a greater superiority in the Warsaw Pact artillery versus the number of NATO artillery pieces than in main battle tanks or divisions. One need not necessarily agree with the Soviet ratio of artillery weapons to tanks and troops, but their emphasis cannot be ignored. It seems clear that artillery, whether cannon or missiles, should be analyzed as a separate factor and not simply be subsumed under manpower numbers.

Current U.S. Army attention to weaponry for forward air defense should not preclude the simulation or war-gaming of situations in which ground units are subjected to severe losses or become tactically immobile as the result of superior enemy tactical air.

Figure 9.1.   Causes of Defeat

	Yalu	Gumbinnen	2d Ypres	Tunisia
A. Unfavorable Circumstances Beyond Control of Commander				
1. Overpowered by Superior				
a. Numbers			X	X
b. Armor				X
c. Fire support: (1) Artillery	X		X	X
(2) Air				X
d. Skill				
2. Unfavorable environment				
a. Weather				
b. Terrain				
c. Road/LOC				X
3. Hostile Fortifications		X		X
4. Inferior Technology			X	
5. Chance				
	(1)	(1)	(3)	(6)
B. Unfavorable Circumstances Commander May Influence				
1. Unprepared for battle				X
2. Inferior quality forces				
a. Quality of manpower			X	X
b. Training/experience				X
c. Doctrine				
3. Poor morale	X			
4. Troops and/or commander fatigued	X	X	X	X
5. Casualties incurred			X	
6. Subordinate error/failure	X			
	(3)	(1)	(3)	(4)
C. Failure of Command				
1. Surprised	X	X	X	
2. Inferior leadership				
a. Self-delusion (perception)	X		X	X
b. Confused mission	X			
c. Weakness of will	X			
3. Inadequate control				
a. Poor reconnaissance/ intelligence	X	X	X	X
b. Poor planning	X			
c. Faulty tactics	X		X	
d. Inadequate logistics				X
e. Breakdown in communications				
	(7)	(2)	(4)	(3)

Inferior troop quality unquestionably played a part in two, possibly three, of the cases studied. Value may be assigned to combat units based on state of training, weaponry, manpower age and physical profiles, and unit homogeneity or lack thereof. In World War II the Wehrmacht used a four-category rating system in which the rated unit was qualified or unqualified for given missions.

As can be seen in all four of the case studies, physical fatigue has a direct and telling effect on combat effectiveness. Historical factors do exist to measure this—generally days in combat and the severity of that combat. Modern techniques of human engineering might provide such a quantification for war-gaming, command post exercises (CPXs), field exercises, and—ultimately—planning for combat.

The effect of casualties upon both physical force strength and the behavioral reaction of troops cannot be ignored. As intensive combat extends beyond a period of twenty-four hours, the force ratio is likely to change as one side incurs a higher proportion of casualties than the other. This historical phenomenon should be represented in the simulation of combat as well as in the actual tactical control of a battle. In this connection, read the official British World War I analysis of the butchery on the Western Front: ". . . once a certain proportion of casualties were sustained—*a proportion which depended very much on the unit's morale*—the survivors fled or surrendered" [emphasis added].[7]

It should not be ignored that surprise played a role in three of the four case studies—and even in Tunisia, the Allies were to some extent surprised by the speed and effectiveness of the German reaction. In two of the other three instances (the Yalu and Gumbinnen), the surprise was the direct result of a command failure: inadequate reconnaissance.

Clearly—and the matrix analysis emphasizes this—the critical factor of defeat is the quality, or lack thereof, of the leadership. Much attention is being given these days to the possible simulation of the mind of the commander and the process of command decision by Artificial Intelligence. The historical cases cited above suggest that a major role of the commander in battle is to determine the distribution, movement, and employment of reserve units. It is possible to replicate this role in war-gaming, and certainly (to the extent permitted by "the state of the art") as a routine part of combat simulation.

Failures in intelligence of enemy strengths and intentions appear in all the cases of defeat described above. The promises made for future electronic battlefield surveillance can be nullified by electronic countermeasures

(ECM), darkness, bad weather, and accidented terrain. Computer simulations and map exercises should therefore routinely provide for the degradation of combat intelligence.

In only one of this particular selection of case studies was the logistic factor important. But in this one case (Tunisia) it was possibly the most important contributor to the Allied defeat. American military experience since World War II has tended to stultify interest in and attention to logistic support factors. The proximity of the Japanese base to Korea, the creation of a huge supply complex under friendly auspices in Vietnam, and our reliance on British and French logistic support in the two World Wars may have given us advantages that will not be repeated in some future theater of operations. In any case, logistic transport and resupply may be difficult in forward areas if enemy air or missile attack is effective—as in the Ypres salient. The play of lines of communications and supply complexes should be regularly inserted into war-gaming.

The historical failure in the dash for Tunis represents a problem that requires the wisdom of Solomon in contingency planning: how much tonnage and manpower shall be given to "the teeth," how much to "the tail." Eisenhower concluded that in planning for TORCH "we should have paid more attention to 'red tape' and 'paperwork' " rather than relying on the gut reaction of combat commanders such as Patton. War games supported by computers represent an obvious approach to this problem in that variables of "tail" and "teeth" may be introduced.

The battles at the Yalu and in the Ypres salient suggest the importance of the C^3 (command, control, and communications) problem during the confusion of battle and in complicated chains of command. These factors were dominant: (1) the time for information to go back, (2) the time consumed in sending orders forward, (3) the remoteness of the higher command from the actual conditions obtaining, and (4) the probability that orders would be misunderstood and plans miscarry. Those factors routinely should be considered and replicated in war-gaming.

Finally, consideration must be given to the ubiquitous problem so often referred to in the four cases: the ratio of troops to space. This problem is not included in the causes of defeat listed in Chapter 2, although it is implicit in the question of numerical strength. This is a particular problem when defense *in depth* replaces *linear* dispositions. Many years ago Basil Liddell Hart proposed the concept of "The Expanding Torrent," a descriptive title for the manner in which attacking troops may alter their course when diverted by enemy resistance or obstacles and be reinforced by more advancing troops until the "torrent" grows stronger and sweeps the opposition away. Attempts to relate battlefield geometry and changing troop ratios have had only limited success. Using Sir Basil's concept of the expanding torrent, one may perceive an analogy in calculations on the flow of fluids. Is it possible that the new and more powerful computers in the service of new branches of theoretical physics now being developed to calculate the flow of fluids can be applied to the simulation of the changing battlefield?

Chapter 10

"The Division Has Bled to Death"

For about six months—from the middle of July 1943 to the middle of January 1944—the German 16th Panzer Grenadier Division was almost constantly in combat in the southeastern Ukraine, just north of the Crimean Peninsula, along the southern portion of the long Russo-German battle line. The division, commanded by Lt. Gen. Count Gerhard von Schwerin, was a part of the XXX Corps, under the command of General of Artillery Maximilian Fretter-Pico. The XXX Corps was in turn an element first of Col.-Gen. Eberhard von Mackensen's First Panzer Army and later Col.-Gen. Karl Adolph Hollidt's Sixth Army. (This, of course, was a newly created Sixth Army, established after the surrender of Gen. Friedrich Paulus' original Sixth Army at Stalingrad early in 1943.) These armies were elements of Field Marshal Eric von Manstein's Army Group South during most of these operations, although in January 1944 the Sixth Army (including the XXX Corps and the 16th Panzer Grenadier Division) was shifted to the control of Army Group A, under Field Marshal Paul L. E. von Kleist.

During this six-month period the XXX Corps, and its 16th Panzer Grenadier Division, were being almost constantly battered by elements of the Soviet South Front (or army group)—later (20 October) redesignated the 4th Ukrainian Front—commanded by Gen. F. I. Tolbukhin. As Soviet units became depleted and exhausted, Tolbukhin would pull them out of the line and feed in fresh divisions and armies. The overextended Germans, however, were rarely able to withdraw units from the line for rest, and though individual replacements were received from time to time, these were never enough to bring the dwindling German units back to strength. In a book written after the war, Fretter-Pico also complained about the quality of those few replacements who were received; he said that his infantry divisions received only the manpower dregs, after the requirements of the Navy, the Luftwaffe, the SS, and technical services had been met.[1]

In mid-January Fretter-Pico requested each of his division commanders—four infantry, one panzer-grenadier—to submit to him a report about the status of their units. In response, on 20 January General von Schwerin reported on the status of the 16th Panzer Grenadier Division. He enclosed reports he had received from two of his subordinate commanders.

THE REPORT

Schwerin's report, verbatim, follows:

Report from Commander, 16th Panzer Grenadier Division, to the Commanding General of Artillery Fretter-Pico, 20 January 1944

The division was cited three times in the Wehrmacht Report during the great defensive battles of last summer. Committed repeatedly at decisive points of combat—on the Mius, the Donets, and at Zaporoshye—the division suffered extremely heavy casualties three times. In these battles, the division lost 9411 men; consequently, in relation to its former infantry combat strength, the division was almost destroyed three times. By using its own reserves and by the arrival of replacements, the division still managed to maintain its combat effectiveness. After the end of the battle of Zaporoshye, however, this could no longer be achieved. The combat strength and combat effectiveness of the division—especially, of course, of the infantry—had been decisively weakened at this point. The reserves for regeneration had been exhausted.

At this point—20 October 1943—the division went into combat in the area southwest of Dniepropetrovsk without any prior refreshening [rest and reorganization]. During the following period, from 20 October 1943 to 14 January 1944, the division suffered additional casualties of 5120 men—killed, wounded, missing, and sick—and once more was committed, without pause, to the following main sectors of combat:

> 20–30 October: Battles in the Zakhagan sector;
> 1–12 November: Battles north of Goloye Pole;
> 11–30 November: Battle for Goloye Pole;
> 4–7 December: Battle for Nazarovka;
> 1–2 January: Battles south of Nazarovka;
> 10–14 January: Battles for Novo Nikolyaevka.

Considering the present combat strength of the infantry, this again is equivalent to being destroyed at least three times. The division infantry has lost its complement of personnel at least six times since the start of the battles last summer.

Now the division has bled to death. The combat effectiveness of the infantry—I must make a very difficult, painful, but true report—has dropped below the current general standard of infantry divisions. Battalions from other infantry divisions committed recently in the sector of this division have fought better than my own battalions.

For amplification, I attach special condition reports from the grenadier regiments. . . .

The division's combat effectiveness currently lies only in the artillery and the armored units. The infantry is no longer able to stand up to a major attack.

[MAJ. GEN. COUNT GERHARD VON SCHWERIN]

Enclosure: Report on the Combat Effectiveness of the 156th Grenadier Regiment

The strong decline in combat power is apparent not only in the statistical decrease, but especially in the considerable deterioration in the personnel complement. During its commitment at the Mius, from 17 July to 15 August 1943, the regiment lost 1850 NCOs and men who had been brought to a high state of combat effectiveness in the preceding training period. This loss was partially compensated for by the subsequent assimilation of 1222 NCOs and men who had had brief training in the field replacement battalion. The battles at Isyum and the withdrawal to the Dnieper caused the regiment 856 losses of NCOs and men. It was no longer possible to make up for these losses by fully qualified replacements; in the following allocations of replacements of at most 317 men, there were a few returning from convalescence, but most of them were older men who had been "combed out," men with only a minimum of combat effectiveness.

After the Zaporoshye casualties (342 NCOs and men) the last well-trained people were gone. An especially unfavorable factor in this situation was the completely inadequate number of men capable of rising to officer status; the reason for this was that the allocated replacements of NCOs had had no experience at the front at all, and the heavy casualties among the older men made it impossible to find potential officers in the companies.

Battles in the Zakhagan sector cost the regiment 1366 more casualties of NCOs and men up to 31 December 1943. In the light of already weak combat strengths, this became more and more of a burden. The 1311 NCOs and men who arrived as replacements in this period were unable to receive any training, since they were constantly needed to keep the greatly debilitated companies to some degree ready for combat. Consequently, there was a constant turnover within the companies, which meant that there could be no close personal ties maintained at that level.

The 300 replacements who arrived at the beginning of January were immediately used in the fight for the area Ternovatka–Orlova–burial mound, which resulted in 485 casualties of NCOs and men. This means that currently the regiment has a battle strength of 85 NCOs and 484 men who have been heavily committed in Russia for only a relatively short time and whose combat effectiveness is extremely slight. The physical strength of individuals has also been greatly diminished by the past hard battles. Constantly exposed to inclement weather, the grenadiers have had their capabilities strained to the utmost. In addition, there has been the adverse effect on morale of being incessantly under fire and of the enemy's great numerical superiority.

Since 18 July 1943, the regiment has suffered 4701 casualties of NCOs and men, amounting to about 200 percent of its authorized combat strength; or, based on a battalion battle strength of 1200–1500 men, the regiment has been destroyed about four times since September 1943. Against this loss, there have been 3209 allocations of NCOs and men; about one-third of these are soldiers returning from convalescence, while the remaining two-thirds have completely inadequate training and experience. This is particularly true of the noncommissioned officers.

This minimal combat strength also has an effect on weapons, particularly since possibilities for manning heavy weapons are totally inadequate.

These conditions indicate that the combat effectiveness of the regiment is no longer adequate for a successful major battle.

Signed FISCHER

Enclosure: Report on Combat Effectiveness of the 60th (Motorized) Grenadier Regiment

The combat elements of the companies have changed several times within half a year, so that cohesion has been lost; the soldiers in the companies scarcely know one another. The few good replacements that have arrived are gone, and the replacements who have had no experience at the front are only poorly trained, or not trained at all, in handling automatic weapons and close-range weapons.

It is impossible for the remaining young officers and the "combed out" inexperienced potential officer candidates to give the soldiers the necessary backbone. They do not have the requisite combat experience; they become casualties themselves after a short time; and therefore they can have no effect on the soldiers.

After long major engagements, and casualties experienced again and again, the soldiers themselves are crushed in spirit and currently hardly can be expected to withstand or hold out against a major attack after strong artillery preparation. Most of them are lethargic and apathetic, and can be led only by the greatest personal commitment of the few officers available.

In the current condition, the regiment is qualified only to a limited degree to undergo and endure a major battle.

Signed as deputy—MAJOR GROLLMANN

ANALYSIS

The internal evidence of the report indicates that on 17 July the division was about 10,000 strong, close to 90 percent of its T/O&E (Tables of Organization and Equipment) strength. During the thirty days between 17 July and 15 August, engaged in constant defensive combat, the division suffered about 8000 losses. Apparently some of these were men hospitalized due to illness. In the months of July and August in temperate climates, expected losses (mostly to the hospital) for injuries and illness are about 0.15 percent per day. If (to be on the safe side) that normal loss rate is doubled, it can be assumed that not more than 900 of the division's losses were due to illness (and probably not more than 500). Thus casualty losses were at least 7000, or more than 233 men per day.

It is clear from the report that the division received some replacements during this time—but nowhere near enough to make up for losses incurred. On the basis of the start strength on 17 July, this is an average percent loss of more than 2.3 percent per day and closer to 4.0 percent at the end of the period. Because of the inevitable fluctuations of intensity of battle, this means that there were certainly days when the division suffered more (on some days much more) than 5 percent casualties per day. (In comparison, the average loss of U.S. divisions in Europe in World War II on *intensive* days of combat was almost exactly 1 percent per day. It has been estimated that on the Eastern Front during World War II the average loss of German divisions on intensive days of combat was less than 2 percent per day.)

By 15 August the division strength was less than 6000 men, or probably close to 60 percent of its start strength. There were obviously times during the previous month that the division was less than 50 percent of its start strength.

General von Schwerin's report states: "In relation to its former infantry strength [about 3500 men] the division was almost destroyed three times. . . . By using its own replacements [transferring men from other units into the infantry regiments] and by the arrival of replacements, the division still managed to maintain its combat effectiveness."

What was the breakpoint, or the threshold of effectiveness, of the 16th Panzer Grenadier Division? What of its regiments, one of which suffered close to 70 percent casualties during those thirty days? Obviously that breakpoint or threshold was more than 30 percent, since the division commander says the division remained combat-effective.

General von Schwerin continued: "20 October 1943 [after another battle with heavy losses] the division went into combat . . . without any prior refreshening [rest and reorganization] . . . From 20 October 1943 to 14 January 1944, the division suffered additional casualties of 5120 men. . . ." He then lists six battles and adds "Considering the present combat strength of the infantry [about 1800 men], this again is the equivalent of being destroyed at least three times."

Using the same basis for calculation as before, it can be assumed that in the winter weather the sick loss was about 0.30 percent (twice that of summer), or about 1600 men. Thus battle casualties in those 90-odd days were probably about 3500 men, no less. This is about forty men per day, or (considering declining strength) an average of probably slightly more than 1 percent per day for ninety days. Again considering lulls in battle, there were days the division must have suffered more (and, again, probably much more) than 3 percent casualties. Considering the bitterly cold weather and the very short days (both circumstances that historically reduce combat casualty rates), this was an extremely high loss rate.

The effect on the division was succinctly summarized by Schwerin: "The division has bled to death." In other words, he considered that the division had passed the threshold of adequate combat effectiveness. At exactly what point, and for exactly what reason, the threshold was passed can only be guessed from the report. But clearly it was a combination of casualties (particularly the losses of trained and experienced soldiers), inadequate numbers and quality of replacements, and probably sheer exhaustion.

No simple breakpoint percentage is applicable to the case of the 16th Panzer Grenadier Division. However, possibly Schwerin's report, considered in combination with other examples in a reasonably adequate sample of experience, can shed light on the breakpoint phenomenon, to which more attention is given in Part IV of this book.

POSTSCRIPT

Not long after Lieutenant-General von Schwerin submitted his report to his corps commander, General of Artillery Fretter-Pico, these two generals were together at a conference with the army commander, Colonel-General Hollidt. (At that time a German lieutenant-general was the equivalent of an American two-star [major] general; a general of artillery—or cavalry or infantry—was the equivalent of an American three-star [lieutenant] general; and a colonel-general was the equivalent of an American four-star general.) During the conference a heated argument broke out between Schwerin and Fretter-Pico, very possibly over the casualties and replacements of the 16th Panzer Grenadier Division. General Hollidt resolved the argument by relieving General von Schwerin of his command on the spot.[2]

It is indicative of the way in which the German army operated that, not long after this, Schwerin was placed in command of another division and early in 1945 was placed in command of the LXXVI Panzer Corps with the rank of General of Armor, the equivalent of a lieutenant general in the American army. He had been properly relieved of command for insubordination, but due consideration was given to the stress under which he had been operating; his superb performance as a division commander was recognized, and he was eventually rewarded for his ability.

Chapter 11

The 28th Division
in the Huertgen Forest

BY CHARLES B. MACDONALD

SETTING THE STAGE

All through the fall of 1944—from mid-September to mid-December—
American soldiers fought to conquer a great forest south and southeast of
the German border city of Aachen, a forest twenty miles wide and ten miles
deep. The forest got its name from a village near the eastern extremity, the
village of Huertgen. To American soldier and German soldier alike, the
name Huertgen Forest came to symbolize a special grim way of fighting a
war, a special grim way of dying.

Five American infantry divisions and a combat command of armor
fought full-fledged battles inside the Huertgen Forest, plus supporting
tank, tank destroyer, chemical, medical, engineer, and artillery units,
approximately 120,000 men augmented by hundreds of replacements. On
the German side, six understrength divisions plus supporting units, around
80,000 men plus replacements.

Americans killed, missing, captured, and wounded in the forest totaled
24,000 men. Another 9000 succumbed to so-called nonbattle causes:
trench foot, respiratory diseases, combat fatigue. The total: 33,000. On the

Western Front in World War II, losses of 10 percent of a unit's strength in a three-month period were considered high. These were losses of more than 25 percent.

It was the most prolonged and one of the more costly battles fought by American forces on the Western Front. For the most part, the battle was fought in separate division actions and, despite the heavy losses, all but one of the divisions eventually either succeeded or reached a stalemate. The story of that one division's defeat (the 28th Infantry Division in the battle for the town of Schmidt) is replete with starkly vivid examples of what can go wrong in battle.

BACKGROUND OF THE BATTLE

As Allied armies in September 1944 drew up to the German frontier after a 500-mile pursuit across France and Belgium, they were short of almost every commodity needed for battle—rations, artillery ammunition, and gasoline—and the men and machines were exhausted.

Yet Allied commanders were reluctant to break the momentum of their drive at least until they had breached the border fortifications, known to the Germans as the West Wall, to the Allies as the Siegfried Line. In the vicinity of the border city of Aachen, the commander of the U.S. First Army, Lt. Gen. Courtney Hodges, authorized one of his corps to breach the Siegfried Line before pausing. In rolling countryside south and east of Aachen, the corps accomplished that until a fresh German division arrived to impel a halt. Yet nobody saw that as more than a temporary delay; as soon as the Allied armies could replenish their supplies and concentrate their forces they could get on with a drive to the Rhine River and beyond.

A special problem existed in the vicinity of Aachen in the form of the vast, almost trackless woodland known as the Huertgen Forest. General Hodges considered that before renewing the offensive on the open ground near Aachen he needed to clear that forest, else the Germans might assemble under concealment of the dense firs for counterattack. As badly beaten as the Germans appeared to be, clearing the forest looked like no major assignment in any case. While the rest of the First Army paused to build up supplies, the 9th Infantry Division was to sweep the forest.

The job turned out to be far more difficult than anybody had foreseen. The Germans had no major reinforcements to throw in, but they committed hastily formed small units—a battalion here, a battalion there—and amid the thick foliage of the Huertgen Forest a resolute small unit could do the work of a much larger force. Through the last days of September and through much of October, the 9th Division worked to clear the forest, but when the division at last ground to a halt spent and exhausted, most of the forest still belonged to the Germans.

The 9th Division had created a salient in the forest not quite two miles deep but was far short of high ground on the far fringes of the forest needed to anchor the First Army's flank, in particular high ground marked by the town of Schmidt. And the cost had been high: more than 4500 casualties.

By that time, the First Army's logistical situation had improved to the point that General Hodges contemplated renewing his main offensive in conjunction with another American force, the Ninth Army, which had entered the line north of Aachen. He planned a jump-off early in November, but first he wanted that high ground at Schmidt in order to anchor his flank.

Hodges called on a veteran division that had been resting since the fighting in Normandy, the 28th Infantry Division; but, seemingly ignoring the difficulties the 9th Division had experienced in the forest, Hodges assigned the 28th Division a second mission. Once the high ground at Schmidt was in hand, the division was to turn southwest and with the help of a combat command of armor was to clear fairly open ground just south of the Huertgen Forest known as the Monschau Corridor, which would afford the First Army a second avenue of advance.

That added assignment, plus a reaction to a counterattack that had struck the 9th Division during its advance, left the 28th Division commander, Maj. Gen. Norman D. Cota, with little initiative. By order from above, one regiment was to drive north to the woodline overlooking the village of Huertgen, thereby blocking the route the Germans had used earlier for counterattack. A second regiment was to drive south to seize a road junction deep in the forest from which eventually to open roads into the Monschau Corridor. That left only one regiment to make the main effort to take Schmidt.

Displaying at least some concern for the possible difficulty of the tasks, Hodges did provide the 28th Division strong reinforcements. In addition to the usual attached medium tank battalion and self-propelled tank-destroyer battalion, he afforded the division an entire engineer combat group of three engineer battalions and provided strong artillery reinforcements: a 4.2-inch chemical mortar battalion and eight battalions of corps artillery.

Providing engineer support was a bow to the dearth of roads through the forest. In the salient forged by the 9th Division there was no road, only muddy firebreaks and trails. There was a road leading north to Huertgen and another south toward the Monschau Corridor, but the regiment making the main effort against Schmidt faced a particular problem. From the jump-off point on the fringe of the forest at the village of Germeter, a dirt road led into the next village of Vossenack, but from Vossenack across the deep wooded gorge of the little Kall River leading to the village of Kommerscheidt and thence to Schmidt there was only a narrow cart track, whose existence could not be verified—because of the foliage—by aerial photographs. Schmidt itself was a crossroads town, but three of the four roads leading into Schmidt would still belong to the Germans: a principal highway leading to Schmidt from the Monschau Corridor and out the other side and another leading downhill to the southeast to a big dam on the upper reaches of the little Roer River, the Schwammenaüel Dam.

The Schwammenaüel Dam was one of two big dams on the upper Roer River designed to prevent flooding farther north after the river emerged from the Huertgen Forest into flatlands east of Aachen. It was over those flatlands that the big offensive by the First and Ninth armies was to pass.

As early as October the 9th Division's G-2 had noted the existence of the dams. They were clearly discernible on a map and somebody found a description of them in a Baedecker travel guide (which somebody thereupon stamped TOP SECRET). Yet nobody appeared to take note of the peril the dams might pose if they remained in German hands. If the Germans controlled the dams, they could either demolish them or release the waters in a calculated flow, in either case to cause widespread flooding of the flatlands to the north. If by that time troops of the First and Ninth armies had crossed the Roer River, the flooding would wipe out their tactical bridges and expose the troops on the east bank of the river to defeat in detail.

Although German commanders were expecting the Americans to renew their attack from Germeter (not toward Schmidt but to the northeast through the village of Huertgen), they were keenly aware of what a tactical ace they possessed in the Roer River dams. Indeed, at the top level of German command, the commander in chief in the West, Field Marshal Gerd von Rundstedt, had a special interest in the dams. Unlike his subordinates, he had been let in on a secret, that the German Führer, Adolf Hitler, was planning a major offensive for late November or early December in the region south of the Huertgen Forest in eastern Belgium and northern

Luxembourg, the Ardennes. If conditions were to be right for that offensive, he had to prevent the Americans from crossing the Roer River.

As a corollary to the Ardennes offensive (the purpose still known only to von Rundstedt) the Germans were preparing to relieve the division that had been holding the Monschau Corridor, the 89th Infantry Division, so that it could be rebuilt for the offensive. Otherwise, only a weak 275th Infantry Division stood in the 28th Division's path, but in the restricted confines of the Huertgen Forest that weak division had been sufficient to create real problems for the U.S. 9th Division.

The 28th Division commander, General Cota, was unhappy with the plan of attack, but there was nothing he could do about it. He was also unhappy that the 28th Division was to attack one day in advance of the main First Army–Ninth Army offensive. That was designed to attract German reserves from the main front, but for the 28th Division there was a built-in peril in the plan: The 28th Division was to attack on 2 November, no matter what the weather, whereas the main offensive was to delay until the weather turned favorable for air support. Regardless of the weather, the main attack was to begin no later than 16 November; but should that prove to be the case, the 28th Division would be attacking alone for more than two weeks, a cynosure for all German reserves along that entire sector of the front, more than 170 miles.

Nobody intended it, but the 28th Division was to be thrown to the wolves.

THE BATTLE IN THE NORTH

The target date of 2 November dawned cold and misty. A heavy artillery preparation preceded the attack, but the weather denied help from fighter bombers.

In the north, two battalions of the 109th Infantry headed for the woodline overlooking the village of Huertgen. One battalion advancing through the forest gained the woodline with surprising ease, but another, advancing along the Germeter–Huertgen highway, ran into a minefield. Early the next day, 3 November, that battalion was trying to outflank the minefield when a small German force attacked the other battalion at the woodline. Although noisy, the attack posed no real threat, but through a garbled radio message the commander of the battalion along the highway thought he was supposed to send help. He dispatched two companies that soon became enmeshed in the other battalion's fight, and the attempt to advance on Huertgen via the highway came to a halt.

Although the 109th Infantry still had a reserve battalion, attempts to thwart German infiltration in the forest had virtually tied up that battalion—that plus the necessity to contain a German salient along fire-breaks and trails deeper inside the forest. By the end of 3 November, the mold of the 109th Infantry's positions had almost set. For several more days the regiment tried to eliminate the German salient and to advance along the Germeter–Huertgen highway, but to no avail. Every movement served only to increase already alarming casualties and to ensnare the companies and platoons ever more inextricably in the coils of the forest.

On the German side, even as the 28th Division's attack began, the commander of Army Group B, Field Marshal Walter Model, was convening his subordinate commanders for a map exercise based on a theoretical American attack in the vicinity of Huertgen. The exercise was barely under way when a telephone call told of the actual American attack. Sending the responsible corps commander back to his post, Model continued the map exercise with the actual situation as subject. When it became apparent that the main American thrust seemed to be against Huertgen, Model ordered a portion of the panzer grenadiers of a reserve division, the 116th Panzer Division, to move immediately to Huertgen and counterattack.[1] That was the force that hit the 109th Infantry early on 3 November. In the meantime, Model ordered the rest of the 116th Panzer Division to head for Huertgen.

THE BATTLE IN THE SOUTH

Back on the American side, on the jump-off day of 2 November the 110th Infantry had attempted to drive south from Germeter through the woods to seize a forest-cloaked road junction known as Raffelsbrand. Yet no sooner had men of the two attacking battalions risen from their foxholes than a rain of machine-gun and mortar fire brought them to earth. By painful, costly infiltration one battalion finally reached the triple concertina wire encompassing pillboxes of the Siegfried Line at Raffelsbrand, but the enemy gave no sign of weakening. In late afternoon, both battalions reeled back, dazed and stricken, to the line of departure. As with the 109th Infantry, continuing efforts by those two battalions got nowhere, resulting only in ever-increasing casualties.

On the third day of the attack, 4 November, General Cota approved releasing the 110th Infantry's third battalion from division reserve to bypass the German positions and take the village of Simonskall, which would put an American force in the rear of the pillboxes at Raffelsbrand. The battalion gained Simonskall with little difficulty, but there the battalion remained, making no effort to move against Raffelsbrand, and at Raffelsbrand the enemy held firm.

THE ADVANCE ON SCHMIDT

The situation was at first far less gloomy in the center, where the 112th Infantry was making the main effort against Schmidt. With tanks in close support, one battalion advanced rapidly from Germeter along an open ridgeline into the village of Vossenack, then all the way through the village to an open nose of ground beyond it. There the men began to dig in, undeterred by German fire but uncomfortable in the knowledge that just beyond a wooded draw to the north there was high ground still in German hands, the Brandenberg–Bergstein ridge.

Why those men had to dig in on open ground when they might have defended just as well—perhaps better—from positions among the houses of Vossenack, nobody bothered to say. Possibly for the simple, inane reason that somebody back in the G-3 operations section had drawn a goose egg with a grease pencil on a map, meaning the objective, and that was what the men were to gain and there they were to stay.

The commander of the 112th Infantry, Lt. Col. Carl Peterson, had in the meantime begun the advance on Schmidt along a wooded draw just south of the Vossenack ridge. It was difficult going in the thick woods, so when word came of the swift advance into Vossenack Colonel Peterson called off the attack and made plans to move the next morning through Vossenack and down the cart track leading across the Kall River to Kommerscheidt and Schmidt.

Although Peterson's decision delayed an advance on Schmidt by a day, it otherwise proved fortuitous. When Peterson with two battalions began to advance from Vossenack into the Kall gorge, not a German stood in the way. Beyond the deep gorge of the Kall, the leading battalion entered Kommerscheidt, quickly dispatched a group of rear-echelon Germans, and proceeded on to Schmidt.

Because Schmidt sprawled spread-eagled across a bald ridge, defending the town with a single battalion was more a matter of outposts than of a solid line, yet Colonel Peterson wanted to retain his other battalion at Kommerscheidt to afford a defense in depth. No doubt lulled by the ease of the advance, the men at Schmidt made little effort to dig foxholes but instead holed up in the buildings. They placed daisy chains of antitank mines across the three main roads leading into Schmidt but made no effort to dig them in. The battalion commander himself was not at hand to demand more, for he was setting up his headquarters in a pillbox midway between Schmidt and Kommerscheidt.

Taking Schmidt had been easy. Too easy.

At headquarters of the 28th Division, General Cota was amazed at the facility with which his men had captured the division objective. So many telephone calls of congratulations did he receive from corps and other division commanders that he began to feel (in his words) like "a little Napoleon." Yet, like his subordinate commanders, Cota was sharply conscious of how exposed and isolated were the two battalions beyond the Kall and was anxious to assure that tanks and tank destroyers reach them during the night.

Getting that support across the Kall gorge along what turned out to be a narrow, precipitous little cart track proved a difficult and frustrating assignment. As determined by attached engineers, the track was in effect a narrow shelf, limited abruptly on one side by a clifflike wall of dirt studded with rock obstructions and on the other by a sheer drop down into the gorge. When the tank company commander arrived in his tank to try to negotiate the shelf, the shoulder above the gorge began to give way, and the rock obstructions on the other side denied movement in that direction. Managing to save his tank by backing up quickly, the tank commander returned to his men and reported the trail impassable. Word came down that the engineers were to work on the trail through the night, and the tanks were to be ready to move through at dawn.

It was still dark on the morning of November 4, when a platoon of Sherman tanks set out to negotiate the little trail across the Kall. The platoon leader's tank in the lead almost immediately set off a mine, damaging the tank and partially blocking the trail, but with the aid of a winch the tankers finally got four other tanks past. They got past the spot where rock outcroppings sharply constricted the trail, but they left the left shoulder of the trail torn and crumbling. At the little Kall River, one of the four tanks stuck in the mud and threw a track, but the three others continued on to Kommerscheidt.

Close behind these tanks, the tank company commander tried to get the rest of his tanks through. The first to try plunged off the trail but came to rest in a position where it could be used as a buffer for the other tanks to pass. Two got past, but at the rock outcroppings both slipped off the trail and threw their tracks. Nothing—not even a dexterous jeep—could get past.

THE GERMAN REACTION

At Field Marshal Model's map exercise on 3 November, Model and his subordinate commanders had been quick to note the American advance on Schmidt. The Germans had clearly been wrong about the American main effort: The attack was aimed not at Huertgen but at Schmidt. Model promptly ordered the 89th Infantry Division, which was pulling back from the Monschau Corridor, to halt in place and prepare to recapture Schmidt. One battalion had already passed through Schmidt and halted less than a mile beyond the town, while another battalion had yet to reach the town and halted on the western approaches. Nobody in Schmidt was aware of the close proximity of those two German battalions, for nobody did any patrolling.

Confronted with the new direction of American attack, Field Marshal Model also ordered the 116th Panzer Division's panzer regiment to back-track on its route to Huertgen and go instead to Schmidt. At daybreak the next morning, 4 November, the panzer division's Mark IVs and big Mark V Panthers were to help men of the 89th Division retake Schmidt and drive the Americans back across the Kall gorge.

The German artillery preparation began at Schmidt just as day was breaking. The shelling quickly knocked out telephone lines, and sleepy radio operators to the rear failed for a long time to discern the break and turn on their radios, so that more than an hour passed before any American artillery support came through. In the meantime, the German Mark IVs and Panthers were bypassing the exposed antitank mines and shooting up the landscape. Among the defending Americans confusion mounted. Somebody said the word was to withdraw. Somebody else passed the word along. Before long, men were grabbing wildly at weapons and equipment and streaming from the town. Most headed for Kommerscheidt, where with difficulty the men defending that village managed to stop some of them, sometimes at gunpoint. Some 200 others headed into the woods southwest of Schmidt, where the Germans were eventually to round them up.

In less than three hours, it was over at Schmidt.

DISINTEGRATION OF THE 28TH DIVISION

Reorganizing quickly, the Germans continued against Kommerscheidt, but the defenders there had the support those at Schmidt had not had. They had artillery support on full alert and they had three Sherman tanks. Those tanks knocked out three of the German tanks, a rocket from a bazooka accounted for a fourth, and in clearing skies a bomb from a P-47 accounted for a fifth. In midafternoon the Germans fell back to take cover amid the buildings of Schmidt.

General Cota promptly ordered Colonel Peterson to retake Schmidt, which demonstrated how far out of touch with reality Cota was. He was out of touch with reality about the situation along the Kall trail as well, for all through the day word at division headquarters was that the trail was open, but nobody sent anybody to investigate. The engineers working along the trail actually were accomplishing little, wary of using explosives against the rock outcroppings lest they damage the nearby tanks. It was after midnight before Cota finally learned of the impasse along the trail. Either clear the trail by daybreak, he ordered, or roll the tanks over the cliff. That turned out to be their fate.

Soon after daylight on 5 November nine self-propelled tank destroyers and six remaining tanks crossed the Kall gorge to join the defenders of Kommerscheidt. There the defenders were holding their own, for a clear day enabled the American fighter-bombers to set upon anything German that moved from Schmidt toward Kommerscheidt.

That night of 5 November the Germans made what would have appeared from the outset an obvious move. They sent the 116th Panzer Division's reconnaissance battalion to cut the trail in the Kall gorge. Although the engineers working there had been charged with defending the trail, they had done precious little toward that end, and the Germans moved almost with impunity. Once again, nobody could get through to Kommerscheidt.

Fortunately for the men beyond the Kall, the German occupation of the gorge was to be short-lived. Early on 6 November a depleted battalion of the 110th Infantry, removed from the terrible fighting for the Raffelsbrand road junction, marched under orders from General Cota to reinforce the troops at Kommerscheidt and retake Schmidt. Learning that the Germans were blocking the Kall trail, the battalion advanced along a parallel fire-break. There were Germans there, too, but the battalion fought its way through and the panzer division's reconnaissance battalion fell back from the gorge. Yet when Colonel Peterson saw the pitiful condition of the battalion that reinforced him, he knew it would still be impossible to retake Schmidt. He sent the battalion to dig in at the woodline behind Kommerscheidt, thereby again to provide a defense in depth.

At the same time, more trouble was developing elsewhere for the 28th Division, this time on the Vossenack ridge. There, each day, men of the battalion of the 112th Infantry on the exposed nose of the ridge had undergone heavy shelling from German guns whose fire was obviously directed from the Brandenberg–Berstein ridge overlooking Vossenack. Although the men were well dug in and casualties light thus far, it was a terrible strain on a man's nerves, particularly just after dawn each morning when, without fail, the Germans delivered a heavy pounding.

So concerned about those men was the assistant division commander, Brig. Gen. George A. Davis, that he ordered a platoon of tanks to stay in Vossenack at all times to bolster morale. The company commanders were also deeply concerned about their men and reported their concern to their battalion commander, telling him that some men had to be ordered to eat, that others cried like children. But the battalion commander did nothing; he was sitting in his basement command post, his head in his hands. Nobody took any step to pull those men back from the exposed ridge to the shelter of the houses in Vossenack.

On the morning of 6 November, what might have been seen as inevitable at last happened. That morning it was strangely quiet, no early-morning bombardment. Off to the left, a German machine gun fired. Somebody screamed. Then, finally, the accustomed shelling.

The men could stand no more. Panic-ridden, some grabbed at their equipment and broke for the rear. Others saw what was happening and joined the exodus. Soon it was a *sauve qui peut*: every man for himself.

At the battalion command post near the center of Vossenack officers of the battalion staff tried to halt the flight, but few of the men would heed them, and some who did soon took flight again once the officers turned their backs. Said a platoon leader: "It was the saddest sight I have ever seen. . . . [Men] pushing, shoving, throwing away equipment, trying to outrace the artillery and each other, all in a frantic effort to escape. . . . It was a heartbreaking, demoralizing scene."

Nobody saw any Germans. In fact, there were no Germans, but the Germans were quick to follow up on the retreat. Panzer grenadiers moved quickly into the fringe of Vossenack, prompting General Davis to call on the attached engineers to send a battalion to clear the village. Still wearing rubber hip boots used against the mud in the forest, the engineers the next day joined a platoon of tanks to drive the Germans out.

News of the debacle at Vossenack prompted immense concern at higher levels of the American command. Disturbed lest the Germans push on to Germeter and split the 28th Division, the corps commander called upon the 4th Infantry Division, then moving to join the First Army's main offensive, to send a regiment to relieve the 109th Infantry, which then was to help retake Schmidt. That hope proved as elusive as the others before it, for whether anybody was ready to admit it or not, the 28th Division was no longer an effective offensive force; and just what the division still might accomplish on the defense was soon to be tested again.

Soon after daylight on 7 November German tanks and infantry, advancing behind an hour's artillery preparation, moved from Schmidt against Kommerscheidt. Although American tanks and tank destroyers knocked out five German tanks, they paid with three tank destroyers and two tanks of their own. The American infantrymen began to give—not in panic as at Schmidt and Vossenack but to give nonetheless. Individually and in small groups, the men who could escape the German fire fell back to seek refuge in the reserve position at the woodline.

The 28th Division's holdings beyond the Kall were reduced at that point to a small defensive perimeter at the woodline where the Kall trail emerges from the gorge. Nobody on the scene had any real hope of holding that little perimeter for long, and, for once, those away from the scene saw it the same way. Cota telephoned the corps commander, who telephoned General Hodges, and in time permission came for the 28th Division to pull back behind the Kall.

Although parts of the division continued to attack for another five days in an effort to seize the rest of the woodline overlooking Huertgen and to conquer the pillboxes at Raffelsbrand, those were prodigious assignments far beyond the means of a unit that had taken such a physical and moral beating as had the 28th Division. When the division at last was relieved and moved to the Ardennes (there to be hit by the big German offensive in December) the lines remained much as they had been after the third day's fighting, except at that point nobody was on the other side of the Kall River.

ASSESSMENT

So much went wrong in the 28th Division's attack that it is difficult to pin down all the reasons for failure. In the end, attrition certainly had much to do with the failures of the 109th and 110th infantry regiments, but at the start there were other factors: in the case of the 109th Infantry, a garbled radio transmission; and in the case of both regiments, failure to provide close-in mobile fire support from tanks or tank destroyers, which the experience of the 9th Division had shown was essential for any real progress in the dense forest, particularly where prepared defenses such as pillboxes were involved. The commitment of a battalion to get in behind the Raffelsbrand defenses at the village of Simonskall might well have turned that position anyway, but that battalion failed to take advantage of its position once Simonskall was in hand.

The reason for the failure of the battalion of the 112th Infantry on the Vossenack ridge was obvious: faulty position. That battalion clearly could have defended the ridge better from the fringe of Vossenack and, amid the concealment of the buildings, the men would have suffered no such malaise from the observed German shelling as they experienced on the open ground. A battalion commander, cowering in a basement, his head in his hands, obviously contributed to the failure.

At Schmidt the battalion well might have been doomed in any case by the superior strength of enemy forces, including tanks, but the battalion contributed to its problems by failing to organize an adequate defense, to conceal its antitank mines, and to patrol. A battalion commander on the scene rather than in a pillbox well out of town also might have helped. Failure to obtain timely artillery support also contributed to the failure.

At Kommerscheidt eventual defeat was preordained, for in view of the difficulties along the Kall trail, German strength, particularly in armor, was far too superior.

Clearly the 28th Division failed to pay sufficient attention to opening the Kall trail and defending it. Of three attached battalions of engineers, only one worked on what was in effect the lifeline for the troops beyond the Kall, and seldom did that battalion have more than a single company working on the trail at any one time. So too the failure of the engineers to defend the trail.

All these local failures obviously contributed to the overall failure of the 28th Division. But there were broader reasons for the overall failure, matters over which the division commander, General Cota, had no control.

First, a failure by higher commanders to appreciate the importance of the objective of Schmidt and its relationship to control of the Roer River dams. As it turned out, the Germans had to commit only one reserve division—the 116th Panzer Division—to maintain control of the dams, but had more been required, Field Marshal von Rundstedt no doubt would have committed them as needed.

What a tactical ace the Germans had in the Roer River dams was demonstrated later, in February 1945, when the First and Ninth armies had at last drawn up to the Roer River downstream and were preparing to cross. At that point the Germans destroyed the penstocks in the Schwammenaüel Dam, releasing no major cascade of water but instead a gradual flow calculated to produce a long-lasting flood in the valley of the Roer downstream. For eleven days the First and Ninth armies had to sit idly until the waters at last began to recede, and even then the crossing of a swollen river was more difficult than it would have been had there been no flood.

Second, by assigning the 28th Division subsidiary tasks of taking the woodline overlooking the village of Huertgen and taking the Raffelsbrand road junction, higher commanders so reduced the strength available for taking Schmidt that it was markedly inadequate. It should have been at least a two-division attack, with the second division moving up the Monschau Corridor.

Third, by ordering the 28th Division to attack well in advance of the main American offensive, higher commanders practically assured the division's defeat. Had the attacks gone off simultaneously, the 116th Panzer Division, for all the importance of the Roer River dams, probably would have been used not at Schmidt but against the greater threat to the north. Had that been the case, there would have been no German tanks to overrun Schmidt and Kommerscheidt.

Fourth, who in his right mind would assign an objective accessible only by a trail whose very existence nobody could confirm?

And yet another consideration: What if the Americans had early made a concerted effort to capture the Roer dams, an effort—given the paucity of German strength in September—that surely would have succeeded? The Germans then would have faced the same situation that would have confronted any American force that might have crossed the Roer while the dams were in German hands. With a flooded river at their backs (or even the threat of a flooded river) would the Germans have risked a sturdy defense along the approaches to the Roer?

Had that been the case, there might have been no battle of the Huertgen Forest, none of those dreadfully high casualties, which in the case of the 28th Division were the most costly to befall an American division in offensive action on the Western Front: counting attached units, a shocking 6184.[2]

And with the dams in American hands, putting American forces in position to drive deep into the Rhineland, what effect would that have had on Hitler's plans for a grand offensive in the Ardennes region of Belgium and Luxembourg?

Part IV

THE SIMULATION OF DEFEAT

Chapter 12

The Planning and Simulation Dilemma

THE BREAKPOINT MECHANISM

One of the many problems that have plagued the designers of computer models of combat is how to bring about a realistic conclusion of a simulated battle or engagement. Unlike flesh-and-blood soldiers, who are quick to realize when they are approaching or have reached the limits of human endurance or capability, computer warriors are willing and able to continue to fight to the last man on one side or both. This, of course, is not the way it happens in the real world.

In order to approximate reality, therefore, the modeler must put into the program some trigger mechanism that will automatically be activated at that point in the simulated battle when a real-life soldier would be likely to conclude that he cannot or should not fight further.

Most model designers operate on the often-unstated but nonetheless generally accepted assumption that battles are driven (or their outcomes determined) by casualties or attrition. To deal with this problem of battle termination they have inserted into their models arbitrary breakpoints or thresholds triggered by numbers or percentages of casualties incurred. A commonly accepted breakpoint, or threshold, for acknowledgement of defeat is 30 percent casualties. In other words, the computer program will cause an attacker to stop attacking or a defender to withdraw from the field when the casualties of either the attacking or defending force reach 30 percent of starting strength.

Many military men and operations research analysts have doubted the validity of the 30 percent value—or any other arbitrary proportion of strength—as a determinant of defeat or a reason to terminate ongoing combat. Any competent military historian knows that, for a variety of reasons, such a value (whatever it may be) cannot be correct, since it bears no relationship to historical experience. But until or unless such soldiers and/or scholars come up with a more realistic—and quantifiable in some fashion or other—alternative means of assessing or determining success or failure in battle, attrition and an attrition-related breakpoint will remain the basis for determining success or failure in computer simulations of combat.

DOROTHY CLARK AND BREAKPOINTS

Some thirty years ago a significant effort was made to examine the relationship between casualty rates and battle termination (the "breakpoint" issue). This was a study by Dorothy Kneeland Clark of the Operations Research Office (ORO) of Johns Hopkins University.[1] The critical elements of her conclusions:

> The statement that a unit can be considered no longer combat effective when it has suffered a specific casualty percentage is a gross oversimplification not supported by combat data. . . .
> The very wide individual differences in the ability of infantry battalions to carry out a given mission cannot be accounted for in terms of casualties alone, no matter how the data are presented.
> Of the variables other than casualties which may affect the ability of an infantry battalion to carry out its mission, it is believed that failures and breakdowns in leadership, fire support and reinforcement, and communications are the most frequent and powerful influences.

Clark did present some quantitative conclusions, very cautiously hedged with qualifications. These can be interpreted and summarized as follows:

The data indicated that, on the average, a U.S. infantry battalion in World War II became ineffective after suffering, in a few days, cumulative casualties of about 30 percent. Clark noted that rates were likely to be different for units of other size and type. And the 30 percent average that could be inferred from her findings was an average of some forty-four different loss rates between about 10 percent and 70 percent, with rather uniform distribution.

There was nothing in Clark's data, however, to suggest whether the *rate* at which casualties were incurred was significant. Some historians and analysts suspect that 30 percent casualties incurred in a short period of time may affect a division's effectiveness more than the same number of casualties incurred over a longer period of time.

THE RELEVANCE OF HISTORICAL EXPERIENCE

Many operations research analysts are reluctant to rely upon historical experience in considering the effects of weapons on attrition rates or on combat outcomes of the future. History is interesting, but (say these forward-looking scientists) its examples are not really relevant to war in the future. War today is so different from World War II and the Arab–Israeli wars as to make their lessons of dubious value; war in the future will be even more different, making past experience largely irrelevant.

This is an argument that cannot lightly be disregarded. Nor, on the other hand, can it be accepted without question. Before looking further at the evidence of history, therefore, we should try to satisfy ourselves that it really *is* relevant.

Three major bases are cited in support of the argument that historical experience, even recent historical experience, is irrelevant:

a. Weapons in use today are far more lethal than those used in past wars. Thus attrition rates will be much different, and will, of course, be much higher than in the past.

b. Added to the effectiveness of the weapons will be the nature of the modern battlefield, often referred to by operations research analysts as "a target-rich environment." In other words, there are more highly visible weapons, vehicles, and installations on the modern battlefield than in the past, and so the increasingly lethal weapons will have more targets than did the less powerful weapons of the past, further changing the nature and extent of battle lethality.

c. Finally, movement on the modern battlefield will be much faster, because of the greater speed of armored and unarmored vehicles on the earth's surface and of fixed wing and rotary wing aircraft overhead in the skies. There does not seem to be a consensus among operations research analysts as to how this greater speed and mobility will affect attrition rates and battle outcomes. But it is obvious to most analysts that movement rates will be so different that historical statistics based upon previous movement and advance rates will be unrelatable to future battlefields.

These arguments appear quite reasonable and are accepted by many scholars, scientists, and soldiers concerned with planning for and simulating modern war. There is only one problem with the arguments. Overwhelming evidence demonstrates that they are almost totally erroneous conclusions drawn from superficial consideration of the relevant facts.

Let me deal with these arguments very quickly.

First, let's look at the conventional wisdom regarding the effect of increasingly lethal weapons on attrition rates. Yes, the weapons have unquestionably become more lethal. Figure 12.1 shows that the power of weapons has increased tremendously since gunpowder weapons became really effective early in the seventeenth century.

This, of course, will explain why there have been steadily increasing casualty rates in battles since about 1600. Right? No, wrong! Figure 12.2 shows how casualty rates have rather steadily declined, not increased, during these centuries in which weapons lethality has risen so sharply. This might seem to be counterintuitive. Or the reader may wonder if he is being subjected to some clever sleight-of-hand with statistics.

No, this is straightforward, unequivocal statistical fact. The reason is explained in Figure 12.3, which shows that as weapons lethality has increased over the past four centuries, dispersion of troops on the battlefield has increased at least equally rapidly. The weapons are more lethal, but the forces have become so dispersed that most of the increased weapons effectiveness is dissipated harmlessly over empty space. Figure 12.4 demonstrates this effect of dispersion in another fashion, by showing how typical military forces, 100,000 men in strength, have occupied increasingly large areas in each successive period of history. How long such a trend can continue is a matter for conjecture. That there has been such a trend, and that it has yet to bottom out, is undeniable.

But again some may demur. Isn't the argument about declining casualty rates refuted by the evidence of the recent Arab–Israeli wars, particularly 1973, where the combat was more intensive than in World War II and casualty effects much greater?

No, it is not, as will be seen below.

Well, what about the "target-rich environment," with its likelihood that

Figure 12.1

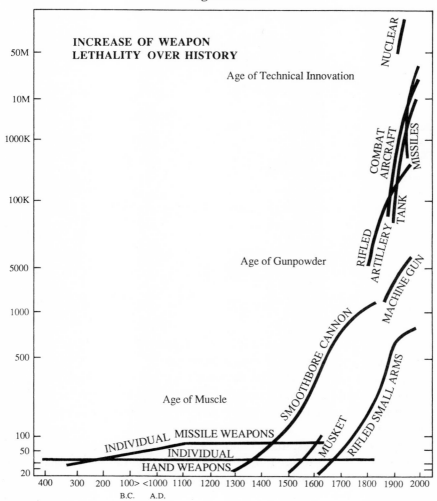

INCREASE OF WEAPON
LETHALITY OVER HISTORY

Age of Technical Innovation

Age of Gunpowder

Age of Muscle

more numerous weapons will be more concentrated on the modern battle-field and more easily taken under fire by more accurate weapons?

The target-rich environment is a myth, as can be seen from Figure 12.5, which is an elaboration of part of Figure 12.4. It shows how the actual number of large, not easily concealed weapons has increased to some extent in wars of the twentieth century. However, because of the steady increases in dispersion of troops and vehicles over the same time period,

Figure 12.2

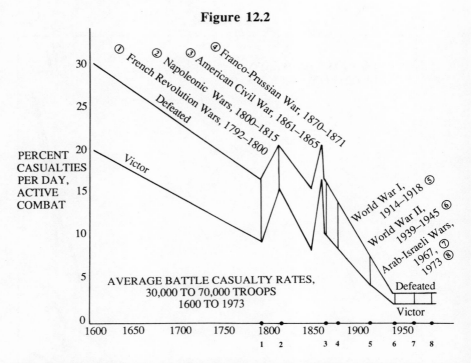

the density of targets has declined rather steadily. The battlefield is increasingly lonely and deserted; it is *not* target-rich.

Historical trends and patterns have been quite consistent over long periods, and this has been true during modern history, when the industrial revolution has caused revolutionary changes in weapons and other military technology.

This is not to suggest that technology has not had an enormous effect on the ways in which wars are fought. There are many examples, in addition to the revolutionary changes in weapons effects already cited. But the point is that the humans fighting the wars have adjusted to these technological changes in such a way that the patterns have been consistent, and the trends quite steady and predictable.

Just because this has been so in the past is no guarantee that there will not be major changes in the future. But past experience suggests that such changes are quite unlikely.

The most dramatic effect of technology on the battlefield was not the tank, the machine gun, or the airplane. It was a very simple technological modification of a weapon more than a century ago. And the perturbation in battle-

Figure 12.3

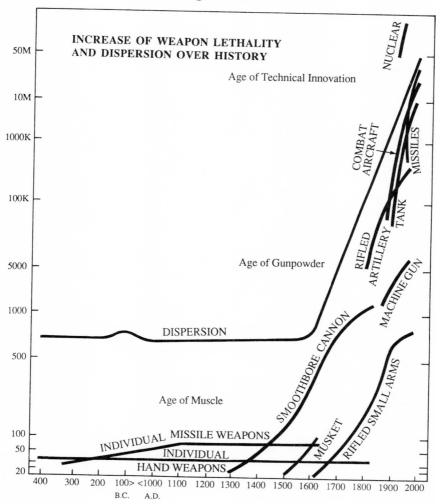

INCREASE OF WEAPON LETHALITY
AND DISPERSION OVER HISTORY

field patterns caused by that technological weapons change was redressed in less than half a century by a totally nonlethal technological innovation.

Figure 12.6 shows the relative effectiveness of the three major kinds of weapons in use in the early nineteenth century and the relative effectiveness of these same kinds of weapons ten years after the introduction of the conoidal bullet in the rifled musket. This was because the increased range and accuracy of the infantryman's major weapon had a deadly effect upon

Figure 12.4.　Historical Army Dispersion Patterns
(Army or Corps of 100,000 Troops)

	Antiquity	*Napoleonic Wars*	*American Civil War*	*World War I*	*World War II*	*1973 October War*
Area occupied by deployed force, 100,000 strong (sq km)	1.00	20.12	25.75	248	2,750	3,500
Front (km)	5.00	8.05	8.58	14	48	54
Depth (km)	0.20	2.50	3.00	17	57	65
Men per sq km	100,000	4,970	3,883	404	36	29
Square Meters/ Man	10.00	200	257.5	2,475	27,500	35,000
Football Fields/ per Man	1/500	1/25	1/20	1/2	5+	7

artillery gun crews and charging horsemen. These statistics applied to the U.S. Civil War, the Danish-German War, the Austro-Prussian War, and the Franco-Prussian War in a ten-year period from 1861 to 1871. But by World War I, artillery was again inflicting about 50 percent of the casualties, simply by adaptation of the invention of Alexander Graham Bell to the battlefield. The field telephone permitted indirect fire, so gun crews were no longer exposed to the aimed fire of hostile infantrymen.[2]

This has not really been a digression. It is important to demonstrate quantitatively and scientifically that history is indeed relevant to modern war, that historical trends are likely to persist, and that the patterns of history are likely to be repeated in the future, regardless of the technological tools of the men waging war.

The historical relationship of losses to defeat (and to success) can be summarized in a number of specific examples, then in terms of average experience culled from a relatively large data base of combat experience.

RELEVANT GERMAN EXPERIENCE IN WORLD WAR II

We begin with the German experience. One example of such experience is that of the 16th Panzer Grenadier Division in Russia from 17 July 1943 to 14 January 1944. That is discussed in some detail in Chapter 10, so here it is only alluded to in passing. For our purposes it is enough to note that no simple breakpoint percentage is applicable to the case of the 16th Panzer

**Figure 12.5.   Twentieth-Century Army Dispersion Patterns
(Average Corps or Army of 100,000 Troops)**

	World War I	World War II	October War 1973	Europe Deployment c. 1990
Area of 100,000 Men (sq km)	248	2,750	3,500	6,000
Number Tanks	100	266	961	2,000
Number APCs	—	589	1,464	2,000
Number Guns	400	537	435	750
Number Other Crew-Served Weapons	4,000	5,694	5,524	7,500
Number Major Weapons	4,500	7,086	8,384	12,250
Square Meters/Man	2,475	27,500	35,000	60,000
Major Weapons/sq km	18.15	2.58	2.40	2.04
Men/sq km	404	36	29	20

Grenadier Division. Possibly, however, General von Schwerin's report, considered in combination with other examples in a reasonably adequate sample of experience, can shed light on the breakpoint phenomenon.

One other such case in German World War II experience is that of the 362d Infantry Division in Italy in May 1944.

On 23 May the 362d Division was in the path of the U.S. 3d Infantry and 1st Armored divisions as they smashed their way out of the Anzio beach-head in a surprise attack. That day and the next two the division, which had been around 12,000 strong at the beginning of the breakout battle, suffered about 3.4 percent casualties per day—something close to 1200 men in all—for an overall total loss of at least 10 percent. Late on the twenty-fifth the daily U.S. VI Corps G-2 report said that the 362d was "broken."

What the VI Corps G-2 did not know was that Maj. Gen. Heinz Greiner, the commander of the 362d Division who had been on leave in Germany, had arrived back at his division command post the evening before. Even as the battle raged on, he spent the next thirty-six hours preparing his shaken troops for the inevitable Allied exploitation thrust.

That exploitation was undertaken by the U.S. 1st Armored Division, which jumped off shortly after dawn on 26 May. Neither Maj. Gen. Ernest Harmon, commanding the division, nor his men were expecting serious opposition. How serious that opposition was is evident from the casualties the two divisions suffered in the next fourteen hours. The 1st Armored Division suffered about 770 casualties, or 5.25 percent, one of the highest single-day losses suffered by any U.S. division during the war. The 362d

**Figure 12.6.   Nineteenth-Century Causes
of Battlefield Casualties**

	Before 1850	After 1860
Artillery	40–50%	8–10%
Infantry Small Arms	30–40%	85–90%
Saber and Bayonet	15–20%	4– 6%

lost about 960 men killed, wounded, and missing, a whopping 10.7 percent loss, the largest one-day loss of a World War II division in HERO's data base.[3]

At dusk General Harmon called off the attack. He relieved the commander of one of his combat commands and wrote some bitter comments in his diary. On the basis of the record of that single day, we might assume that the one-day breakpoint of General Harmon and his men was about 5 percent casualties. It would appear, however, that it was not the casualty rate that caused General Harmon to break off the battle. It was the fact that he could not accomplish his mission under the existing circumstances and probably could not have accomplished it no matter how many more casualties he incurred.

As to the 362d Division, it had incurred about 17 percent casualties over a four-day period, culminated by more than 10 percent in one day. Furthermore, the division had concluded these terribly costly four days of battle with a successful defense. Certainly that division had not reached its breakpoint.

SOVIET EXPERIENCES IN WORLD WAR II[4]

Next let us look briefly at Soviet experiences in World War II.

According to prewar Soviet unit replacement doctrine, based on the experience of the Imperial Russian Army during World War I, a loss of 30–35 percent of a division's manpower called for its replacement and withdrawal from combat. In practice, however, the Soviets in World War II seldom replaced a combat unit that had suffered fewer than 70 percent losses. There were cases, especially during 1941 and 1942, when the strength of a division had dropped below 500 effectives and it was still in combat.

According to Marshal of the Soviet Union Konstantin Rokossovsky, in the winter of 1942 Soviet divisions of the Western Army Group usually had about 3500 men, sometimes only 2000 or less; on rare occasions there might have been one of 4000 men, but this was speedily brought down to par with others after one or two engagements. In December 1941 and January 1942, the divisions of the Sixteenth Army fighting near Moscow numbered no more than 1200 to 1300 men each. The situation in the neighboring armies was not better.

According to *50 Years of Soviet Armed Forces* (Moscow, 1968), the prewar Soviet rifle division was set up in April 1941 to be 14,183 men strong. During the war it never reached this strength. In the second half of 1942 it was set at 12,974. In December 1942 the authorized strength of the rifle division was 9435 men (in guards divisions 10,670). *The Great Soviet Encyclopedia* (Vol. 8) gives the same figures for 1943 and 1944. The Soviet "shortened" division, often mentioned in memoirs of Soviet generals, had about 8000 men. However, in the summer of 1943, shortly before the Kursk battle, the rifle divisions of the Central Army Group were built up only to a strength of 4500 to 5000 effectives; only three or four had as many as 6000 to 7000.

There was no standard or previously agreed-on percentage of losses that required a withdrawal of a formation (division or higher) from combat commitment. In extremely difficult situations, such as during all of 1941, at Stalingrad in 1942, or in the Caucasus in 1942, sometimes divisions with fewer than 500 effectives were not withdrawn and replaced, although their combat effectiveness was less than that of a battalion. Marshal Grechko calls some of them relatively battleworthy. Under more "normal" conditions, however, it appears that the Soviets considered a loss of 70 percent the maximum a division could suffer and still be suitable for combat use, although not fully effective. At that point, all-out efforts were to be made to replace the division, or at least to supply it with a considerable number of individual replacements. In case of low morale, on the other hand, the Soviets considered replacing divisions that had suffered losses of only 40 to 50 percent.

During September and October 1943 the 322d Rifle Division was attached to the Thirteenth Army and took part in offensive operations. By the end of October the division had lost two-thirds of its manpower. Its rifle battalions had no more than eighty to a hundred men left. For all practical purposes the division had lost its combat effectiveness, but it was not replaced since there was no replacement division to take its place. Instead, in November the 322d received several thousand fillers and continued to advance in spite of heavy casualties. Again, it was not replaced. Not until

December did the division receive enough individual replacements to bring its strength to some 8000 effectives. This enabled the 322d to break through the German defense lines in the Krasnoselka–Mirch sector and to destroy the German 208th Infantry Division.

It is important to note Soviet motives behind choosing the right time for a formation to be replaced. A division was seldom replaced simply because it was battle-weary. Usually such a move was related to a specific change in an army group or army mission, such as a turn from defense to an offensive or an increase in the defense effort in a particular sector.

In other words, the concept of a breakpoint or a threshold related to unit strength had little or no meaning in the Red Army in World War II.

AMERICAN EXPERIENCES IN WORLD WAR II

In several instances during World War II American divisions appear to have reached a breakpoint. We will look at a few here.

We have already noted that the 1st Armored Division called off its attack at Velletri on 26 May 1944 after suffering 5.3 percent casualties in one day.

Earlier in the Italian campaign, 20–22 January 1944, the 36th Infantry Division was repulsed in an unsuccessful assault crossing of the Rapido River. The division suffered 12.0 percent casualties in a period of about forty-eight hours, for a daily loss rate of almost exactly 6.0 percent.

Later, in the bitter battle of Schmidt, 2–13 November 1944, the 28th Infantry Division suffered 25.4 percent casualties in twelve days, for an average daily loss rate of 2.1 percent. It is worth noting, however, that the heaviest single-day loss rate, on 10 November, was 6.7 percent and that on at least two occasions individual battalions of the division suffered losses at rates exceeding 40 percent per day.

It should be noted that these operations of the 1st Armored, 36th Infantry, and 28th Infantry divisions were all attacks, in which the attacker had the option of calling off an attack (subject to approval of higher authority) when success seemed remote or losses seemed too high.

Let us look at two cases of U.S. units on the defense and the losses they suffered, as well as the outcome of the defense.

There is the epic stand of the 30th Division at Mortain, when the Germans were desperately attempting to thwart Operation Cobra, the Allied breakout from Normandy in July–August 1944. The Germans made a major thrust westward across the Cotentin Peninsula, to cut off and isolate those units of General Patton's Third Army that had already debouched into the German rear areas. In five days the 30th Division held open the narrow line of communications at the western edge of the peninsula against desperate German attack. They held successfully, with a casualty rate for five days of 12.2 percent, or a daily loss rate of 2.5 percent per day. There was no breakpoint, nor does it appear that the division was close to a breakpoint during the period. On the other hand, on 7 August one of its battalions suffered more than 20 percent casualties and apparently reached its breakpoint.

Finally, there was the U.S. 99th Division, which got in the way of the main effort of the German Sixth Panzer Army on 16 December 1944, the first day of the Battle of the Bulge. The relatively green 99th, abreast of the veteran 2d Division, was actually engaged in an offensive operation of its own when the German blow fell. On that short day, the 99th suffered 9.56 percent casualties, apparently the heaviest one-day loss of any U.S. division in World War II.[5] Since loss rates are usually higher on warm days, with more hours of daylight, this casualty rate is even more exceptional.

The 99th was driven back, but was not broken. Assisted by the stand of the 2d Division on its left (which became the anchor for the northern shoulder of the Bulge), the 99th continued to fight effectively in containing German efforts to widen the penetration.

BRITISH EXPERIENCES IN WORLD WAR II

Finally, let's look at some British divisional operations that are comparable to the American examples.

In many ways the assault crossing of the Volturno River by the British 56th Division on 13 October 1943 at Capua was very similar to that of the U.S. 36th Division across the Rapido about three months later. Both were river assault crossings attempting to dislodge a determined enemy from the far bank. Both failed. The American 36th Division tried for two days, suffering 6.0 percent daily losses. The British 56th Division gave up a few hours after launching its attack, having suffered 2.5 percent casualties in that shorter-than-normal day of fighting.

One reason for the apparently less-determined British effort was that the 56th Division was assessed by the British high command in the Mediterranean as its worst division. However, on that day it was commanded by a very capable general who was later to win considerable distinction. Any comparison of the British failure at the Volturno with the U.S. failure at the Rapido must take into account that the British (remembering the bloodbath of World War I) were much more concerned about casualty rates than their American counterparts. Gen. Gerald Templar undoubtedly had this in mind when it became obvious after a few hours that a successful crossing was probably not possible and that the time had come to cut his losses. In this he may have shown better generalship than the American division commander who kept disastrously reinforcing failure at the Rapido.

Certainly the British did not shrink from losses when this was necessary. The performance of the British 1st Infantry Division in the early days of the Anzio operation provides an example. In a valiant and successful stand against a determined German effort to drive the Allies off the Anzio beachhead, between 3 and 5 February 1944, the British 1st Division took about 22.1 percent casualties in three days for the horrendous daily loss rate of 7.35 percent per day, a rate all too reminiscent of World War I losses. Then, just a few days later, 7 and 8 February, the division took 8.2 percent losses (a daily rate of 4.1 percent) in a successful defense against another desperate German effort.

So, in these two examples, one British division reached a breakpoint in an attack after incurring 2.5 percent casualties. Another British division, in defensive posture, did not reach a breakpoint after incurring more than 30 percent casualties over a period of six days, with the daily casualty rate exceeding 7.4 percent on at least one of those days.

Before drawing any conclusions from this examination of a rather small number of samples from the experiences of four national military forces in World War II, it will be helpful to look at a statistical survey from a larger data base.

THE HERO/DMSI DATA BASE

Recently a new analytical tool has become available to enable analysts to test the relevance and validity of historical experience. This tool is the Land Warfare Data Base (LWDB) of the Historical Evaluation and Research Organization (HERO). That data base provides detailed statistical information, and a number of historical judgmental assessments, for 604 battles or engagements from 1600 through 1973. About three-fifths of these engagements—363—are from the twentieth century, the majority of these (217) from World War II and the 1967 and 1973 Arab–Israeli Wars. Theoretically, there can be about ninety entries for each battle or engagement; practically, however, there are about sixty entries for each battle since, for instance, there were no tanks or aircraft in battles before World

War I, and there have been few instances of employment of horse cavalry since that time.

In a recent study, all battles or engagements in major campaigns recorded in the data base (at division level or lower) were reviewed for the following wars: World War I, World War II, the 1967 Arab–Israeli War, and the 1973 Arab–Israeli War. The casualty rates (percent casualties per day) for both sides in each battle were examined as follows:

a. Maximum loss rate
b. Minimum loss rate
c. Overall average loss rate
d. Average loss rate for successes
e. Average loss rate for failures
f. Average loss rate for draws

To make a meaningful analysis, it was necessary to look at these statistics for both attacker and defender, for each national force engaged. A summary of the data retrieved from the data base is shown in Figures 12.7, 12.8, and 12.9. Figure 12.7 shows comparisons of statistics for Germans and Western Allies in World War I in six campaigns in Italy and Northwest Europe in World War II. Figure 12.8 provides similar comparative data for the Eastern Front and the conflict between Japan and the United States in World War II. Figure 12.9 presents similar data for the 1967 and 1973 Arab–Israeli wars. For purposes of comparison, the tables include average attrition statistics for the major national forces involved, in both the attack and defense posture.

A few observations on the figures displayed in these two tables:

a. Attrition rates for World War I were approximately four to seven times as great as for World War II.

b. Note the comparative loss rates of Germans to Allies before mid-1944 (Rome campaign) and after; before mid-1944 the German rates were lower; subsequently they were higher. This is a reflection of the fact that prior to May–June 1944 the Germans had dominated the battlefields in Italy; subsequently the allies were dominant.

c. The loss rates for both sides in the Volturno campaign were substantially lower than the average Allied and German loss rates; the Volturno campaign was fought in miserable weather in very rugged terrain.

d. The loss rates for both sides were somewhat lower for the Lorraine campaign than the average Allied and German loss rates; this campaign

Figure 12.7. Modern Casualty Rates, Attackers vs Defenders, by Nationality (I)

	ATTACKERS							DEFENDERS						
	No.	Max	Min	Av	Av Suc	Av Fail	Av Dr	No.	Max	Min	Av	Av Suc	Av Fail	Av Dr
W. ALLIES VS GERMANS														
WWI 20,000	52	45.3	0.7	7.0	3.5	9.0	12.5	2	3.7	2.3	3.0	2.3	3.7	—
WWII, Salerno	5	3.9	1.0	2.2	2.0	2.0	—	4	3.6	0.7	2.0	2.0	—	—
Volturno	19	2.5	0.1	0.7	0.7	0.8	0.3	1	2.0	2.0	2.0	—	2.0	—
Anzio	3	3.0	0.4	1.6	2.2	0.4	—	8	7.4	0.3	2.6	1.6	4.5	0.7
Rome	23	5.5	0.3	1.1	1.1	1.8	0.8	0	—	—	—	—	—	—
Lorraine	13	1.3	0.2	0.6	0.6	—	0.6	0	—	—	—	—	—	—
Other NWE	22	1.9	0.2	0.7	0.7	1.1	0.6	5	9.6	0.6	2.5	3.4	0.8	1.4
Average	85	5.5	0.1	1.2	1.2	1.2	0.5	18	9.6	0.3	2.3	2.3	2.4	1.1
GERMANS VS W. ALLIES														
WWI 20,000	2	11.1	4.1	7.6	4.1	11.1	—	52	66.5	1.2	12.5	3.2	13.8	26.5
WWII, Salerno	4	2.4	1.5	1.8	—	1.8	—	5	0.9	0.7	0.8	0.7	0.9	—
Volturno	1	0.1	0.1	0.1	0.1	—	—	19	1.5	0.1	0.6	0.5	0.6	0.5
Anzio	8	2.5	0.6	1.4	1.7	1.2	0.8	3	1.5	0.5	1.1	1.5	0.8	—
Rome	0	—	—	—	—	—	—	23	10.7	0.5	2.8	4.7	3.0	1.6
Lorraine	0	—	—	—	—	—	—	13	4.1	0.9	2.0	—	2.0	1.9
Other NWE	5	3.1	0.8	2.1	1.3	2.8	0.8	22	7.0	0.5	2.4	0.9	2.4	2.9
Average	18	3.1	0.1	1.4	0.7	1.9	0.8	85	10.7	0.1	1.6	1.7	1.6	1.7

Figure 12.8. Modern Casualty Rates, Attackers vs Defenders, by Nationality (II)

		ATTACKERS							DEFENDERS					
	No.	Max	Min	Av	Av Suc	Av Fail	Av Dr	No.	Max	Min	Av	Av Suc	Av Fail	Av Dr
WWII, E. Front														
GERMANS VS RUSSIANS	6	2.3	0.4	1.1	1.3	0.7	—	22	21.8	0.3	4.6	2.0	4.8	4.7
RUSSIANS VS GERMANS	22	7.0	0.1	2.4	2.1	2.9	6.3	6	11.7	1.0	5.4	2.9	6.7	—
WWII, Pacific														
US VS JAPANESE	26	1.3	0.2	0.6	0.6	0.7	0.5	2	1.5	1.1	1.3	1.3	—	—
JAPANESE VS US	2	31.7	27.0	29.4	—	29.4	—	26	96.0	5.0	20.6	11.9	24.0	17.0

Figure 12.9. Modern Casualty Rates, Attackers vs Defenders, by Nationality (III)

	ATTACKERS							DEFENDERS						
	No.	*Max*	*Min*	*Av*	*Av Suc*	*Av Fail*	*Av Dr*	*No.*	*Max*	*Min*	*Av*	*Av Suc*	*Av Fail*	*Av Dr*
ISRAELIS VS ARABS														
1967 War, Sinai	9	3.6	0.2	2.4	1.2	—	0.6	2	1.7	1.2	1.5	1.5	—	—
W. Bank	5	4.7	1.5	2.8	2.8	—	—	0	—	—	—	—	—	—
Golan	3	5.6	2.8	4.1	4.1	—	—	0	—	—	—	—	—	—
Average	17	5.6	0.2	3.1	2.7	—	0.6	2	1.7	1.2	1.5	1.5	—	—
1973 War, Suez–Sinai	10	2.7	0.4	1.1	0.9	1.6	—	6	7.4	0.9	3.7	0.9	5.1	—
Golan	8	2.6	0.8	1.3	1.0	2.3	—	9	5.0	0.3	2.7	2.2	5.0	2.8
Average	18	2.6	0.6	1.2	1.0	1.3	—	15	7.4	0.9	3.2	1.6	5.1	2.8
ARABS VS ISRAELIS														
1967 War, Sinai	2	12.9	2.5	7.7	—	7.7	—	9	18.3	1.2	8.4	—	7.6	15.0
W. Bank	0	—	—	—	—	—	—	5	4.6	1.8	3.5	—	3.5	—
Golan	0	—	—	—	—	—	—	3	10.4	5.8	7.7	—	7.7	—
1973 War, Suez–Sinai	6	2.3	1.3	1.7	1.1	1.8	—	10	4.4	1.0	2.5	1.8	2.9	—
Golan	9	3.9	1.0	2.7	1.8	2.4	1.0	8	6.3	1.6	3.2	5.3	2.6	—
Average	15	3.9	1.0	2.2	1.5	1.8	1.0	18	6.3	1.0	2.9	3.6	2.8	—

was fought in miserable weather over terrain that was relatively good for combat operations.

e. The average loss rate for U.S. infantry battalions in the Dorothy Clark study was greater than the loss rates for U.S. divisions that failed to accomplish their missions in the LWDB by a factor of approximately 12.0, more than an order of magnitude.

f. German rates on the Eastern Front in World War II appear to be slightly higher than German rates in Italy and Northwest Europe.

g. Soviet rates on the Eastern Front were approximately twice as great as German rates.

h. U.S. rates against Japan were slightly lower than were U.S. rates against Germany.

i. Japanese rates against the United States were about twice as great as Soviet loss rates against Germany.

j. Israeli rates for the 1967 and 1973 Arab–Israeli Wars are very similar to those for the Western Allies and Germany in World War II.

k. Arab and Israeli rates in the 1967 war were approximately twice as great as in the 1973 war; this is apparently due to the fact that engagements in the 1967 war were mostly at brigade level; those in the 1973 war were mostly at division level.

l. Arab rates in the 1973 war were approximately the same as Soviet rates at the same level of aggregation in World War II.

m. Note that the Arab loss rates were consistently higher than Israeli rates in all circumstances.

CONCLUSIONS

The above analysis of consolidated data from the LWDB appears to be generally consistent with the findings of the earlier examination in this chapter of a few selected examples of German, Soviet, British, and American experience in World War II. Several conclusions can be drawn:

1. Casualties and casualty rates have little, if anything, to do with determining the point—or breakpoint—at which a military force is defeated or is constrained to change its posture.

2. If there is such a thing as a breakpoint, and if casualties have anything to do with it, defenders seem to be able to sustain higher casualties than attackers before acknowledging defeat. This is to some extent due to the fact that they have less option to end a battle than does the attacker, who holds the initiative.

3. In seeking to determine a logical rationale for representing battle termination in analyses or combat simulations, the following considerations must be explored:

   a. The nature of the terrain in which combat takes place.
   b. The nature of the weather during the period of combat.
   c. The posture (offense or defense) of a military force engaged in combat.
   d. The relative combat effectiveness of the opposing forces engaged in combat, based on some rational assessment in terms of national origins of the forces or other logical assessment process.
   e. The size or strength of the force; daily loss rates are higher for smaller forces than for larger forces.
   f. Other battlefield circumstances that could influence a commander, or his troops, to abandon the pursuit of an assigned mission.

4. The approach to battle termination on most current models and simulations has been shown to be historically invalid, thus emphasizing the need of all combat models for a mechanism for battle termination that will approximate reality.

As can be seen from Appendix C, an important step has recently been taken to do something about these conclusions. Much more needs to be done.

Chapter 13

Casualties and the Statistics of Defeat (1941–1982)

B Y   R O B E R T   M C Q U I E

Three generations of American military men seem to agree on at least one point: "It is dangerous to be in the infantry. A battlefield is a good place to get your head blown off." This bit of folk wisdom has been reinforced by most theories of land combat, which have tended to view war as essentially a process of inflicting casualties. From Clausewitz to Westmoreland, the framework for analysis of combat has been related to the actions of a force that is trying to destroy its opponents.[1] It certainly is the analytical framework used by the vast majority of operations research analysts today. Consequently, such theories of combat have had as their principal, and often their only, insight an explanation of the process by which casualties were produced. When Thomas Livermore accumulated data about the Civil War, his concern was casualties.[2] When Frederick Lanchester described the mathematical processes of World War I, he expressed them in terms of casualties.[3]

Although theorists like Antoine Jomini[4] and Charles Ardant du Picq[5] tended to view war from a different viewpoint, their thoughts today are not widely quoted. These days, when the results of the most recent war game analysis are presented to generals in the Pentagon, the first question usually is: "What were the casualty rates?"

This chapter attempts to throw some light on the casualty-oriented convictions of both folk wisdom and military theory. The following pages examine what the actual casualties have been at the time a commander has recognized that he has been defeated. From this, one may possibly be able to infer the extent to which casualties have actually influenced the commander's decision to give up. Since battles tend to be terminated by the loser, the examination will be of casualties sustained by defeated forces.

SYMPTOMS AND CONSEQUENCES OF DEFEAT

During a battle, commanders of the opposing forces are frequently faced with the question "Have I lost?" If the answer for either side is yes, they must do something about it. For an attacker, the choices are a shift to the defense or a call for reinforcements. For a defender, the choices are a call for reinforcements or a withdrawal. If large reinforcements are introduced by either side, new tactics and different opportunities will have been introduced, and a new battle will have arisen. But if there are no reinforcements, the loser must terminate the battle by changing his offensive or defensive posture.

What aspect of the battlefield situation makes one side or the other conclude it is losing a battle? What was it that influenced a commander to resort to one of the two relatively simple options just described? If it has been casualties, as is commonly believed, then what particular aspect of casualties led to the conclusion? Has it been their number? Has it been the rate at which they have been incurred? Has it been the relative losses of one side to the other? Has it perhaps been the comparative strengths remaining in the two forces? Or has it been something else?

EVIDENCE FROM ACTUAL BATTLES

For answers to these questions, data were examined from eighty defeats that actually took place between 1941 and 1982. These defeats consisted of both unsuccessful attacks and unsuccessful defenses. They took place in

World War II and in the 1967 and 1973 Arab–Israeli wars. The battles were located in the Far East, the Near East, in Eastern and in Western Europe. All of the battles were combined-arms engagements, involving infantry, artillery, and in most cases armor and airplanes. The number of battles and the categories under which they were examined are:

	World War II	Arab– Israel War
Defender Defeated	25	24
Attacker Defeated	23	8

The data used here have been assembled over the years by the Historical Evaluation and Research Organization.[6]

The median attacking force, in these data, involved about 22,000 troops, while the median defending force consisted of about 12,000. In the tank battles that were examined, a median of about 360 attacking armored vehicles were employed against about 260 defending tanks. The median battle resulted in twenty hours of combat over a period of two days.

Has It Been the Number of Casualties?

We may first ask "Has the recognition of defeat in battle been due to the total number of troops lost during the entire course of an engagement, be they killed, wounded, or missing?" As an example, at the Battle of the Chinese Farm in 1973, did the Egyptians withdraw because their cumulative casualties during the battle had reached, as it did, 1 percent of their total troops? Figure 13.1 summarizes historical data that attempt to answer such a question. It shows the medians and ranges of the percent of casualties incurred during the entire course of battles by the losing sides. As may be seen, in half the battles, an attack was recognized as a failure when casualties had reached less than 4 percent of the attacking force. The median defense was abandoned when casualties of the defending force reached less than 8 percent. A point to note, however, is that when combat was broken off, casualties had ranged widely; some forces admitted defeat when their losses were negligible, while others (if the doubtful records are taken literally) fought to the last man.

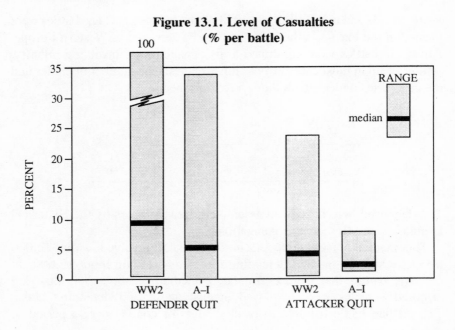

**Figure 13.1. Level of Casualties
(% per battle)**

HAS IT BEEN INTENSITY AT WHICH CASUALTIES WERE INCURRED?

It may have been not total casualties, but rather the rate per hour or per day at which they were incurred that has triggered a recognition of defeat. As an example, during the U.S. breakout at Anzio in May 1944, the Germans withdrew when their casualties had reached about one-third of 1 percent per hour. Figure 13.2 summarizes the historical data on casualties per hour of actual combat; that is, excluding lulls of at least one hour in the battles. As may be seen, the median attack was recognized as unsuccessful with casualties of less than one-fifth of 1 percent per hour. (For the average combat day, that would have been about 2 percent per day.) The median defense was recognized as a failure when casualties had reached approximately two-fifths of 1 percent per hour, or 4 percent for the average day of combat. Figure 13.3 shows intensity measured per day of combat rather than per hour. As may be seen, the median casualty rate at which unsuccessful engagements were terminated was from 2 to 3 percent per day. A perplexing feature of these data is the variation of intensity of casualties at

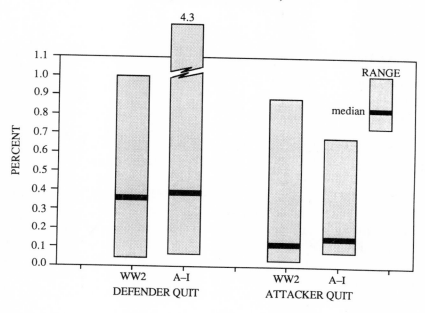

Figure 13.2. Intensity of Casualties
(% per hour of combat)

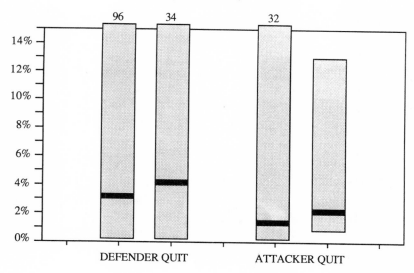

Figure 13.3. Intensity of Casualties
(%/day of combat)

which the losing side gave up. It ranged from almost no casualties to as high as 4 percent of the force per hour, in a rare instance, to nearly 100 percent for a day.

HAS IT BEEN RELATIVE CASUALTIES?

Perhaps it was not total casualties or the intensity of casualties that triggered recognition of defeat, but rather a sensing of how one's losses compared with those of the enemy. This was examined by calculating the ratio of the attacker's to the defender's casualties during a battle. An example is the Israeli attack at Kantara–Firdan in 1973, the most severe defeat that army has ever suffered. The Israelis withdrew when their casualties were about one-third those of the Arab defender. A broader insight into this relation is provided by Figure 13.4, which summarizes the casualty exchange ratios of attacker to defender for the eighty battles under examination. As may be seen, the median ratio at which an attacker terminated a battle was approximately 2 to 1, while for defenders the median ratio was approximately .8 to 1. To put this in another way, the median attacker gave up where his casualties had reached twice those of the defender, while the median defender gave up when his casualties were

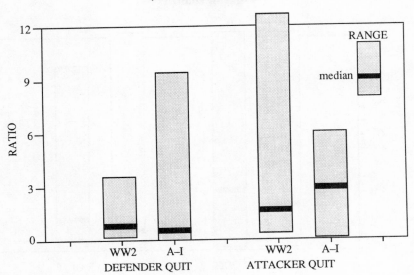

Figure 13.4. Relative Casualties
(attacker/defender)

no more than 25 percent greater than the attacker. The range here is intriguing. Some forces gave up with casualties less than one-twentieth those of their opponent. Others took more than ten times the casualties of the opponent before admitting defeat. These extremes, however, almost invariably reflect two things: special circumstances in a battle or/and greatly differing qualities of the opposing forces.

HAS IT BEEN THE FINAL FORCE RATIO?

Perhaps casualties have influenced the recognition of defeat in an indirect fashion. Perhaps it is not the casualties themselves, but the change they produce in the force ratio for the battle. If the force ratio drops to a certain point, for example, a sense of defeat or impending defeat might have developed that led the commander to terminate an attack. This possibility was examined by calculating the final force ratio considering casualties incurred for each of the eighty battles under consideration. The results are summarized in Figure 13.5. The median attack was terminated when the

**Figure 13.5. Final Force Ratio
(attacker:defender)**

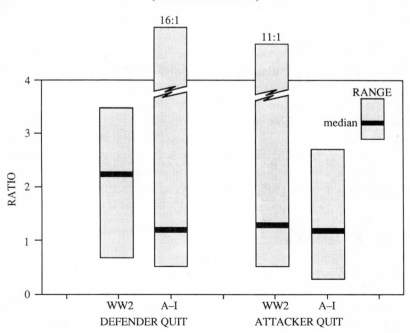

ratio was about 1.3 to 1; that is, when the attacker had about 30 percent more troops than the defender. The median defense was terminated when the force ratio was about 2.1 to 1. As with the previous measures of casualties, however, the ratio at the point of defeat ranged widely. Some attacks were terminated when the attacker had eleven times the strength of the enemy. Some defenses were abandoned when a defender had twice the strength of an enemy. Again, the extremes reflected other special circumstances, great differences in combat effectiveness, or both.

To summarize what has been observed so far: there seems to be no pattern of influence. No matter how casualties are measured, battles have been given up as lost when casualties ranged from insignificant to overwhelming.

A SUBJECTIVE CRITERION

Perhaps now is the time to pose a question to the reader. "If you were fighting a losing battle, at what level would casualties make you quit?" Would you call off an attack, or withdraw from a defense, with casualties as low as many of the battles in the charts just presented? The casualty levels they show are certainly much lower than the ones that are seen as a matter of course in most current military planning and analysis studies. There does not appear to have been any research about unacceptable losses in combat. Until very recently, the last examination of breakpoints, for example, was published more than thirty years ago.[7] Before the most recent study, and lacking a casualty guideline, a consensus of professional judgment was sought. A group of combat-arm officers ranging from major to lieutenant general were asked individually: "If you were a division commander, how high would casualties have to be in your division for you to quit?" Their answers, while qualified, suggested that most of them would recognize defeat on taking perhaps 50 percent casualties.

MORE EVIDENCE

The large difference between these professional opinions and the actual combat discussed earlier led to a further review of the battles in question. An attempt was made to identify for each battle the reason, other than casualties, why the loser gave up. While multiple factors appeared to have

Figure 13.6.   Reasons for a Force Abandoning an Attack or a Defense

Maneuver by Enemy		
Envelopment, Encirclement, Penetration	33	
Adjacent Friendly Unit Withdraw	13	
Enemy Occupied Key Terrain	6	
Enemy Achieved Surprise	8	
Enemy Reinforced	4	64%
Firepower by Enemy		
Casualties or Equipment Losses	10	
Heavy Enemy Artillery and Air Attacks	2	12%
Shortages of Resources		
No Reserves Left	12	
Supply Shortages	2	14%
Conditions External to the Battle		
Truce or Surrender	6	
Change in Weather	2	
Orders to Withdraw	2	10%

influenced the losing side, the most likely reason could be identified in fifty-two of the eighty battles, and the results are tabulated in Figure 13.6.

To the extent that these fifty-two battles are representative of war in our lifetime, then the principal condition associated with defeat appears to have been the use of maneuver by an enemy, which was present in 64 percent of the cases. It does not seem to have been the result of the intensity of the enemy's firepower, which was associated with only 12 percent of the defeats. Where maneuver was the decisive influence, moreover, recognition of defeat appears to have arisen from a look toward the future and an enemy's potential capabilities for inflicting casualties rather than toward the past and the casualties he has already inflicted.

IMPLICATIONS

It appears, then, that casualties (or a commander's perception of casualties) are not often the reason battles are lost. This fact that defeat is not usually related to casualties or casualty rates has implications for understanding war. It leads to the conclusion, tentative perhaps, that Lanchester's equations—at least as they are generally interpreted and used—present a completely inaccurate description of combat, at least as practiced since 1941.

SUMMARY OF LANCHESTER'S LAWS

Frederick W. Lanchester, as implied by the title of the original article on his mathematical theory of combat, was attempting to show mathematically the effect of application of the principle of Mass or Concentration upon battle outcomes. He did this in terms of force strengths and the changes that occur in force strengths as these are affected by casualties incurred in combat. He produced two equations, known variously as Lanchester's Equations or Lanchester's Laws. These equations are, in effect, a mathematical theory of combat, focused on the process of attrition during the course of a battle.[8]

Lanchester postulated two different sets of circumstances. In one set, one or both opposing sides can see the opponent, and thus is (or are) able to aim at enemy targets. In the other case, each side is generally aware of the location of the opponent but not precisely enough for aimed fire, thus the fire at the enemy is unaimed.[9]

In either case, Lanchester viewed the battle as proceeding in accordance with the concept of differential equations, or a change of state related to the progression of time. In the case where one side can see the other, he applied what has come to be called the Linear Equation:

$$dR/dt = K(RB), \text{ or}$$
$$dB/dt = K'(BR)$$

when R = strength of the Red force
B = strength of the Blue force
t = time interval related to force strength changes
K = a constant coefficient
K' = another constant coefficient

In instances in which a force cannot see the opponent clearly or precisely enough for aimed fire, Lanchester's Square Equation is applicable, as follows:

$$dR/dt = CB$$
$$dB/dt = C'R$$

when C and C' are still different constant coefficients.

Thus, in the Linear Equation, when aimed fire is used, the change that occurs (i.e., the casualties) is a function of the product of the strengths of the opposing sides. In the Linear Equation the casualties incurred by one side are a function of the strength of the other side.

The Lanchester Equations are the principal tool for calculating the destruction of one unit by another in most computerized war games and simulations of combat in use in the United States today. Even where not employed directly, they provide the frame of reference within which the war gaming community thinks about combat, and papers are continually being written about variations on the basic equations. The standard reference on Lanchester's equations has more than 200 items in its bibliography.[10]

However, given the evidence in Figure 12.6, there must be doubts. The issue is not whether Lanchester's "square" law is right, or his "linear" law, or some other law. It is rather whether the Lanchestrian formulations of battle describe an event that has ever taken place.

The reason for this uncertainty may be summarized as follows. The outcome of battle modeled by the Lanchestrian equations postulates a development of combat in response to casualties incurred. During the last fifty years, however, battles appear to have been resolved largely on the basis of other considerations. The laws state that (with a knowledge of the strength of two opponents) we can anticipate which of two opposing forces will kill the most people and therefore win a battle. The laws state that, given rates of attrition, the outcome of an engagement can be anticipated. This just does not appear ever to have been the case, at least not in the eighty battles examined here. On the contrary, the resolve of the defeated force appears to have been shaken by completely different types of events.

Exactly why the process Lanchester suggested as a theory has not eventualized as a fact can at present only be a speculation. Not enough is understood about the processes of command in battle to make a definite statement. There is the possibility that a Lanchestrian attrition process has always been present in combat, but that it has never been allowed to reach a point where it influenced the outcomes of a battle. Commanders or their troops could have stopped such a process, even though it had begun, by calling off the battle for other reasons. In any event, men in combat do not appear to have been the foolhardy and suicidal opponents that Lanchester's laws suggest; they appear to have been both prudent and very, very cautious, a fact amply supported by folk wisdom even if ignored by most current military theory.

A second implication of the evidence just examined concerns not war itself but the tools used to analyze it. War games and simulations employ casualties as an internal criterion for terminating simulated battles. Casualty rates of from 15 percent to 30 percent per day are not unusual in the big simulations of combat in use in the United States military establishment today. This extremely high level of casualties is accompanied by a tempo of combat—in the games—however, that has not actually occurred in the past and might not be sustainable in the future, given the limits of human nature. The reasons war games generate such high casualty rates, while widely discussed, remains obscure. One reason may be that combat simulations do not reproduce the decision to desist from a faltering attack or to withdraw from hopeless defenses. This defect, happily, has not been observed in those doing the actual fighting.

SUMMARY

In general, then, the casualties incurred by losing forces in historical modern battles appear to have been much lower than usually envisaged by those of most military analysts concerned with either command of troops or analysis of war. It also appears that Lanchester's equations—at least as they are currently used—present a drastic misstatement, inconsistent with the fact that in most cases a force of about division size has quit when its casualties reached less than 10 percent per battle or 3 percent per day. In most battles, moreover, acknowledgment of defeat does not appear to have been caused by casualties.

Part V

CONVERTING DEFEAT TO VICTORY

Chapter 14

PLANNING UNDER PRESSURE

A commander defeated on a battlefield rarely has an opportunity for immediate recovery, either to turn the tables and win that presumably lost battle, or without delay to win a new battle emerging from that which was lost. Napoleon's refusal to accept defeat at Marengo was an example of a skillful, determined leader converting apparent defeat into victory. This was also the case with Sheridan, after a twenty-mile ride, at Cedar Creek. Generals Eisenhower and Bradley clearly lost the first round in the Ardennes in late 1944, even though their formidable combat power superiority limited the German offensive within the confines of the so-called Bulge. Their massive counteroffensive, begun shortly after Christmas, was a new battle, in which—with the assistance of Field Marshal Montgomery —they marshalled an even greater superiority to smash the attackers back out of the bulge salient in early January 1945.

Usually, however, when a military force or its commander recovers from defeat to gain an ultimate victory, it has been after a period of retrospective analysis, combined with a major effort to accumulate resources that will— hopefully—result in combat power superior to that of the originally successful enemy. Representative of this process was the earlier-cited example of General Stilwell, who took more than a year to recover from his "humiliating" defeat in Burma and convert it to eventual victory.

But both forms of conversion of defeat to victory—the "quick conversion" of Napoleon at Marengo or Sheridan at Cedar Creek and the "deliberate conversion" of Stilwell in Burma—can be instructive to those who have tasted the bitter draught of defeat.

QUICK CONVERSION AT SHILOH

There is probably no better example of a quick conversion than the recovery made by Union General Ulysses S. Grant at the Battle of Shiloh, 6–7 April 1862. A surprise dawn attack by Confederate General Albert Sidney Johnston's army of 40,000 men threw Grant's army, about equal in strength, into great confusion, driving the Northerners back toward the unfordable Tennessee River and almost certain disaster. In a demonstration of the importance of personal leadership and presence in the front line as well as considerable tactical skill, Grant rallied his troops and halted the Confederates just short of the river bank. Early the next morning, with about 20,000 reinforcements from the nearby Union Army of Gen. Don Carlos Buell, Grant counterattacked and drove the Confederates off the field. Through his coolness, his ability to reorganize his army in a situation of disaster, and his sheer obstinate determination, Grant had retrieved the battle by nightfall of the first day. With reinforcements (available due to his thoughtful prior preparation) he won it the next morning.

DETERMINATION AT COPENHAGEN

A comparable, at least equally remarkable, victory was won by Horatio Nelson at Copenhagen on 2 April 1801. Nelson was second-in-command of a British fleet under Adm. Sir Hyde Parker, sent to the Baltic to compel the Neutral League of Russia, Prussia, Sweden, and Denmark to abandon neutrality in the long-drawn-out war between Britain and revolutionary France. Deciding to place pressure on Denmark first, the British fleet approached Copenhagen. There they found that the Danish fleet, somewhat smaller than that of the British, had withdrawn behind a sandbar into Copenhagen harbor. There it was drawn up in a formidable defensive position, the ships' broadsides integrated with coastal fortifications and floating batteries.

Nelson obtained Admiral Parker's reluctant permission to take the twelve smallest British line-of-battle ships—light enough to get across the sandbar—to attack the Danes, who had about twice the gunpower of Nelson's squadron. The ensuing battle raged for about four hours, with heavy British loss and no apparent weakening of the Danes. At this time, through the smoke of the battle Nelson's flag captain saw signal flags flying on Admiral Parker's flagship, ordering Nelson to discontinue the engagement and withdraw. Nelson realized that, if he withdrew, the Danes would catch his ships as they tried to get back over the bar and that he would lose half or more of his vessels. He put his telescope to his eye and looked in the direction of Parker's flagship. "You know, Foley," he said to the captain, "I do not see the signal. Renew the attack!" He had, as most British schoolboys know, placed the telescope to the eye that had been blinded in a battle many years before. A few minutes later one of the Danish ships surrendered, then another, and another. At the end of an hour all Danish resistance was smashed and Denmark was suing for peace.

Nelson expected to be court-martialed, more than likely convicted of disobedience of orders, and hanged from the yardarm of Admiral Parker's flagship. (The British Royal Navy was known for rough treatment of recalcitrant admirals.) However, the Admiralty in London—not far away—learned about the affair; before Parker could take action, he was relieved and Nelson promoted to take his place. A fighting admiral—particularly a successful fighting admiral—was much admired by the Admiralty.

"I HAVE NOT YET BEGUN TO FIGHT"

Twenty-two years earlier an American commodore had taught the British a lesson about tenacious fighting in another sea battle, actually within view of the British coast. This was Capt. (acting Commodore) John Paul Jones who, in command of a small Franco-American squadron in the North Sea, on 23 September 1779 attacked a British convoy, protected by a British squadron of comparable size. It was soon evident that the outcome of the battle would be determined by the result of the encounter between two frigates: Jones' flagship, the USS *Bon Homme Richard*, and the largest of the British ships, HMS *Serapis*. It was also soon evident that the American ship, an old, rotten, converted merchantman, was no match for the newer, stronger British frigate. However, despite terrible punishment from the British guns, through superior seamanship Jones was able to pull alongside the British vessel and get the bowsprit of his ship tangled in the British rigging, so that the two were stuck together. The broadsides of the two ships now smashed into each other, only a few feet apart, causing havoc on both gun decks.

The flag of the *Bon Homme Richard* had been shot away during these maneuvers, and British Captain Richard Pearson thought that Jones had pulled down his flag in surrender. "Have you struck, sir?" he shouted at Jones through a speaking trumpet. (In other words, "Have you struck—pulled down—your flag in surrender?") Jones grabbed his own speaking trumpet and shouted back: "I have not yet begun to fight, sir!" He then ordered the two ships to be grappled together and led his sailors and marines in a charge over the rails of the two ships. At first the Americans were repulsed, and the deadly struggle continued for another hour. Finally, with the mainmast of the *Serapis* shot away and her gun deck cleared by a powder explosion touched off by an American grenade, Captain Pearson surrendered. Jones, his own ship sinking, then transferred the survivors of his crew to the British vessel and limped back to a friendly Dutch seaport.

(There is a story about this battle, unquestionably apocryphal but worth recounting, that has presumably been handed down from generation to generation of U.S. Marines. It seems that when Jones was hailed by Captain Pearson, a mortally wounded Marine was lying on the quarterdeck of the *Bon Homme Richard* beside Jones, amid the wreckage of the mizzenmast that had just been shot down by British gunfire. The Marine had been in a fighting top on the mast, firing a rifle at targets on the deck of the *Serapis*, when the mast was shot down. Already wounded, he had been crushed by the wreckage of the mast but was still conscious. When he heard Jones shout "I have not yet begun to fight," the marine shook his head. "There's always some son-of-a-gun," he muttered, "that doesn't get the word.")

Let's look at one more example of cool, calm professionalism combined with iron determination, winning an apparently lost battle.

COMBINED ARMS RECOVERY AT BUENA VISTA

In 1846 and early 1847, Gen. Zachary Taylor and his small American army fought their way about 200 miles deep into northern Mexico, to Saltillo. Here the central Mexican desert blocked further advance toward Mexico

City, 600 miles away. Taylor was reluctant to attempt to cross this formidable obstacle in the heart of a hostile country. The U.S. government then approved the plan of General-in-Chief Winfield Scott to invade central Mexico by a seaborne expedition through the port of Vera Cruz. Taylor was ordered to send most of his veterans to join Scott's army and was left with a handful of regulars plus about 4500 raw militiamen in five Volunteer infantry regiments.

At this point the senior Mexican military commander, who was also the President of Mexico, Gen. Antonio Lopez de Santa Anna, recognized how vulnerable were General Taylor and his little army, exposed without support in north-central Mexico. He led an army of 20,000 men from San Luis Potosí to Saltillo—losing 4000 men in the grueling march across the desert in midwinter. Nonetheless, as he approached Saltillo, Santa Anna's army outnumbered Taylor's by more than three to one.

Taylor, although surprised by the arrival of the Mexicans across the inhospitable desert, had plenty of time to take up a defensive position in a narrow mountain gap eight miles south of Saltillo, near a ranch called Buena Vista. Santa Anna, on 22 February 1847, sent a cavalry brigade on a wide northeastern detour to cut Taylor's line of communications near Saltillo. Then, late in the afternoon, he attacked and drove in Taylor's outposts. The Mexican attack was renewed the following morning; by noon the Mexicans had driven three of Taylor's five Volunteer infantry regiments off the field and captured two of his guns.

To Santa Anna victory now seemed certain, particularly since he expected his enveloping cavalry brigade to appear soon in the rear of the American army. The center of Taylor's position was held, however, by three batteries of Regular Army artillery. His left was protected from a threatened Mexican envelopment by the 3rd Indiana Volunteer Infantry Regiment and the 1st Mississippi Volunteer Regiment, commanded by Col. Jefferson Davis. As the Mexican main body approached, Taylor was calmly sitting sidesaddle on his horse, saber in hand, behind his massed artillery. At this point he is reputed to have said to the closest artillery battery commander, Capt. Braxton Bragg: "A little more grape [grapeshot], Captain Bragg." It is more likely, however, that he really said: "Double-shot your guns, Bragg, and give them hell!"

Whatever Taylor may have said, the American artillery fire was devastating. The Mexican attack faltered. At that point Taylor ordered Davis to counterattack against Santa Anna's right. The sight of the gleaming bayonets carried by the charging, cheering, Mississippi and Indiana volunteers was simply too much for the already-shaken Mexicans. They fled. Meanwhile the cavalry brigade, for which Santa Anna waited in vain, had been driven off from Saltillo by the rear guard Taylor had thoughtfully left to protect his rear and his line of communications. Santa Anna had no choice but to retreat southward, to face Scott's invasion.

"NEXT DAY" RECOVERY ON THE MARNE

At the outset of World War I, both the major alliances (the Triple Entente, and two thirds of the Triple Alliance) mobilized and moved their forces into battle in accordance with long-standing, carefully prepared plans, which each side was sure would bring quick victory in a war that all of the high commands knew would be violent but therefore inevitably short. (They were correct in predicting violence; they were all very wrong in assuming consequent brevity.) The most important of these plans were the German Schlieffen Plan and French Plan XVII which, between 14 and 25 August 1914, interacted to throw nearly three million men into an extraordinarily bloody conflict along an arc of about 300 miles stretching southeastward from Mons in Belgium to Belfort in France, near the intersection of the French, Swiss, and German borders. At the end of twelve days of the violent battles of the Frontiers, French Plan XVII was in ruins and the German Schlieffen Plan completely victorious. Just as Schlieffen had envisaged it, the German right-wing armies, having won the opening battles, were marching in their giant sweep toward Paris in pursuit of badly defeated French and British forces. And also, as Schlieffen had envisaged it, the left-wing German forces held the fortified line of the Vosges Mountains, having thrown back in bloody defeat the expected French effort to invade the lost provinces of Alsace and Lorraine.

However, as has been noted in an earlier chapter, the Schlieffen Plan was not going exactly as its designer had anticipated, due to errors of both planning and execution by the German high command. Although the Germans had been victorious across the entire front, there was some disarray in General von Moltke's headquarters. The situation was quite different in the French high command.

The Allied generalissimo was French general Joseph J. C. Joffre, a somewhat overweight gentleman whose kindly, avuncular appearance was deceptive. "Papa" Joffre was a tough, pragmatic, intelligent—and very professional—realist. He quickly realized how he and French intelligence had misinterpreted the German plan and objectives and also recognized that Plan XVII had actually played into the German hands and had contributed to their initial victories. Yet he knew that, despite the sharp defeat, his well-trained troops were still full of fight and all was not necessarily lost. Without a moment's hesitation he threw Plan XVII into the wastebasket and created a new plan from scratch.

While the German right-wing armies continued their giant wheel—only briefly set back by an unexpected French counterattack at Guise on 29 August—Joffre began stripping most of his troops from his right wing in the Vosges, going on the defensive there, as the Germans already were. He used these troops to form two new armies. With one (the Ninth) he filled a gap between his Fourth and Fifth armies as they reeled back from their initial defeats west of Verdun. The other army (the Sixth) was established south of the Somme River, and north of Paris, as a counterattack force. As Joffre visualized it, the further the German right wing marched into central France, the more vulnerable its right flank would become. When these two new armies were ready and in place, and as the Germans advanced toward the Aisne and Marne rivers, he intended to have the Sixth Army strike the exposed German right flank, while the Fourth, Ninth, and Fifth armies, plus the British Expeditionary Force, would stop their retreat and turn in a counteroffensive.

It was a bold, brilliant, hastily extemporized plan. And it worked! No plan ever goes exactly as it is envisaged, and the Germans—who were at least the equal of the French as soldiers—did not cooperate readily. The battle began just east of Paris on 5 September, as the French Sixth Army advanced against the right rear of the German First Army. By that time the First Army, and most of the Second and Third armies, were crossing the Marne River, only to be struck by the Allied counteroffensive from the south. At the height of the battle the commander of the new French Ninth Army, Gen. Ferdinand Foch, is reputed to have sent a message to Joffre: "My center is giving way; my right is withdrawing; the situation is excellent; I attack!" By 10 September the Germans were in full retreat to the Aisne River. Joffre had converted total defeat to stunning victory.

Chapter 15

Fighting Back

TACTICS CONTRIBUTE TO STRATEGY

A survey of twenty-six major wars of the nineteenth and twentieth centuries shows that in fourteen instances the side that ultimately won the war also won the first battle. In twelve instances the side that lost the first battle won the war. This does not strongly suggest that a defeat in the initial battle of a war is likely to lead to defeat in the war. On the contrary, it implies that the outcome of a war is more likely to depend on other considerations than on the mere fact that one side had the initial military strength or ability to win the first battle.

Fifteen of those wars lasted more than one year. When one examines the first battle that took place in the last calendar year of those fifteen wars, it is a different story. In thirteen of those wars the side winning the first battle of the last year of the war also won the war. This suggests that if the opponents are closely enough matched that the war is not won quickly by one side or the other, and the hostile motivations are strong enough for both sides to persevere in major war efforts, a trend will be established that, by the beginning of the last year of the war, clearly indicates the likely outcome of the war. This was true, for instance, in the U.S. Mexican War, the American Civil War, the Franco-Prussian War, the Russo-Japanese War, and World War II—whether one looks at that latter conflagration as one enormous war or as several large component wars.

The two exceptions to this pattern are interesting and have some features in common. The first of these was the Sixth Coalition against Napoleon, 1812–1814. Napoleon won the first battles in Russia in 1812, and—after several defeats in Russia and Germany in 1812 and 1813—had been driven back into France by the beginning of 1814. The odds against Napoleon were so great that—so long as the alliance against him held firm—there was really no chance that he could win. Yet his personal genius was such that—after losing the first battle in 1814—he won a series of remarkable victories over far larger forces and held the Allies at bay for several weeks. He was also inspired by the example of Frederick the Great, which we shall examine shortly. There was always the possibility that one or more of the discouraged Allies would abandon the struggle, in which case Napoleon might even had had some chance of success. When, however, the Allies finally coordinated their operations, the game was up for the French Emperor. The Allies took Paris, and he was forced to abdicate.

In World War I the Germans won the initial battles in 1914. Then came the Battle of the Marne and a three-year stalemate on the Western Front. By the beginning of 1918, however, it had become obvious to both Germans and Allies that the odds against an ultimate German victory were increasing, with the tightening of the Allied blockade and the addition of American economic and military strength on the Allied side. Leaders on both sides recognized that Germany's only real hope of winning the war would be to inflict a crushing military defeat on the Allies before the Allied naval blockade of Germany, increasing Allied economic preponderance, and the commitment of American troops, brought Germany to her knees.

Germany acted accordingly. General Ludendorff was convinced that the West Front stalemate could be broken and that the Allies could be so badly defeated that the war-weary British people would make peace. After careful preparation, he launched the German Somme Offensive of March 1918. The Germans smashed through the British armies, broke the trench-war stalemate, and as a result came close to winning the war. They were contained just short of Allied disaster, but barely.

The Allies, however, had learned a lesson from the German victory at the Somme. The Germans had struck against the British right flank, where it joined the French left. When a breakthrough became imminent, the

French pulled back to the southwest, to protect Paris; the British pulled back to the northwest, to protect their lines of communications to the Channel ports. The breakthrough was not quite achieved, but if it had been, the Allied front would have been split irretrievably.

Both sides assessed the situation at the end of the German offensive and both reached similar conclusions. Germany had the resources for one or more comparable offensives, and still might achieve a battlefield success before the trickle of arriving American troops could become enough to influence the outcome. Until that occurred a solid Allied front was necessary, and this was impossible so long as the British army took its instructions from London and the French army from Paris. The Allied Supreme War Council met and appointed French General Ferdinand Foch—completely respected and trusted by the British—as the Allied commander in chief. That was the answer.

The Germans did mount further offensives. In July, after two more partially successful drives, they launched still another that—at least for a few days—threatened to break through to Paris. But Allied resources, coordinated by one commander, were adequate to contain those offensives. By mid-July, as the fifth German offensive was halted, Foch decided that the Germans had so depleted themselves, and the Americans were present in sufficient numbers, that the Allies could undertake a counteroffensive. For nearly four months, from 15 July to 11 November, under the direction and inspiration of Foch, an unceasing barrage of Allied counteroffensives converted the Allied defeat on the Somme to an Allied victory in the war.

There have been, of course, a number of instances in which a commander has been defeated, has learned from his defeat, and has come back to victory. These are more valuable as lessons, of course, than are the ultimately unsuccessful efforts of Napoleon in 1814 and of the Germans in 1918. We will look at four examples: a Byzantine emperor, an English king, a Prussian king, and an American general.

HERACLIUS THE RESTORER

Heraclius became emperor at Constantinople in 610, when it appeared that the Byzantine Empire was about to disintegrate from a combination of internal decay and corruption and apparently irresistible external threats from east and west. When he died thirty-one years later, he had eliminated both of the external threats and established a sound administrative system as a basis for a sturdy military organization and political regional control. A new external threat had appeared, but the system bequeathed to them by Heraclius enabled his successors to hold that threat at bay for more than eight centuries.

Shortly after he became emperor, the eastern dominions of the empire were overrun by the Persians, while the Avars ranged across the European territories, south of the Danube, their armies camping boldly in sight of the walls of Constantinople. The Byzantine Army, ruined by decades of defeat, corruption, and misadministration, offered only halfhearted resistance to either invader. In 616 the Persians drove Heraclius and his dispirited troops inside the city walls east of the Bosporus, then besieged and captured the fortress of Chalcedon, a scant mile from Constantinople. They would remain there for ten years.

Heraclius was then defeated by an Avar army just outside the city walls on the European side. Unable to gain the popular support necessary to reorganize the Byzantine Army effectively, in 619 he was about to abandon the city and take his navy and his court to the Byzantine province of Africa (modern Tunisia and Algeria). At this point he was persuaded to remain in his capital by Sergius, the Patriarch of Constantinople. Over the next three years Heraclius and Sergius inspired a popular resurgence of patriotism inside Constantinople. With the somewhat reluctant approval of Sergius, the emperor emptied the overcrowded monastaries to recruit monks for the army and seized much of the wealth of the churches of the city. With the support of the church, he instilled a new discipline into his troops.

The Byzantines retained control of the sea. In 622 Heraclius sailed from Constantinople with a small army and landed a few days later at the junction of Cilicia and Syria, near Alexandretta and ancient Issus. This was the beginning of six years of campaigning in which Heraclius fought the Persians across eastern Anatolia, Armenia, Mesopotamia, Media, and Persia itself. He won battle after battle, of which the most noteworthy were Issus (622), the Halys (622), Sarus (625), and the decisive Battle of Ninevah (627). In 628 he finally dictated peace with Persia in the ancient capital of Media at Ctesiphon, then returned in triumph to Constantinople. In six campaigns he had led his army from total disaster to glorious victory.

During this time he had not neglected the Avar threat. He returned frequently to Constantinople to supervise the construction of new fortifications to cover the approaches to the city from the north and west and to conduct occasional raids against the Black Sea coast of the Avar kingdom. While he was away campaigning in the east, he left his son Constantine in command of the city's defenses. In 625 and 626 the Avars and Persians formed an alliance against Heraclius. While the Persians mounted an offensive against Heraclius in eastern Anatolia, Persian and Avar armies besieged and assaulted Constantinople. Hard-pressed in the east, Heraclius nevertheless sent 12,000 of his best veterans to help Constantine defend the city. This they did in six weeks of desperate, almost incessant fighting, during which Chalcedon was recaptured from the Persians. After having suffered terrible losses, the Persians and Avars retreated, never again to threaten the city.

After his return from his victorious campaigns in the east, Heraclius supervised a series of campaigns that soon cleared the Avars from the region south of the Danube. Late in his reign the Arabs appeared out of the desert and overran some of the territories Heraclius had recently recon-quered from the Persians. Apparently too worn out for more arduous campaigning, Heraclius contented himself by organizing the security of Anatolia with the theme system, which was to become the basis for Byzantine military organization and regional government for centuries to come. The Arabs, not eager for more encounters with the new Byzantine Army, found easier lands to conquer. Heraclius died peacefully in 641, leaving a viable, prosperous empire.[1]

EDWARD THE PRESERVER

Edward I was one of England's greatest kings, renowned as an efficient administrator, a gifted and prolific lawmaker, and a great contributor to the development of the system of parliamentary government. He was also one of Britain's greatest generals, arguably the greatest. However, his first military experience was disastrous.

Through his father, King Henry III, young Prince Edward was a land-holder in Wales. Some of the fiercely independent barons of that region of Britain paid reluctant homage to the English king, but most did not. In 1256, when Edward was barely seventeen years old, he got into a quarrel with Llewelyn ap Gruffyd, the leading Welsh baron, who was about to declare himself the independent Prince of Wales. Edward received no help from his father or from the English border barons. He was badly defeated by Llewelyn and driven from his holdings in Wales.

In the next few years Edward earned a deserved reputation as a young scoundrel, was widely unpopular, and became an associate of Simon de

Montfort, Earl of Leicester, who was the leader of the baronial party involved in a dispute with inept King Henry. It is likely that Simon and Edward were conspiring to overthrow the king so that Edward could take the throne, with Simon as his chief minister. However, in 1260 Edward suddenly broke off with Simon and was forgiven by his father. Thus, when the barons rebelled against the king in 1264, Edward was his father's chief lieutenant in the army that took the field against the barons. The royalists won the first battle, at Northampton on 5 April, but were surprised by an army of barons and Londoners at Lewes on 14 May. Edward, commanding the right wing of the royal army, drove the Londoners off the field, pursued and butchered many of them, then looted the baron's camp. Meanwhile Montfort and the other barons defeated Henry and the remainder of the royal army. Both Henry and Edward became prisoners, and Simon established himself as the dictator of England.

A year later Edward escaped and joined and took command of a group of royalist barons in rebellion against Simon in southwest England. Edward quickly outmaneuvered Simon and isolated him and his smaller army west of the Severn River. Edward's efforts to bring Simon to battle were frustrated by the Welsh under Llewelyn, who entered into an alliance with Simon. Meanwhile Simon's son, Simon de Montfort the Younger, was marching west from London with a large army to join his father. At that time Edward had about 20,000 men, Simon the elder had about 10,000, and Simon the Younger about 30,000; thus the strength of the combined armies of the two Montforts was about double that of Edward. He boldly marched to Worcester to place himself between the two Simons while guarding the Severn crossings to keep the elder Simon from moving east to join his son. Learning that the younger Simon's army was encamped near Kenilworth, late on 31 July Edward made a remarkable afternoon and night march of forty miles from Worcester to Kenilworth. Without waiting to rest his tired army, at dawn on 1 August Edward attacked the unsecured camp of the younger Simon. There was scant resistance from the surprised Montfort army; most of them were killed or captured.

Edward wasted no time in rest. Early on 2 August he was marching back to Worcester, where he discovered that the elder Simon had taken advantage of his absence to cross the Severn. Late next day Edward again put his soldiers on the road for another night march, planning to intercept the elder Simon near Evesham. Next morning, as the two armies approached each other, Edward's troops displayed Montfortian banners captured at Kenilworth. Montfort at first thought this was his son's army. Before he realized his mistake it was too late to escape. He and his army were trapped in a bend of the Avon River near Evesham. His Welsh allies fled and were ignored by Edward, who closed in on Montfort and his remaining troops. In the ensuing battle every man in the Montfort army was killed or captured, Simon being among the dead. King Henry (who had been kept a prisoner with Simon's army all this time) was slightly wounded by royalists by mistake before he was freed.

(It is worth noting, in the light of his previous unsavory performance, that Edward placed his father back on the throne and remained his loyal first minister until Henry died seven years later.)

This campaign, probably the most brilliant ever fought on the island of Britain, would have done credit to a Napoleon. It is in itself enough to rank Edward among the greatest soldiers in the history of England. There are other reasons, but they are beyond the scope of this book.[2]

FREDERICK THE SURVIVOR

Frederick II, King of Prussia, is one of the most controversial figures of history. His father, King Frederick William, considered him an effeminate intellectual, and when Frederick as a youth rebelliously attempted to escape his father's tyranny, the king had him tried by court-martial for desertion and sentenced to death. The sentence probably would have been carried out had not other members of the royal family intervened. History would have been much the poorer.

Here we shall consider only a few months in 1757, when Frederick was disastrously defeated, his kingdom invaded from east, west, and south by four armies, each larger than his own, and his capital occupied by the enemy. (A fifth enemy army, smaller than his, was also invading from the north.) No one would have ever thought ill of Frederick had he sued for peace. Instead, in a series of lightning movements, he inflicted overwhelming defeats on two of his larger enemies and frightened the other three into withdrawing. A brief chronology tells the story.

April. With 65,000 men, the largest field army he ever commanded, Frederick invaded Bohemia and sought battle with an Austrian army of 70,000 men under Prince Charles of Lorraine.

May 6. Battle of Prague. In a hard-fought battle Frederick defeated the Austrians and threw them back into Prague, which he invested.

May–June. An Austrian relief army of 60,000, under Marshal Leopold J. von Daun, approached Prague.

June 16. Leaving about 15,000 men investing Prague, Frederick marched with 34,000 to meet Daun's army.

June 18. Battle of Kolin. Frederick was disastrously repulsed from an attack on Daun's entrenched camp. He was forced to raise the seige of Prague.

July. A French army of 100,000 men under Marshal Louis d'Estrées invaded Hanover, defended by a Prussian-English army of 50,000 under Duke William Augustus of Cumberland. Simultaneously, an Austro-French army of 84,000, under French Duke Charles of Soubise and Austrian Prince Joseph of Saxe-Hildberghausen, also advanced into Hanover to join d'Estrées; the combined armies then intended to march east into central Prussia. The Austrian army in Bohemia, now 110,000, under Prince Charles and Marshal Daun, advanced north over the mountains, following Frederick's retreat into Prussian Silesia, prepared to drive him back toward Berlin from the southeast. A Russian army of 100,000 under Marshal Stepan Apraksin was advancing west into East Prussia. An army of 16,000 Swedes landed in Pomerania, prepared to join either the Russians or the Austro-French army. The Prussian and English forces defending Prussia and Hanover were less than 200,000 men. The converging, invading armies totaled more than 400,000.

July 26. Battle of Hastenbeck. The Duke of Cumberland was defeated by Estrées and driven from Hanover. The road to Berlin from the west was open.

July 30. Battle of Gross Jagersdorf. A Prussian army of 30,000, protecting East Prussia, was defeated by Apraksin's Russians. The road to Berlin from the east was open. However, the Russians were slowed by poor supply arrangements.

August–September. Harassed ineffectually by small Prussian delaying forces, the French army (now under the Duke of Richelieu), the Austro-French under Hildberghausen and Soubise, and Apraksin's Russians converged toward Berlin.

September–October. Leaving about 20,000 men in front of Prince Charles' Austrians in Silesia, Frederick took 23,000 northwest to join the Prussians that were attempting to delay the two armies converging from the west on Berlin. But Richelieu's army did not move, and as

Frederick approached, now with about 40,000 men, Hildberghausen and Soubise retreated from Magdeburg. Frederick rushed back to Silesia, since Prince Charles and Daun were beginning to march north.

October 16. Austrian raiders occupied and plundered Berlin.

October 18. Sending a small detachment to rescue his capital and leaving a small force to delay the Austrians in Silesia, Frederick again marched northwest with 20,000 men to block the renewed advance of Hildberghausen and Soubise through Saxony toward Berlin.

November 4. Hildberghausen and Soubise with 64,000 men approached Frederick with 21,000, near Rossbach.

November 5. Battle of Rosbach. Frederick lured the allies to move to envelop his left flank, near Rossbach. As the enveloping columns, 41,000 strong, swung around behind Rossbach, they were ambushed by most of the Prussian army and completely routed, with the loss of 8000 men. Frederick had 500 casualties.

November 6–December 5. Frederick marched back rapidly to Silesia, where Charles and Daun had defeated the Prussian delaying force and had captured Breslau. With the defeated survivors, Frederick had 36,000 men. The Austrians, deployed just north of Breslau, were 80,000 strong.

December 6. Battle of Leuthen. Frederick used part of his cavalry to demonstrate in front of the Austrian right wing. At the same time he utilized terrain to screen the approach of his main body against the Austrian left wing. His infantry, in his favorite echeloned formation with left flank refused, unexpectedly emerged from a line of hills to attack the Austrian left wing. He smashed this portion of the Austrian army, then continued on to drive the remainder of the Austrians off the field. The Prussians captured 20,000 Austrians, 6750 were killed or wounded. Frederick lost 6150 killed and wounded. This was perhaps the greatest tactical masterpiece in all military history.

December. All the invading armies withdrew. They and the Prussians went into winter quarters. Defeat had been converted into victory.

The war lasted five more years, and Frederick was often in desperate straits. But how could the man who had won Rossbach and Leuthen ever give up hope? With skill and determination—and just a bit of luck—he outlasted his enemies. When the war ended, tiny Prussia shared with mighty Austria the power balance in central Europe.

STILWELL: ILLEGITIMATI NON CARBORUNDUM

That was Joseph W. Stilwell's personal motto; "Don't let the bastards grind you down!" was his free translation of this bit of outrageous dog Latin.

During the years following World War I Stilwell served in China on three different occasions—first as a language student, twice later as a military attaché. During those years he came to know the Chinese people, and particularly the Chinese soldier, as have few other Occidentals.

When World War II broke out, Stilwell was a major general commanding the U.S. III Corps on the West Coast. The United States government decided to send a senior American general to China to establish an enlarged military mission in that country and take over the functions of the air-training mission and military Lend-Lease mission already there. Since Stilwell, a general officer with thirty-seven years' service, probably knew more about China than any other man in the United States Army, he was a logical choice for the task. He was to assist in the training and supply of the Chinese Army and to advise Generalissimo Chiang Kai-shek and his military subordinates on overall matters of strategy and tactics. At the same time he would become chief of staff to the Generalissimo, who had accepted the invitation of the Anglo-American Combined Chiefs of Staff to assume the post of Allied Commander in Chief of the China Theater.

Early in March, one month after his appointment, Stilwell reported to Generalissimo Chiang in Chungking. En route he had been promoted to lieutenant general. During that month much had happened in the Far East. Singapore had surrendered to the Japanese on 15 February. Allied naval forces in the Far East had been practically annihilated in the Battle of the Java Sea, 27–28 February, and on 9 March the Dutch formally surrendered the Netherlands East Indies to Japan. The Malay barrier, which had been expected to limit Japanese advances in Asia and the Pacific, had been irretrievably lost, the Allies split in twain.

Even more serious so far as Stilwell's interests were concerned, the Japanese had started a vigorous offensive in Burma and seemed to have the disorganized, outnumbered British defenders on the run. With Burma in Japanese hands, the Allies would be split once more. China, its artery for

Lend-Lease supplies lost, would be cut off from all land contact with its allies. There could be no land lines of communications worthy of the name over the Himalayas from India, or across the deserts and mountains of Turkestan from Russia—even if stricken Russia could have diverted any supplies from its own death struggle with Hitler. It was doubtful, therefore, whether China could remain in the war if Burma were to fall into enemy hands.

In this desperate crisis the Generalissimo offered to send troops into Burma to help in its defense. The British, distrustful of Chinese intentions in that region, had refused an earlier offer of such assistance, but now, with the Japanese in possession of Rangoon, Burma's capital, and with enemy columns driving deeper into the country so as to threaten India itself, they were ready to accept.

So down the Burma Road poured two Chinese armies, the Fifth and the Sixth. In actual combat strength the Fifth Army was perhaps comparable to a Western or Japanese division; the Sixth Army was scarcely better than a rabble, with little significant combat potential. The commander of this Chinese Expeditionary Force was Lt. Gen. Joseph W. Stilwell, as he learned to his surprise when he reported to Chiang in Chungking.

Silwell promptly left for Burma to assume his new command. At Maymyo, the beautiful summer capital, he reported to Gen. Sir Harold Alexander, the overall British commander in Burma. No unified Allied command organization had been established, and command relationships were unclear. But for the moment the tactical situation was fairly obvious.

There was a lull as the Japanese reorganized themselves in the Rangoon area for a further advance. The Allied defenders were busily organizing a defensive line across the narrow portion of south-central Burma, about a hundred miles north of Rangoon. On the right was the exhausted British I Burma Corps, holding the Irrawaddy Valley, under the firm leadership of a new commander, Maj. Gen. William Slim. In the center the Chinese Fifth Army held the Sittang Valley and had moved a division south of Toungoo. On the left the Chinese Sixth Army was holding the most easily defensible position, athwart the deep, narrow valley of the Salween.

Stilwell moved promptly to Pyabwe, headquarters of the Chinese Fifth Army, roughly 130 miles north of the leading Chinese division south of Maymyo. He gravely disapproved this location of the army headquarters so far to the rear of the fighting troops, but the army commander ignored his hints to move forward. Stilwell began to realize that his authority over his command was far from complete.

Japanese pressure against the three major Allied elements began to mount. In mid-April they made a bold bid for quick victory in Burma. Initially the main Japanese effort was thrown against the tired British, and their almost precipitate retreat forced Stilwell and his Fifth Army to withdraw promptly up the Sittang to keep from unduly exposing his right flank. He sent a regiment from the newly arrived veteran Chinese 38th Division to help cover the British withdrawal through the Yenangyaung oil fields. As Japanese pressure increased, he sent two more divisions over to the Irrawaddy front to attempt to retrieve the desperate situation, thus dangerously weakening his own Fifth Army front. To the surprise of most of his American staff but not to Stilwell, these outnumbered Chinese troops responded magnificently in the face of defeat and disaster. With Stilwell constantly and courageously exposing himself to enemy fire and the attacks of the enemy fighter planes that now dominated the air, the tough, disciplined Chinese *lao bing* (literally "old soldier," equivalent of the American "GI") smiled approvingly at this unusual Occidental commander and carried out his orders. It looked as though the front might be stabilized below Mandalay, despite the apparent collapse of the British, of whom Stilwell was now openly, and somewhat unjustly, contemptuous.

Then, about 21 April, the Japanese struck a powerful blow to the unprepared Chinese 55th Division of the Sixth Army. The division simply evaporated.

With Alexander's approval Stilwell moved the hard-fighting 200th Division from the British front and rushed it to Taunggyi, a critical road junction 150 miles south of Lashio. But misunderstandings and missing trucks delayed the movement. The 200th reached the vicinity of Taunggyi just one day after the Japanese had seized the town. Stilwell rushed to the front and personally took command of a company under heavy Japanese fire. When reinforcements arrived, he led a counterattack that pushed the enemy back for more than twenty miles, and for a short time the Chinese actually held Taunggyi, cutting the Japanese lines of communication.

But the Japanese commander of the flying column, displaying first-rate leadership on his own part, ignored the situation in his rear. He was living off the countryside, getting plentiful supplies from Allied depots, and he swept into Lashio without opposition.

The Burma Road was blocked, China cut off from the rest of the Free

World. But of more immediate concern to Stilwell was the fact that his Chinese Expeditionary Force was isolated in Burma, its only escape route to China cut off. Meanwhile, the continuing Japanese advance up the Irrawaddy Valley was threatening to cut the one remaining road that led from Mandalay through Kalewa across the mountains from Burma to Imphal in India. Since the retreating British were clogging this road, Stilwell had to find another route, or routes, through narrow jungle trails farther north.

Refusing to abandon his troops by flying out of Burma with the last plane to leave Shwebo on 30 April, Stilwell gathered his official household, soon to be augmented by other refugees, and marched northwest. Or, as he reported it, "I then picked up my headquarters group and brought them out."

Thus did Stilwell dismiss, with one curt sentence, a 400-mile trek with 100-odd men and women of various nationalities and races. The route lay up the Irrawaddy Valley, then over steep jungle hills to the Chindwin Valley, across the Chindwin, and finally up and over the 8000-foot range of mountains disarmingly known as the Chin Hills, to Imphal and safety. The last 150 miles was all done on foot and completed in the amazing time of 14 days. During this anabasis the irrepressible fifty-nine-year-old veteran outmarched men half his age, and by sheer personal leadership coaxed, bullied, jollied, and dragged with him his heterogeneous group through dense jungle, across wide, swift rivers, and over unmapped jungle-mountain trails. His own weight dropped from 140 pounds to 120 during those terrible two weeks.

On 20 May he arrived at Imphal. Resting only overnight, early the next morning he proceeded by automobile and train to Dinjan, the nearest airfield, whence he could fly to New Delhi. And at Dinjan, on 22 May, he made his famous, honest, offhand evaluation of the first Burma campaign, voicing his grim determination to "find out what caused the loss of Burma" and to "go back and retake it."

Stilwell, in fact, already had a pretty good idea of what happened, and how. He was even at that early date planning what to do about getting ready to "go back." He plunged at once into the task he had laid out for himself.

The first job was to reorganize the scattered elements of Chinese troops who had fled into India. Stilwell brought them to a training center he established at Ramgarh, some 200 miles west of Calcutta. The Ramgarh training center was staffed with a group of the best young American officers that Army Ground Forces could send in response to Stilwell's urgent request. Here the Chinese, who had already proved their worth as soldiers, were issued new American and British equipment and put through an intensive course in the employment of modern arms. To these veterans of the Burma campaign, Stilwell was able to add thousands more Chinese soldiers—mostly untrained recruits—shipping them in on the supply planes that would otherwise have returned empty across the Hump from China.

During the latter part of 1942 and in early 1943 three Chinese divisions went through the Ramgarh training center. The veteran 38th, brought up to full strength of about 11,000 men by recruits flown in from China, was issued brand-new weapons and equipment. As soon as it had completed its training course, it was shipped back to the Burma–India border, with headquarters near the town of Ledo in Assam. Next was the experienced 22nd Division, which in August 1943 arrived rejuvenated near Ledo, to join the 38th.

The next task of the Ramgarh training center was to use the recruits and a few veterans from China to build up a new division, the 30th plus a number of independent units—artillery, armor, infantry, engineer, quartermaster, and others—to round out a balanced, modern army corps.

Stilwell was not able to spend much time at Ramgarh—though that was where his heart lay, and that was where he went whenever the heavy burden of his other duties would allow. He now had four widely dispersed headquarters, and at each of these he exercised a different responsibility. As Chief of Staff of the China Theater—an Allied command—under the Generalissimo, his headquarters were in Chungking, China. As Commander in Chief of the American China–Burma–India Theater, his headquarters were in New Delhi, India. As Deputy Supreme Allied Commander of the Southeast Asia Command, under Lord Louis Mountbatten, he had to spend a great deal of his time at SEAC headquarters at Kandy, Ceylon. And as the Commanding General of the Northern Combat Area Command—from which he exercised his operational control over the New Chinese Army in India—his headquarters were initially in Ledo, India, and later moved to Burma behind the fighting front.

The Northern Combat Area Command (NCAC) was under the operational direction of the British Fourteenth Army, which was in charge of all Allied ground operations in Burma. As Deputy Supreme Allied Commander of SEAC, Stilwell frequently *issued* orders to his old friend, British General Slim. (Slim, incidentally, was one of the very few Britishers

Stilwell liked; the feeling was mutual between two splendid fighting men.) But as Commanding General of NCAC, Stilwell *received* his orders from Slim.

As he tried to wear all of these hats and to meet the demanding and challenging requirements of his many responsibilities, Stilwell really had only one main thought in his mind: to carry out his mission by driving the Japanese from Burma and reopening a land route to China. Dangling at the end of a 10,000-mile supply line, realizing that his command was lowest on the priority of the Combined Chiefs of Staff when they parceled out Allied resources, Stilwell found himself plunged into a maelstrom of inimical political forces, buffeted by conflicting interests of the United States, Great Britain, China, and the seething unrest of independence-minded India. As if this were not enough, he was inevitably and inextricably involved in jealousies both within and without his command, finding himself at cross purposes with other American, as well as with British and Chinese, military men. Finally, vacillating policies in Washington were transmitted down that long line of communications as along a rope, with Stilwell at the end in a gigantic game of crack the whip.

These circumstances, the likes of which no American soldier had ever been faced with before, would have taxed the patience and finesse of even the most able diplomat. And Stilwell was not a diplomat; he was a field soldier. It is beyond the scope of this book to discuss Stilwell's stormy relationship with the second senior American in China, Maj. Gen. Claire L. Chennault, who commanded the U.S. Fourteenth Air Force.

The second Burma campaign began in November 1943. The spearhead of the drive was the 38th Division. The veterans of this division knew the enemy well. Many of them had been fighting the Japanese since the Battle of Shanghai in 1931. It could not be said that they feared the Japanese; it was merely that in their experience, their lack of equipment and inferior mobility had always forced them to go on the defensive. And so, as they met the old enemy once more in North Burma's densely jungled Hukawng Valley, they automatically went on the defensive. It didn't matter that they had new and improved equipment; they did not care what their American instructors had taught them at Ramgarh; here were the Japs, and there was only one way to fight Japs. They dug in. The enemy immediately took advantage of this immobility, and promptly surrounded each of the three leading battalions.

As soon as he learned of this setback, Stilwell flew to the Hukawng Valley, to supervise and direct the relief of the surrounded units and to encourage the Chinese forward. He was successful and the division began to move again. Slowly, but it moved.

There was an interesting pattern of Chinese reaction to Stilwell—and his undiplomatic, direct, blunt, aggressive attitude—from fighting front in Burma to Chinese Army headquarters in Chungking. It ranged from adoration by the *lao bing*, through admiration by junior officers and grudging respect by slow-moving generals in Burma, to fear, opposition, and downright hatred by many of the most senior officers in Chungking. Stilwell, "packing up his divisions on his back," as one observer put it, was winning his battle in Burma, but he was losing a war in Chungking, where that same back was exposed to subtle Oriental knifing.

Having proved to his Chinese troops that they could fight and beat the Japanese on their own terms in the jungle, Stilwell was able to goad the division commanders into a slow but steady offensive. It was not an easy job, for him or for them, and some of the Americans who served with the Chinese in Burma tended to be critical of the apparently leisurely pace. The Japanese were outnumbered, true enough, but on the narrow jungle trails two men with a machine gun could stop a regiment indefinitely. And the Japanese commander, a first-rate tactician named Tanaka, conducted a classic delaying action.

Sometimes Stilwell would use his one regiment of American infantry, Merrill's Marauders, to spearhead an assault. Relying upon the importance of "face" to the Chinese, Stilwell was sure the *lao bing* would not allow himself to be excelled by the GI. The psychology worked, and by the spring of 1944 the advance was accelerating. As the Chinese gained confidence and their commanders gained experience, Stilwell began more daring maneuvers, sending regiments, battalions, and finally entire divisions on sweeping envelopments. By the time the monsoon rains began in June, his troops had reached the Irrawaddy at Myitkyina, and had swept through the cities of Kamaing and Mogaung in north-central Burma.

All this time Stilwell's troops had been supplied almost entirely by air, through the magnificent efforts of Maj. Gen. Howard C. Davidson's Tenth U.S. Air Force. And behind the advance, Chinese and American engineers were building a road—the Ledo Road—that was to become the new land link to China.

When the rains came, everyone—British, Chinese, Japanese, even the Americans—expected military operations to close, as they always had ceased in monsoon season in South Asia. But Stilwell had no intention of stopping. His two leading Chinese divisions, he knew, were exhausted, so he did let them slow down in the early monsoon days, but he maintained the pressure against the valiant Japanese defenders of Myitkyina and, with a fresh British division to lead the way, continued to press the astonished foe.

When the monsoon ended, Stilwell issued new orders. Two new Chinese divisions had been flown in to augment his command, as had another American regiment. He now had a real fighting force of more than six divisions. Striking swiftly, he drove the unprepared foe back to the Irrawaddy between Katha and Bhamo. Then as enemy resistance stiffened on the two main axes of his advance, he threw two divisions and an American brigade across the jungled country toward Lashio. The main Japanese force in North Burma, the Thirty-Third Army, was about to be trapped in a double envelopment—the holding force at Bhamo and Chinese divisions just across the border at Lungling providing the anvil for this hammer swinging down from the Irawaddy—and thrown back against the impassable Salween River. A brilliantly conceived and planned maneuver, its success was inevitable.

Stilwell had kept his promise. He had come back. North Burma was in his grasp. The campaign was about to end in dramatic glory.

In the moment of victory Stilwell was relieved, on 19 October 1944. Cautious higher-ups now canceled his planned double envelopment.

More than six months would elapse before Japanese resistance in Burma would finally collapse, under combined British–Chinese–American pressure. It would be vain to speculate on whether things would have been different either in Burma or in China (where a new Japanese advance was again threatening the Chinese war effort) had Stilwell stayed on. And such speculation would be unfair to his successors, stout Gen. Daniel I. Sultan who took over in Burma and India and brilliant Gen. Albert G. Wedemeyer, who succeeded Stilwell as the chief of staff to the Generalissimo in China. Stilwell's relief, and his departure from the scene, were accompanied by far-reaching political and military reshuffling, which caused both of these capable generals to face entirely different situations in the new theaters they had inherited.

Such speculation, too, would be unfair to the gallant British effort, under Stilwell's old friend General Slim, which in May 1945 gained revenge for the dismal days of early 1942 by a lightning drive to Mandalay and thence onward to Rangoon.

But to the *lao bing* and the occasional American soldier in northern Burma, the change in tempo, the apparent slackening of the effort, and the abandonment of Stilwell's plan to envelop the Japanese Thirty-third Army meant much.[3] These men neither knew nor cared about the political forces that had swirled about Stilwell or the global strategic factors that had affected his roles in Chungking, New Delhi, and Kandy. They would have laughed at suggestions that Stilwell was not an adroit diplomat. So what? Like them he was a soldier. In 1942 he had taken a beating in Burma, had taken it like a man, and had promised to go back and retake it. And he had!

The Principles of War and Battle Analysis

ORIGINS OF THE PRINCIPLES OF WAR

The idea that there are some underlying, fundamental, immutable principles that govern successful waging of war came more or less simultaneously, and quite independently, to two early nineteenth-century military theorists: Antoine Henri Jomini and Carl von Clausewitz. They came to their almost-identical conclusions about principles for the same reason: They could see clear patterns of systematic planning, decision-making, and battlefield leadership in the campaigns and battles of Napoleon. Strangely, however, while both of these brilliant theorists recognized, and wrote about, the principles they observed in Napoleon's operations, neither attempted to prepare a comprehensive list of principles, with carefully thought-out definitions. Neither, unfortunately, did the master of warfare from whom they got the idea, although (one way or another) most of the concepts we now call the principles of war can be found in the *Maxims* of Napoleon.

Following the lead of Jomini and Clausewitz, other military theorists of the late nineteenth and early twentieth centuries were fond of referring to "fundamental," or "immutable," or "well-known" principles of war, and for the most part they had some fairly well-defined concepts in mind for these principles based on reading of the *Maxims* and/or of at least parts of the voluminous works of Jomini and Clausewitz.

Early in the twentieth century a student at the British Staff College at Camberly—Maj. John F. C. Fuller—annoyed his instructors by asking just what were these "well-known" principles of war? If they were so important, why weren't they codified for the benefit of military students? His embarrassed instructors could not give him an answer and tagged him as a troublemaker. Fuller decided he would undertake such a codification and began intensive reading of military history. He was interrupted in this work by World War I, but soon after that war he produced a list of eight Principles of War.

The crystallization of military thought implicit in Fuller's codification of the Principles of War has been almost universally adopted in most of the armed forces of most nations. Minor differences as to number, nomenclature, and relative importance of the several principles are found in the doctrines of the various nations and even among the services of a single nation. But, for the most part, these differences are essentially those of semantics or emphasis. Soon after Fuller's first publication of a revised list of his principles (now nine in number) in the early 1920s, they were adopted with some changes by the United States Army. Over the subsequent decades there have been still further changes in the precise wording of the concepts and in their definitions, but they are still nine in number in official U.S. army doctrine. I personally prefer the discussion of those that appeared in the U.S. Army Field Manual 100-5, *Field Service Regulations: Operations*, in 1954. The list and discussion at the end of this appendix are taken from that manual.

USE OF THE PRINCIPLES FOR BATTLE ANALYSIS

I have found the Principles of War a very useful tool in studying historical military operations and in teaching others how to study them. It was originally my intention to use them in this book as the basis for theoretical analysis of defeat (the concept) and defeats (the events). However, I soon discovered that—useful though they were for general analysis and for studying the reasons for military success—they were not comprehensive enough to deal with the analysis of defeats. This can probably best be demonstrated by analysis of what is probably the best-known defeat of history: Napoleon's at Waterloo.

The use of the principles by the victorious Allies is fairly clear. The most important principles in the Allied success were The Objective, Surprise, Maneuver, and probably Simplicity. It is also easy to see evidence of the other five (Offensive, Mass, Economy of Forces, Security, and even Unity of Command), particularly in the performance of the Prussian Army and the single-minded determination of Marshal Blücher to fulfill his promise of cooperation to the Duke of Wellington.

But what of Napoleon? Is there any way we can see in his performance a violation of any of the principles of war? Quite frankly, no. He was surprised by the arrival of the Prussians on his right flank, but he had adequate security—in the form of reserves—to deal with this. Yet he was defeated, and there are reasons for his defeat independent of the reasons—explicable in terms of the principles of war—for the victory of his opponents.

ANALYSIS USING "CAUSES OF DEFEAT"

It was to deal with, and to analyze, the reasons for defeat that I prepared the list of causes of defeat found in Chapter 4. If we apply them to Napoleon's performance at Waterloo, we can better understand why the French Emperor was defeated.

First there is cause A.1.a, overpowered by superior numbers. The unexpected arrival of the Prussian Army on the battlefield assured allied victory. But why had the Prussians arrived? Hadn't Napoleon considered that possibility? He most certainly had, and had taken what had seemed to him adequate measures to prevent it. After defeating the Prussians at the Battle of Ligny on 16 June, he had sent Marshal Grouchy, with more than a third of his army, to pursue the Prussians and to keep them from joining forces with Wellington. But Grouchy had failed. This was reason B.6, subordinate error/failure. Category B is called unfavorable circumstances commander may influence. Grouchy apparently was not up to the mission he had been given, although one would expect that the nature and significance of the mission should have been evident to, and within the capabilities of, a marshal of France. Nevertheless, Napoleon should have been aware of Grouchy's limitations. What could he have done about this? Possibly he should have chosen a different general for the pursuit mission, or perhaps he should have been more explicit in his instructions to Grouchy.

There are two other reasons for Napoleon's defeat, although the two discussed above are the most important ones.

Had Napoleon attacked Wellington early on 18 June, there is little doubt that he would have driven the Anglo-Allied army off the field before the Prussians arrived, beginning about 2:00 P.M. But it was almost noon before Napoleon attacked. Was this sloth, laziness, or inefficiency? Not at all. There had been a violent rainstorm the preceding evening, and the farmland over which the battle would be fought was too wet to permit the cross-country movement of the French horse-drawn artillery. Knowing that his artillery was superior both in performance and numbers to that of the British, Napoleon waited until the ground had dried sufficiently to permit him to use his guns properly. Thus unfavorable weather—another cause over which he as a commander had no control—contributed to the defeat.

Then, of course, there was the matter of surprise. Napoleon was surprised by the arrival of the Prussians, but it is hard to see what he could have done to prevent this beyond what he had done in terms of Grouchy's mission and holding out reserves for unexpected eventualities.

Finally, there was chance, item A.5 in the list of causes of defeat. The rainstorm the evening of the seventeenth seems to have been a chance event over which Napoleon had no control.

So our skeleton analysis of Waterloo is complete, although it could be elaborated considerably. In brief, the performance of the allies can be given high marks in terms of the Principles of War. Napoleon's defeat is explicable in terms of two causes over which he had no control (outnumbered and bad weather) and one circumstance he might have influenced: the failure of a subordinate. And, in a matrix analysis we might wish to put question marks in the box for chance—another cause over which Napoleon had no control—and that for being surprised—a possible failure in leadership related to Grouchy's performance.

THE PRINCIPLES OF WAR

OBJECTIVE

Every military operation must be directed toward a decisive, obtainable objective. The destruction of the enemy's armed forces and his will to fight is the ultimate military objective of war. The objective of each operation must contribute to this ultimate objective. Each intermediate objective must be such that its attainment will most directly, quickly, and economically contribute to the purpose of the operation. It must permit the application of the maximum means available. Its selection must be based upon consideration of means available, the enemy, and the area of operations. Secondary objectives of any operation must contribute to the attainment of the principal objective.

OFFENSIVE

Only offensive action achieves decisive results. Offensive action permits the commander to exploit the initiative and impose his will on the enemy. The defensive may be forced on the commander, but it should be deliberately adopted only as a temporary expedient while awaiting an opportunity for offensive action or for the purpose of economizing forces on a front where a decision is not sought. Even on the defensive the commander seeks every opportunity to seize the initiative and achieve decisive results by offensive action.

SIMPLICITY

Simplicity must be the keynote of military operations. Uncomplicated plans clearly expressed in orders promote common understanding and intelligent execution. Even the most simple plan is usually difficult to execute in combat. Simplicity must be applied to organization, methods, and means in order to produce orderliness on the battlefield.

UNITY OF COMMAND

The decisive application of full combat power requires unity of command. Unity of command obtains unity of effort by the coordinated action of all forces toward a common goal. Coordination may be achieved by direction or by cooperation. It is best achieved by vesting a single commander with requisite authority. Unity of effort is furthered by willing and intelligent cooperation among all elements of the forces involved. Pearl Harbor is an example of failure in organization for command.

MASS

Maximum available combat power must be applied at the point of decision. Mass is the concentration of means at the critical time and place to the maximum degree permitted by the situation. Proper application of the principle of mass, in conjunction with the other principles of war, may permit numerically inferior forces to achieve decisive combat superiority. Mass is essentially a combination of manpower and firepower and is not dependent upon numbers alone; the effectiveness of mass may be increased by superior weapons, tactics, and morale.

ECONOMY OF FORCES

Minimum essential means must be employed at points other than that of decision. To devote means to unnecessary secondary efforts or to employ excessive means on required secondary efforts is to violate the principle of both mass and the objective. Limited attacks, the defensive, deception, or even retrograde action, are used in noncritical areas to achieve mass in the critical area.

MANEUVER

Maneuver must be used to alter the relative combat power of military forces. Maneuver is the positioning of forces to place the enemy at a relative disadvantage. Proper positioning of forces in relation to the enemy frequently can achieve results that otherwise could be achieved only at heavy cost in men and materiel. In many situations maneuver is made possible only by the effective employment of firepower.

SURPRISE

Surprise may decisively shift the balance of combat power in favor of the commander who achieves it. It consists of striking the enemy when, where, or in a manner for which he is unprepared. It is not essential that the enemy be taken unaware but only that he becomes aware too late to react effectively. Surprise can be achieved by speed, secrecy, deception, by variation in means and methods, and by using seemingly impossible terrain. Mass is essential to the optimum exploitation of the principle of surprise.

SECURITY

Security is essential to the application of the other principles of war. It consists of those measures necessary to prevent surprise, avoid annoyance, preserve freedom of action, and deny to the enemy information of our forces. Security denies to the enemy and retains for the commander the ability to employ his forces most effectively.

Significant Historical Defeats

Listed below are 138 significant defeats in history. For the most part these are also significant victories for the successful side, and thus this list includes most of the truly important battles of history. But they were chosen essentially because of their importance as defeats to the losing side. For instance, the Battle of Arausio and the Battle of the Little Big Horn would not be considered as important battles either historically or militarily had it not been for the effect these defeats had upon the nation whose forces were defeated in the battle. Only one of Pyrrhus' two "pyrrhic victories" is listed, simply because Asculum was a bigger battle than Heraclea; and Beneventum (where the Romans finally defeated Pyrrhus, and which is historically more important than either of the other two) is omitted.

It would be surprising if some scholars did not believe that this list omits some important defeats or if other scholars did not believe that some of the battles listed do not warrant inclusion. Nevertheless, most of the most important defeats in history are without doubt listed below. Certainly (with one exception) all of the battles discussed in the text are listed. That one exception is Gumbinnen, in 1914, one of the four battles discussed in Chapter 9. Gumbinnen was, without doubt, a severe defeat for General von Mackensen's XVII Corps, and is a useful case study of defeat. But overall, mainly because of a successful attack by the German I Corps, Gumbinnen was a drawn battle, and thus is not included.

Battle	Year	Defeated	Successful
Marathon	490 B.C.	Persia: Datis/Artaphrns	Athens: Miltiades
Salamis	480 B.C.	Persia: Xerxes	Athens: Themistocles
Syracuse	413 B.C.	Athens: Nicias	Sparta: Gylippus
Leuctra	371 B.C.	Sparta: Cleombrotus	Thebes: Epaminondas
Arbela	331 B.C.	Persia: Darius III	Macedon: Alexander
Asculum	279 B.C.	Rome: Fabricus/Aemilius	Epirus: Pyrrhus
Lake Trasimene	217 B.C.	Rome: Flaminius	Carthage: Hannibal
Cannae	216 B.C.	Rome: Varro	Carthage: Hannibal
The Metaurus	207 B.C.	Carthage: Hasdrubal	Rome: Nero
Zama	202 B.C.	Carthage: Hannibal	Rome: Scipio
Cynoscephalae	197 B.C.	Macedon: Philip V	Rome: Flamininus
Arausio	105 B.C.	Rome: Mallius Maximus	Cimbri/Teutones:
Pharsalus	48 B.C.	Rome (P): Pompei	Rome (C): Caesar
Actium	31 B.C.	Rome (A): Antony	Rome (O): Agrippa
Teutoberg Wood	9 A.D.	Rome: Varus	Germans: Arminius
Adrianople	378	Rome: Valens	Goths: Fritigern
Ninevah	627	Persia: Rhazates	Byz Emp: Heraclius
Yarmuk	636	Byz Emp: Theodore	Arabs: Khalid ibn al-Walid
Chalons	451	Huns: Attila	Rome, etc.: Aetius
Constantinople	717–718	Arabs: Suleiman	Byz Emp: Leo III
Tours/Poitiers	732	Arabs: Abd er-Rahman	Franks: Charles Martel
Hastings	1066	Eng (Sax): Harold	Normans: William
Manzikert	1071	Byz Emp: Romanus Diogenes	Seljuk Tks: Alp Arslan
Myriocephalum	1176	Byz Emp: Manuel Commenus	Seljuk Tks: Kilij Arslan IV
Arsouf	1191	Ayyubid Emp: Saladin	Crusaders: Richard I
Constantinople	1204	Byz Emp: Alexius V	Crusaders: Theobald et al.
Peking	1215	Chin Emp: Wan-yen	Mongol Emp: Genghis Khan
The Indus	1221	Khwarez Emp: Jellaludin	Mongol Emp: Genghis Khan

Battle	Year	Defeated	Successful
Sajo River	1241	Hungary: Bela	Mongol Emp: Subotai
Evesham	1265	Eng Rebs: Simon deMntfrt	Eng Royalists: Edward I
Crecy	1346	France: Philip VI	England: Edward III
Agincourt	1415	France: D'Albret	England: Henry V
Orleans	1429	England: Salisbury	France: Joan of Arc
Constantinople	1453	Byz Emp: Constantine XI	Ottoman Emp: Mohommed II
Cerignola	1503	France: Nemours	Spain: Gonzalo de Cordoba
Rhodes	1522	Hosptlrs: de L'Isle Adam	Ottoman Emp: Suleiman I
Mohacs	1526	Hungary: Louis II	Ottoman Emp: Suleiman I
Vienna	1529	Ottoman Emp: Suleiman I	HR Emp: Philip et al.
Malta	1565	Ottmn Emp: Mustapha Psha	Hosptlrs: J de la Valette
Lepanto	1571	Ottmn Emp: Ali Monizinade	HR Emp: Don Juan
English Channel	1588	Spain: Medina-Sidonia	England: Howard
Yellow Sea	1592	Japan: Hideyoshi	Korea: Yi Sung Sin
Lützen	1632	HR Emp: Wallenstein	Sweden: Gustavus Adolphus
Rocroi	1643	HR Emp: Melo	France: Enghien (Condé)
The Dunes	1658	Spain: Don Juan, Condé	France: Turenne
Vienna	1683	Ottmn Emp: Kara Mustafa	HR Emp/Poland: Jan Sobieski
Blenheim	1704	France: Tallard	HR Emp/Eng: Eugene/Marlbrogh
Poltava	1709	Sweden: Charles XII	Russia: Peter I
Leuthen	1757	Austria: Pr. Charles	Prussia: Frederick II
Plains of Abraham	1757	France: Montcalm	Britain: Wolfe
Saratoga	1777	Britain: Burgoyne	USA: Gates/Arnold
Camden	1780	USA: Gates	Britain: Cornwallis
The Cowpens	1781	Britain: Tarleton	USA: Morgan
Guilford Cthouse	1781	USA: Greene	Britain: Cornwallis
Yorktown	1781	Britain: Cornwallis	USA: Washington
Rivoli	1797	Austria: Alvintzy	France: Napoleon

Battle	Year	Defeated	Successful
Marengo	1800	Austria: Melas	France: Napoleon
Ulm	1805	Austria: Mack v. Leiberich	France: Napoleon
Trafalgar	1805	France: Villeneuve	Britain: Nelson
Austerlitz	1805	Rus/Aust: Alexander I	France: Napoleon
Jena	1806	Prussia: Brunswick	France: Napoleon
Friedland	1807	Russia: Bennigsen	France: Napoleon
Aspern	1809	France: Napoleon	Austria: Archdk Charles
Wagram	1809	Austria: Archdk Charles	France: Napoleon
Borodino	1812	Russia: Kutusov	France: Napoleon
Queenston	1812	USA: van Rensslaer	Britain: Brock
Leipzig	1813	France: Napoleon	Allies: Blücher et al.
Bladensburg	1814	USA: Winder	Britain: Ross
Waterloo	1815	France: Napoleon	Allies: Blücher/Wellington
Buena Vista	1847	Mexico: Santa Anna	USA: Taylor
Mexico City	1847	Mexico: Santa Anna	USA: Scott
Sevastopol	1855	Russia: Gorchakov	Allies: Pelissier/Simpson
Bull Run I	1861	USA: McDowell	CSA: Beauregard/J. E. Johnston
Malvern Hill	1862	CSA: Lee	USA: Porter
Shiloh	1862	CSA: A. S. Johnston	USA: Grant
Fredericksburg	1862	USA: Burnside	CSA: Lee
Chancellorsville	1863	USA: Hooker	CSA: Lee
Vicksburg Cmpgn	1863	CSA: Pemberton	USA: Grant
Gettysburg	1863	CSA: Lee	USA: Meade
Chattanooga	1863	CSA: Bragg	USA: Grant
Cedar Creek	1864	CSA: Early	USA: Sheridan
Nashville	1864	CSA: Hood	USA: Thomas
Cold Harbor	1864	USA: Grant	CSA: Lee
Königgrätz	1866	Austria: Benedek	Prussia: Moltke

Battle	Year	Defeated	Successful
Gravelotte-S. Prvt	1870	France: Bazaine	Prussia: Moltke
Sedan	1870	France: Wimpffen	Prussia: Moltke
Little Big Horn	1876	USA: Custer	Sioux: Crazy Horse
Ulundi	1879	Zululand: Cetawayo	Britain: Chelmsford
Majuba Hill	1881	Britain: Colley	Boers: Joubert
Adowa	1896	Italy: Baratieri	Abyssinia: Menelek
Omdurman	1898	Dervishes: Abdullah	Britain: Kitchener
Colenso	1899	Britain: Buller	Boers: Botha
The Yalu	1904	Russia: Zasulich	Japan: Kuroki
Port Arthur	1904	Russia: Stoesel	Japan: Nogi
Mukden	1905	Russia: Kuropatkin	Japan: Oyama
Tsushima	1905	Russia: Rozhdestvenski	Japan: Togo
Frontiers	1914	France: Joffre	Germany: Moltke (Yngr)
Tannenberg	1914	Russia: Samsonov	Germany: Hindenburg
The Marne	1914	Germany: Moltke (Yngr)	France: Joffre
Ypres II	1915	Britain: French	Germany: Falkenhayn
Gallipoli	1915	Britain: Hamilton	Turkey: Liman von Sanders
Kut el Amara	1916	Britain: Townshend	Turkey: von der Goltz
Jutland	1916	Germany: Scheer	Britain: Jellicoe
The Somme I	1916	Britain: Haig	Germany: Falkenhayn
Verdun	1916	Germany: Falkenhayn	France: Petain
Chemin des Dames	1917	France: Nivelle	Germany: Boehn/Below
Gaza-Beersheba	1917	Turkey: Kressenstein	Britain: Allenby
The Somme II	1918	Britain: Haig	Germany: Ludendorff
Amiens	1918	Germany: Ludendorff	Allies: Foch/Haig
Meuse-Argonne	1918	Germany: Ludendorff	Allies: Foch/Pershing
Megiddo	1918	Turkey: Liman v. Sanders	Britain: Allenby
Warsaw	1920	Russia: Tukhachevsky	Poland: Pilsudski

Battle	Year	Defeated	Successful
Inonu	1921	Greece: Papoulas	Turkey: Kemal/Ismet
Suomussalmi	1939	USSR: Meretskov	Finland: Mannerheim
Flanders/Ardennes	1940	France: Gamelin	Germany: Brauchitsch
Rovno	1941	USSR: Budenny	Germany: v. Rundstedt
Moscow	1941	Germany: Leeb	USSR: Zhukov
Pearl Harbor	1941	USA: Short/Kimmel	Japan: Nagumo
Clark Field	1941	USA: Brereton	Japan: Tsukahara
Bataan	1942	USA: Wainwright	Japan: Homma
Midway	1942	Japan: Yamamoto	USA: Spruance
Stalingrad	1942	Germany: Paulus	USSR: Zhukov
El Alamein	1942	Germany: Rommel	Britain: Montgomery
Tunisia	1942	Allies: Anderson	Germany: Nehring
Kasserine Pass	1943	USA: Fredendall	Germany: Rommel
Kursk	1943	Germany: Kluge/Mannstein	USSR: Zhukov
Hollandia	1944	Japan: Imura	USA: MacArthur
Normandy	1944	Germany: Rommel/Kluge	Allies: Eisenhower
Leyte Gulf	1944	Japan: Toyoda	USA: Nimitz
Ardennes (Bulge) 1	1944	USA: Bradley	Germany: Rundstedt
Ardennes (Bulge) 2	1945	Germany: Rundstedt	USA: Bradley
Osan	1950	USA: Smith (Dean)	N. Korea: Choe Yong Gun
Inchon	1950	N. Korea: Choe Yong Gun	USA: MacArthur
Dien Bien Phu	1954	France: Navarre	N. Vietnam: Giap
Suez Canal	1973	Israel: Gonen	Egypt: Ismail
Chinese Farm	1973	Egypt: Mamoun	Israel: Adan
Falkland Islands	1982	Argentina: Benj Menendez	Britain: Moore
Bekaa Valley	1982	Syria: Berakdar	Israel: Ben Gal

Simulating Defeat with Computers: Forced Changes of Combat Posture[1]

B Y　　J A N I C E　　B .　　F A I N

THE PROBLEM

Designers of combat simulations and war games have long been concerned about the problem of bringing a simulated battle to a realistic conclusion. How can a model determine that the combat has reached the point at which one of the adversaries would, in real combat, shift to a less aggressive combat posture; that is, stop attacking and go on the defensive or stop attempting to hold a position and begin a retrograde movement.

It has long been assumed that equipment or personnel losses are the most useful measures of combat effectiveness degradation, and losses as a percent of authorized or duty strength has been a commonly used indicator that a forced posture change will occur. Some models have considered additional factors, such as supplies remaining and force ratios. However, both factors and parameters have varied widely and have not been based on objective evidence. Thus, there has been considerable concern in the modeling community and the larger defense community that current models do not handle forced posture changes with adequate realism. This study is an attempt to find a way to model such posture changes that is more firmly grounded in the reality of combat experience, with the long-range goal of improving their representation in army combat simulations and war games.

METHODOLOGY AND INFORMATION SOURCES

This project followed the standard pattern for such work: information collection and analysis followed by model design and development.

There were three information sources: historical research, structured discussions with combat veterans, and a search of the literature. The result of the information collection and analysis task was a list of those factors thought to be associated with forced posture changes.

Definitions. For the purposes of this study, the following definitions were used:

• The *combat posture* of a military force is the immediate intention of its commander and troops toward the opposing enemy force, together with the preparations and deployment to carry out that intention. The chief combat postures treated here are attack, defend, and retrograde operations (which include delay and withdraw).

• A *change in combat posture* (posture change) is a shift from one posture to another. It may be either voluntary or forced.

• A *forced posture change* (FPC) is a change in combat posture that is brought about, directly or indirectly, by enemy action. Such posture changes are characteristically changes to a less aggressive posture. The two types of changes considered here are attack-to-defense and defense-to-retrograde operations. (Voluntary posture changes, such as defense-to-attack, are handled by the parent ground combat model or by the war-gamers.)

• The term *breakpoint* has a common meaning of collapse into ineffectiveness or rout. This is not the meaning when the term is sometimes used in this study. While *forced posture change* is the more precise term for the subject of this study, for brevity and convenience, breakpoint is sometimes used in this paper as synonymous with forced posture change.

Historical Data Collection. The Breakpoints Data Base started with 59 engagements drawn from the DMSi Land Warfare Data Base. To that were added 24 new engagements collected specifically for ths project. These 83 engagements all involved U.S. combat units and all took place after 1940. There were 62 divisional-level and 21 regimental-level engagements. The U.S. opponents were German or Japanese. (See Figure C.1.)

Figure C.1.   Engagement in the Breakpoints Data Base

REGIMENTAL ENGAGEMENTS

LWDB#	Id#		Engagement
	1.	15 Feb 43	Sidi Bou Zid II
	2.	20–21 Jan 44	Rapido I North
	3.	21–22 Jan 44	Rapido II North
	4.	20–21 Jan 44	Rapido I South
	5.	21–22 Jan 44	Rapido II South
	6.	7 Aug 44	Mortain II
	7.	2–5 Nov 44	Schmidt I
	8.	2–3 Nov 44	Schmidt II
	9.	2–4 Nov 44	Schmidt III
	10.	17–19 Dec 44	Krinkelt-Rocherath II
	11.	7 Aug 44	Mortain I
5280	12.	4–5 May 45	Jap Counterattack I
5310	13.	24–25 May 45	Jap Counterattack II
4280	14.	7–9 Feb 44	Moletta River Defense
	15.	16–19 Dec 44	Schnee Eifel Center
	16.	14 Feb 43	Sidi Bou Zid I
	17.	19–20 Feb 43	Kasserine Pass
	18.	13–16 Dec 44	Wahlerscheid
	19.	16–17 Dec 44	Krinkelt-Rocherath I
5360	20.	12 Jun 45	Yaeju-Dake
5170	21.	20–24 Nov 43	Tarawa-Betio

DIVISIONAL ENGAGEMENTS

LWDB#	Id#		Engagement
4330	1.	21–23 Feb 44	Fioccia
4300	2.	11–12 Feb 44	Factory Counterattack
3920	3.	23 Mar 43	El Guettar
4610	4.	6–12 Aug 44	Mortain
5260	5.	28–29 Apr 45	Kochi Ridge-Onaga II
5250	6.	25–27 Apr 45	Kochi Ridge-Onaga I
5400	7.	9–12 Apr 45	Kakazu and Tombstone Ridges
5440	8.	14–18 May 45	Attack on the Shuri Line's Eastern Flank II
5470	9.	10–11 Jun 45	Initial Attack on the Yuza-Dake/Yaeju Escarpment
4170	10.	6–7 Nov 43	Pozzilli
5320	11.	26–27 May 45	Shuri Envelopment, Phase II
4820	12.	6 Dec 44	Singling-Bining
5340	13.	6–8 Jun 45	Hill 95-I
4470	14.	26 May 44	Velletri
4740	15.	14–15 Nov 44	Bourgaltroff

Figure C.1. Engagement in the Breakpoints Data Base (*continued*)

DIVISIONAL ENGAGEMENTS

LWDB#	Id#		Engagement
5460	16.	6–9 Jun 45	Advance to the Yuza-Dake/Yaeju Escarpment
4520	17.	29 May–1 Jun 44	Lanuvio
4510	18.	29–31 May 44	Fosso di Campoleone
4310	19.	16–19 Feb 44	Bowling Alley
4160	20.	6–7 Nov 43	Monte Lungo
4480	21.	26–28 May 44	Campoleone Station
3960	22.	11 Sep 43	Sele-Calore Corridor
4780	23.	27–29 Nov 44	Burbach-Durstel
3990	24.	13–14 Sep 43	Tobacco Factory
4690	25.	2–13 Nov 44	Schmidt
4770	26.	26 Nov 44	Baerendorf II
4620	27.	16 Aug 44	Chartres
	28.	16–19 Feb 44	Bowling Alley I
	29.	16–19 Feb 44	Bowling Alley III
	30.	16 Dec 44	Schnee Eifel South
5230	31.	19–21 Apr 45	Tomb Hill-Ouki
5350	32.	9–11 Jun 45	Hill 95–II
5370	33.	15–17 Jun 45	Hills 153 and 115
5330	34.	29–31 May 45	Shuri Envelopment, Phase III
5300	35.	22–23 May 45	Shuri Envelopment, Phase I
5290	36.	6–7 May 45	Kochi Ridge IV
5240	37.	19–23 Apr 45	Skyline Ridge-Rocky Crags
5390	38.	5–8 Apr 45	Advance to Shuri Line Outpost
5420	39.	26–29 Apr 45	Maeda Escarpment
5480	40.	12–17 Jun 45	Capture of the Yuza-Dake/Yaeju-Dake Escarpment
4390	41.	17–19 May 44	Monte Grande (Rome)
4140	42.	4–5 Nov 43	Santa Maria Oliveto
4340	43.	11–14 May 44	Santa Maria Infante
4360	44.	14–15 May 44	Castellonorato
4570	45.	13–17 Sep 44	II Giogio Pass
4530	46.	1–2 Jun 44	Lariano
4080	47.	13–14 Oct 43	Triflisco
4410	48.	22–24 May 44	Terracina
4550	49.	1–2 Jun 44	Valmontone
5380	50.	2–4 Apr 45	Advance from the Beachhead
4580	51.	11–18 Jul 44	St. Lo
5210	52.	2–4 Apr 45	Advance from the Beach
4440	53.	23–25 May 44	Anzio Breakout
4450	54.	23–25 May 44	Cisterna
4460	55.	25–27 May 44	Sezze

DIVISIONAL ENGAGEMENTS

LWDB#	Id#	Engagement	
4630	56.	23–25 Aug 44	Melun
3930	57.	23 Apr–6 May 43	Sedjenane-Bizerte
	58.	16 Dec 44	Schnee Eifel North I
	59.	16–17 Feb 44	Bowling Alley II
	60.	16–19 Dec 44	Schnee Eifel North II
	61.	16–18 Dec 44	Our River Center
	62.	16–17 Dec 44	Our River North

STRUCTURED GROUP DISCUSSIONS[2]

Participants in the discussion groups were combat veterans who had taken part in a military operation in which there had been a forced posture change. In recruiting, we were careful to stress the voluntary nature of the participation. Our standard approach was "We would like to let you know about our study and if you would like to talk with us, we would be happy to talk with you." Response was generally positive, with most veterans who were contacted willing, and some eager, to participate.

A total of thirty-six veterans, including thirteen former officers and twenty-three former enlisted men, participated in the discussions. In addition there were telephone conversations with three former enlisted men who lived outside the Washington, D.C., area. At the time of the engagements, their military ranks ranged from private to brigadier general and their assignments included combat command commander, battalion commander, company commander, platoon leader, regimental staff officer, rifle squad leader, medic, mortarman, cannoneer, armorer-artificer, and rifleman.

It was felt important to have the accounts and judgments of both officers and enlisted men. Only an officer who had been with a regimental commander at the time he surrendered his regiment could have provided convincing testimony as to the reasons that officer gave at the time for his decision. On the other hand, only an enlisted man could have firsthand knowledge of the morale in the ranks before an attack, or could report on the lack of the customary briefing on attack objectives by the squad leader.

A prepared discussion guide was used to encourage consideration of all aspects of the unit's background and circumstances of the operation that might have been related to forced posture changes. Participants were given an opportunity to evaluate their training, their unit's leadership, the strength of the positions they were holding or attempting to capture, and the impact of casualties. It should be noted the role of the discussion guide was to stimulate and focus, rather than restrict, discussion.

The operations are summarized in Figure C.2. The number of participants in each group ranged from 1 to 7, with an average of two and one half.

Figure C.2. Operations Discussed by Groups of Veterans

U.S. Div	Op Name	Location	Date
36 Inf	Rapido River	Italy	Jan 44
45 Inf	Anzio	Italy	Feb 44
28 Inf	Schmidt	Germany	Nov 44
106 Inf	Schnee Eifel	Germany	Dec 44
2 Inf	Krinkelt-Rocherath	Belgium	Dec 44
7 Amd	St. Vith	Belgium	Dec 44
24 Inf	Taejon	Korea	Jul 50
2 Inf	Kunu-Ri	Korea	Nov 50

Figure C.3 shows the factors suggested by the discussion groups as leading to, responsible for, or accompanying forced posture changes.

Literature Search. A survey of the literature revealed very little work directed specifically to the question of posture changes. The most relevant were works by Dorothy K. Clark, Richard C. Adkins, Robert McQuie, and Trevor N. Dupuy.

Figure C.3 Key Factors in Breakpoints as Judged by the Veterans

Force Strength Factors
   High enemy-friendly force ratio
   Low troop-frontage ratio
   High casualty rate

Tactical Factors
   Enemy maneuver/flank/envel
   Force tactically vulnerable
   High-level intelligence failure

Environmental Factors
   Terrain broken by crevasses
   Hills, heavy forests
   Poor roadnet

Means/Materiel Factors

   Poor communications
   No antitank weapons
   Low ammunition
   No air support
   No air supply
   Poor or no maps
   Low/no food

Human Factors

   Poor leadership
   Poor staff work
   Poor cohesion/esprit
   Inexperienced officers and troops
   Poor training/fitness
   Poor training for specific operations
   Poor joint training/coordination
   Lack of combat experience
   High personnel turnover
   Little precombat time in position
   Troop expectation of quiet sector
   Confusion over orders, objective
   Troop exhaustion in combat

Clark's study, the earliest and most detailed, yielded a long list of factors Clark believed to be related to the loss of combat effectiveness. Adkins' thesis on modeling battlefield decision-making provided additional factors. McQuie addressed the question of posture change directly in a study of the causes of defeat in some sixty World War II battles and provided, for the first time, a ranking of the causes of posture changes by frequency of occurrence in battles. Dupuy set forth specific conditions under which, in accordance with historical patterns, he believed attackers and defenders would change posture. Figure C.4 shows the factors gleaned from the literature search.

The results of the information-collection phase was a list of some eighty factors obtained by combining lists from the discussion groups and from the literature survey.

It was noted that there were two modes in which the factors were expressed. Clark and Adkins were listing factors the analyst must think about in creating a breakpoint model. These factors are, therefore, stated in

Figure C.4.   Summary of Factors Mentioned in the Literature as Associated with Posture Changes by Combat Units

Unit strength
Combat power ratio/force ratio
Perception of relative force size
Enemy opposition
Heavy enemy artillery and air attacks
Casualties or equipment losses
Number of casualties (including key personnel)
Casualty rates
Tactical plan/relative tactical posture
Envelopment, encirclement, penetration
Enemy occupied key terrain
Adjacent friendly unit withdrawal
Status of adjacent units/adjacent friendly unit withdrawal
Attacker's advance rate
Fire support and reinforcement
Lack of artillery/air support
No reserves left
Proportion of reserves committed
Supply shortage
Amount of ammunition remaining
Communications
Reconnaissance
Enemy achieved surprise
Enemy reinforced
Condition of troops at beginning
Length of combat experience
Training and experience level
Previous training for current situation
Nature of latest combat experience
Fatigue and motivation
Esprit de corps
Number of new replacements
Leadership
Imperative of the assigned mission
Mission and associated objectives
Unusual environmental stress

Figure C.4.   (*continued*)

Previous experience in this terrain
Previous experience in this climate
Change in the weather
Truce or general surrender
Orders to withdraw

nonspecific, neutral terms. For example, Clark lists the general area of *logistical support* as a factor to be considered.

In contrast to the Clark–Adkins lists, McQuie and the discussion groups were citing factors known, or believed, to have been responsible for posture changes in real engagements. Their factors are generally phrased in specific, negative terms. Thus, while McQuie would agree that *logistical support* is important, it is *supply shortage* that is listed as a contributing factor. Again, Adkins mentions *amount of ammunition remaining* as a factor to be considered, while the discussion groups listed *low ammunition* as responsible for a posture change.

INFORMATION ANALYSIS

The first step in organizing the factors was to pair the general factors of Clark and Adkins with the corresponding specific factors. This pairing is shown in Figure C.5, where the factors in parenthesis, not in the original list, were added to complete the table.

In the next step, the general factors are dropped and the specific factors are evaluated individually as potential building blocks of a breakpoint model, producing the list shown in Figure C.6. This list is based, then, on the literature, the discussion groups, and general considerations of the interactions between the parent ground combat model and the embedded breakpoint model. These factors fall into three general areas of concern:

- The tactical situation
- Relative combat power or strength
- Combat losses

To this point, the treatment of factors has ignored the question of what information about combat engagements is actually available. In starting model development, it was necessary to introduce considerations of the availability of historical data for parameter computation.

Figure C.5.   Separation of Posture Change Factors into General
and Specific Categories

General Factors	Specific Factors
Combat power ratio, force ratio	1. High enemy/friendly force ratio
Perception of relative force	2. (Perception of high enemy/friendly force ratio)
Casualties and equipment losses	3. (Heavy personnel casualties)
	4. (Severe equipment losses)
Tactical plan	5. (Defective tactical plan)
Relative tactical posture and opponent's position	6. Low troops/frontage ratio
	7. Force in tactically vulnerable position
	8. Surprise by enemy
	9. Enemy occupied key terrain
	10. Unfavorable status of unit in adjacent sector
Enemy maneuver; attacker's advance rate	11. Flanking, envelopment, penetration
	12. Unfavorable advance rate by the attacker
Fire support and reinforcement	13. Lack of artillery/air support
	14. Heavy enemy artillery and air attacks
Proportion of reserves left	15. Lack of reserves
Logistical support	16. Supply shortage
	17. Inadequate weapons
	18. Lack of food; hunger
	19. Low ammunition
Communications	20. Communications failure
Reconnaissance, intelligence	21. Poor reconnaissance
	22. Intelligence failure
Condition of troops at the beginning	23. Precombat fatigue
	24. Little time in line before engagement
	25. Hasty unit commitment on new ground
Training and experience	26. Poor overall training and experience
	27. Poor training for specific operation
	28. Inadequate combined arms training
Fatigue	29. Troop exhaustion during combat
Morale and motivation	30. Poor morale
	31. High personnel turnover/replacement
	32. Low mission urgency
Leadership	33. Poor leadership
	34. Poor staff work
	35. Troop confusion over orders, objectives
	36. Poor, or no, maps

Figure C.5.   (*continued*)

General Factors	Specific Factors
Unusual environmental stress	37. Poor roadnet
	38. Weather change
	39. Unfavorable terrain

GENERAL MODEL STRUCTURE

The Breakpoint Model has been developed as a submodel to be incorporated into group and combat simulations and war games for the purpose of terminating combat engagements. The model was developed as a set of factor checks in the form of *if-then* statements. The general form is:

If factor 1 is less (greater) than X1,
Then there is an attacker posture change.

If factor 1 is greater (less) than X2
Then there is a defender posture change.

X1 and X2 are the parameters associated with factor 1. Their numerical values are to be determined from the historical data. (The numerical value of factor 1, which is to be compared to X1 and X2, comes from the parent ground combat model or war game.)

From the data items in the Land Warfare Data Base, factors representing each of the general areas shown above were selected. These factors, shown in Figure C.7, are checked during a combat engagement to determine if either the attacker or the defender changed posture. It would have been desirable to be more discriminating in making such breaks by applying all of the factors listed in Figure C.6. However, the historical data would not always permit this, and few of the existing models (to which the Breakpoint Model would be applied) had outputs to permit such discrimination. It was therefore necessary to proceed with the relatively crude approach dictated by the limited number of factors in Figure C.7.

Two versions of the Breakpoint Model were developed. They share a common view of combat and employ similar, although not identical, factors. They differ primarily in their relationship to simulated time.

The first version is termed the *event* version because it fits most naturally

Figure C.6.   Factors Retained as Potential Elements of the Breakpoint Model

1. High enemy/friendly force ratio
2. Heavy personnel casualties
3. Severe equipment losses
4. Force in tactically vulnerable position
5. Enemy occupied key terrain
6. Unfavorable status of units in adjacent terrain
7. Flanking, envelopment, penetration
8. Unfavorable advance rate by the attacker
9. Lack of reserves
10. Supply shortage
11. Low ammunition
12. Communications failure
13. Poor morale

into an event-sequence ground combat model. It is called once at the end of the engagement to determine which side changed posture. At the start of the engagement, its duration must be determined so that the call to the Breakpoint Model may be scheduled by the parent ground combat model.

The second, the *time-step* version, is called periodically to determine if conditions for a posture change exist. The duration of the engagement is obtained from the (simulated) time at which these conditions are met. How often the time-step version is called depends on the basic time-step of the parent model. The version described here is based on a one-day time-step, since one day is the basic time unit in the Breakpoints Data Base.

Figure C.7.   The Breakpoint Model Factors

General Category	Specific Factor from the Data Base
Tactical Situation	Total Distance Advanced/Width of Front
Relative Combat Strength	Personnel Ratio (Attacker/Defender)
Combat Losses	Attacker Casualties
	Defender Casualties
	Casualty Ratio (Attacker/Defender)

THE EVENT VERSION

Duration Times. Figure C.8 is an operational flow diagram of the event version of the Breakpoint Model showing the factors checked at the end of the engagement to identify the side changing posture. Before a call to this version can be scheduled, the duration of the engagement must be determined. There are several options.

Figure C.8. Operational Flow Diagram of the *Event* Version of the Breakpoint Model

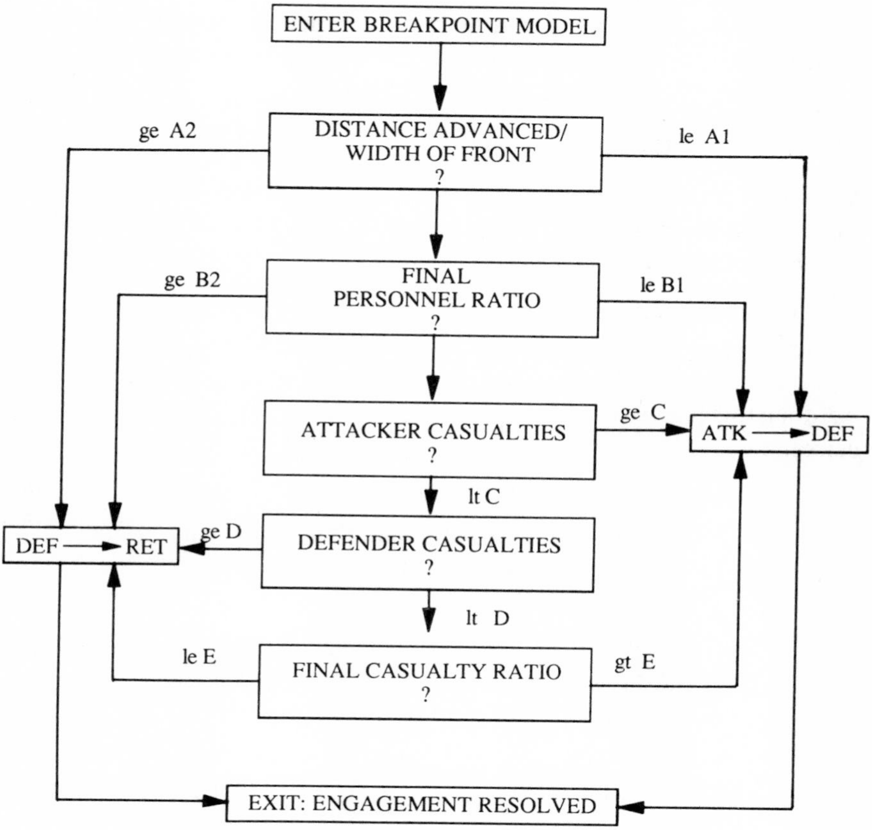

ge=Greater than, or equal to   le=Less than, or equal to
gt=Greater than   lt=Less than

Two options make use of the historical distribution of durations. The first, and simplest, procedure is to set all durations equal to the median value—three days for the divisional-level engagements and one day for the regimental-level engagements. A second option is to choose a random duration from the historical distribution.

A third option is to estimate the duration time on the basis of some piece of information available before the engagement starts. Figure C.9 shows the distribution of durations for the divisional engagments based on the initial personnel ratio. These durations, which are close to the historical distribution, were used here with the divisional-level engagements.

In the regimental cases, the relationship between personnel ratio and duration is too weak to permit such an estimation. For the regimental engagements, then, a constant duration of one day was used.

Model Parameters. The following seven parameters for the event version were shown in Figure C.8.

A1   If the attacker has advanced no farther than this distance (relative to the width of the front), then the attack is essentially halted and the attacker is forced to defend.

A2   If the attacker has penetrated this far (relative to the front width), then the attack is successful and the defender must withdraw.

If the distance advanced (relative to the front width) is between A1 and A2, then this factor is not determining and the model proceeds to check the personnel ratio.

Figure C.9.   Distribution of the Estimated Engagement Durations

Engagement Duration (Days)	NUMBER OF ENGAGEMENTS	
	Estimated	*Historical*
1	3	8
2	12	18
3	21	19
4	14	9
5	7	3
6	5	2
>6	0	3

B1   If the personnel ratio (attacker/defender) is below this value, then the attacker has been halted by superior defensive strength.

B2   If the personnel ratio (attacker/defender) is above this value, then the defender has been overwhelmed by superior attacker strength.

If the personnel ratio (attacker/defender) is between B1 and B2, then this factor is not determining, and the model proceeds to check the attacker casualties.

C   The attacker must change to a defensive posture if his *total casualties* (expressed as a percent of his initial personnel strength) exceed this amount.

D   The defender must withdraw if his *total casualties* (expressed as a percent of his initial personnel strength) exceed this amount.

E   The attacker must take up a defensive posture if the value of the *casualty ratio* (attacker/defender) is equal to, or greater than, this parameter. Otherwise there is a defender posture change.

It can be seen that this last factor, casualty ratio, will assure that no engagement will emerge from the Breakpoint Model without identification of the side changing posture.

The general procedure for obtaining parameter values from the historical combat data consists of the following steps:

1. Sort the engagements on the basis of the factor value. This sorting generally produces a list of engagements with the attacker posture changes clustered together at one end of the list and the defender posture changes clustered together at the other end.
2. Starting at the end of the sorted list favorable to attacker posture changes, go down the list to the first defender posture change.
3. The parameter value is the average of the values for the case of the defender posture change and the adjacent attacker posture change.

To illustrate this procedure, consider Figure C.10, which shows values of the factor *Distance Advanced/Front Width*. Starting at the lowest value of the factor, the run of attacker posture changes (As) is broken at engagement 20. The value of A1 is the average of 0.15 and 0.20 or 0.175. The value of A2 is obtained by starting at the highest values of the factor and going up to

Figure C.10. Sorted Values for the Factor *Distance Advanced/Front Width* for the Regimental Engagements (Parameters for the *Event* Version of the Breakpoint Model)

Id	PC	Value	
1	A	0.00	
12	A	0.00	
13	A	0.00	
8	A	0.15	
			$- - - - - - - - - - - - -$ 0.175 = A1
20	D	0.20	
10	A	0.30	
11	A	0.40	
4	A	0.50	
14	A	0.63	
2	A	0.70	
16	D	0.73	
5	A	0.80	
21	D	0.83	
3	A	1.00	
9	A	1.25	
6	A	1.33	
17	D	1.50	
7	A	2.00	
			$- - - - - - - - - - - - -$ 2.00 = A2
19	D	2.00	
15	D	4.00	
18	D	4.40	

the engagement which breaks the run of defender posture changes. The value of A2 is 2.0.

Figures C.11–C.14 show how the remainder of the regimental parameters are obtained. Parameter values for the divisional-level engagements were obtained by the same procedure. Parameters for the event version are summarized in Figure C.15.

THE TIME-STEP VERSION

Figure C.16 shows a flow diagram for the time-step version of the Breakpoint Model. This version has the following parameters:

**Figure C.11.   Sorted Values for the Factor *Final Personnel Ratio*
(Attacker/Defender) for the Regimental Engagements
(Parameters for the *Event* Version of the Breakpoint Model)**

Id	PC	Value
13	A	0.18
12	A	0.21
1	A	0.28
8	A	1.25
9	A	1.31
7	A	1.33
10	A	1.39
		— — — — — — — — — — — 1.41 = B1
17	D	1.43
16	D	1.44
14	A	1.48
6	A	2.03
11	A	2.26
3	A	3.17
19	D	3.34
2	A	3.47
5	A	3.90
4	A	4.22
		— — — — — — — — — — — 5.56 = B2
18	D	6.90
15	D	9.75
20	D	51.9
21	D	999.

A1   If the attacker has advanced no farther than this distance (relative to the front width), then the attack is essentially halted and the attacker is forced to a defensive posture. While the parameter A1 is a constant in the event version, this time-step parameter is an increasing function of simulated time. Since it represents a cumulative advance that must be attained if the attack is to continue, a value suitable for the first day of the attack would not be appropriate for subsequent days.

There are not sufficient data to determine the proper functional form. The simple linear relationship shown below is assumed:

$$A1 = (M-1) \times A0$$

**Figure C.12.   Sorted Values for the Factor *Total Attacker Casualties*
for the Regimental Engagements
(Parameters for the *Event* Version of the Breakpoint Model)**

Id	PC	Value	
16	D	0.31	
20	D	0.90	
14	A	1.60	
4	A	2.10	
17	D	2.80	
19	D	3.03	
8	A	3.75	
6	A	4.41	
18	D	4.46	
15	D	4.88	
			5.0 = C
2	A	5.10	
9	A	7.07	
5	A	7.63	
11	A	8.59	
3	A	8.76	
10	A	9.89	
7	A	10.3	
1	A	13.4	
13	A	31.7	
21	D	36.5	
12	A	54.0	

where:

A1 is computed by the time-step version of the model to check the factor *Distance Advanced/Front Width* for an attacker posture change

M is the day of the engagement. (First day, $M=1$, second day, $M=2$, etc.)

A0, whose value is determined from the historical data, is used by the model to compute A1.

Figure C.17 illustrates the use of A1 in a hypothetical case in which $A0 = 0.10$ and the attacker is advancing at an average rate of 0.08 km per day across a 1 km front. The column labeled A1 shows the value of the model parameter on each day of the engagement. The next column shows the distance advanced by the attacker through each day. As long as the *distance advanced* is greater than A1, there is no posture change (at least

**Figure C.13.   Sorted Values for the Factor *Total Defender Casualties*
for the Regimental Engagements
(Parameters for the *Event* Version of the Breakpoint Model)**

Id	PC	Value
2	A	0.59
3	A	0.59
1	A	0.60
4	A	0.72
5	A	0.72
14	A	1.40
13	A	1.50
12	A	2.20
8	A	2.90
9	A	5.41
17	D	10.00
11	A	10.81
10	A	10.91
6	A	13.04
7	A	16.92

17.1 = D

Id	PC	Value
16	D	17.20
18	D	17.86
19	D	29.48
15	D	90.24
20	D	96.00
21	D	100

by this factor). At the end of the fifth day, the values are equal and there is an attacker posture change.

A2   If the attacker has penetrated this far, then the attack is successful and the defender must withdraw.

If the *distance advanced* (relative to the front width) is between A1 and A2, then this factor is not determining and the model must proceed to the next factor.

B1   If the change in the personnel ratio since the start of the engagement is above this figure, then the defender has been overwhelmed by the superior strength of the attacker.

Figure C.14. Sorted Values for the Factor *Casualty Ratio* (Attacker/Defender) for the Regimental Engagements (Parameters for the *Event* Version of the Breakpoint Model)

Id	PC	Value	
20	D	0.01	
16	D	0.02	
15	D	0.05	
19	D	0.10	
18	D	0.25	
17	D	0.28	
			0.31 = E
6	A	0.34	
21	D	0.37	
7	A	0.61	
11	A	0.79	
10	A	0.91	
14	A	1.14	
8	A	1.29	
9	A	1.31	
4	A	2.92	
2	A	8.63	
5	A	10.57	
3	A	14.82	
13	A	21.13	
1	A	22.45	
12	A	24.55	

Figure C.15.   Parameter Values for the *Event* Version of the Breakpoint Model

	Unit Level	
Parameters	Divisional	Regimental
A1	0.115	0.175
A2	1.59	2.00
B1	1.53	1.41
B2	7.19	5.56
C	16.6	5.0
D	39.8	17.1
E	0.405	0.31

Figure C.16. Operational Flow Diagram of the *Time-Step* Version of the Breakpoint Model

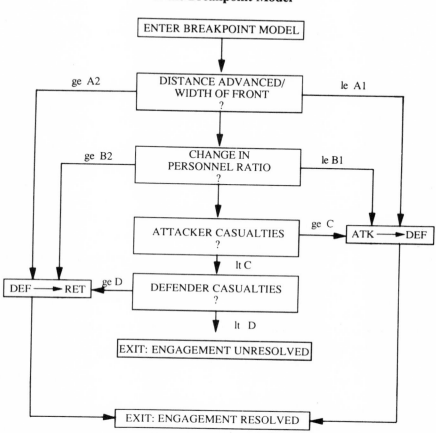

ge=Greater than, or equal to
gt=Greater than

le=Less than, or equal to
lt=Less than

Like A1, this parameter is taken to be a function of simulated time. The same simple linear form assumed for A1 is used:

$$B1 = (M-1) \times B0$$

where:

B1 is computed by the time-step version of the model to check the factor *change in personnel ratio* for an attacker posture change.

M is the day of the engagement (First day, M=1, second day, M=2, etc.)

Figure C.17.   Illustration of the Use of A1 in a Hypothetical Engagement

Simulated Time (Days)	Value of A1	Cumulative Distance Advanced/ Width of Front	
1	0.0	0.08	
2	0.1	0.16	
3.0	0.2	0.24	
4.0	0.3	0.32	
5	0.4	0.4	Atk Pos Chng

Assumptions

0   A1− = (Day − 1) × 0.10

0   Attacker's movement rate = 0.08 (km/day)

0   Width of front = 1 (km)

B0, whose value is determined from the historical data, is used by the model to compute B1.

B2   if the *change in personnel ratio* (since the start of the engagement) is above, or equal to, this value, then the defender has been overwhelmed by the superior strength of the attacker.

If the *change in the personnel ratio* is between B1 and B2, then the posture change has not been determined and the model must proceed to the next factor.

C   If the attacker's *cumulative casualties* equal, or exceed, this value, then the attacker must change to a defensive posture.

D   If the defender's *cumulative casualties* equal, or exceed, this value, then the defender must withdraw.

If the posture change has not been determined after this last factor check, then the engagement continues and the factor checks are repeated during the next time period. Figure C.18 shows the parameter values of the time-step version. Their derivation from the historical data is based on the same principles as the event version parameters.

**Figure C.18.   Parameter Values
for the *Time-Step* Version
of the Breakpoint Model**

Parameters	ENGAGEMENT LEVEL	
	Divisional	*Regimental*
A0	0.089	0.647
A2	1.04	2.02
B0	0.052	0.013
B2	7.05	0.33
C	4.83	4.27
D	36.6	13.6

MODEL RESULTS

Both versions of the Breakpoint Model have been tried on the engagements in the Breakpoints Data Base. In Figures C.19–C.22 the posture changes assessed by the model are compared with the historical posture changes. These results are summarized in Figure C.23.

While the number of correct posture change identifications suggest that this simple, first-order model has captured the essence of the phenomenon, it is the set of cases in which the posture changes were incorrectly identified that is of most interest. These incorrect identifications, of course, were the direct result of the necessarily crude approach required by using only the limited number of factors included in Figure C.7., as discussed above.

Colonel Dupuy has carried out a detailed look at these cases and identified the missing model elements most likely to be responsible for the incorrect posture change identifications. These elements, listed in Figure C.24, are the most likely candidates for the next, and more discriminating, phase of breakpoint model development.

CONCLUSIONS

On the road toward understanding combat dynamics, the loss-based models are the first step. We believe that this model, which has been expanded to include tactical situation and the relative force strength, is a modest second step.

Figure C.19. Breakpoint Model (*Event* Version) Output: Regimental Posture Changes vs History

Eng Id	HISTORICAL		MODEL RESULTS	
	Dur (*Days*)	*Pos* *Chg*	*Dur* (*Days*)	*Pos* *Chg*
1	1	A	1	A
2	1	A	1	A
3	1	A	1	A
4	1	A	1	A
5	1	A	1	A
6	1	A	1	A
7	4	A	1	A
8	2	A	1	A
9	3	A	1	A
10	3	A	1	A
11	1	A	1	A
12	2	A	1	A
13	1	A	1	A
14	2	A	1	A
15	4	D	1	Ⓐ
16	1	D	1	D
17	2	D	1	Ⓐ
18	4	D	1	D
19	1	D	1	D
20	1	D	1	D
21	5	D	1	Ⓐ

A = Posture change by the attacker.
D = Posture change by the defender.
◯ = Posture change identified incorrectly.

We think this project has made four contributions:

1. The addition of the general areas of tactics and force strengths to combat losses as determinants of combat outcomes
2. The selection of specific factors, available both in the historical combat data base and in the most frequently used ground combat simulations and war games, to represent these general areas
3. A methodology for computing numerical values for the model parameters
4. Specific parameter values for the engagements selected for the Breakpoints Data Base

**Figure C.20.   Breakpoint Model (*Time-Step* Version) Output:
Regimental Posture Changes vs History**

| Eng Id | HISTORICAL | | MODEL RESULTS | |
	Dur (Days)	Pos Chg	Dur (Days)	Pos Chg
1	1	A	1	A
2	1	A	1	A
3	1	A	1	A
4	1	A	1	A
5	1	A	1	A
6	1	A	1	A
8	2	A	1	A
9	3	A	1	A
11	1	A	1	A
12	2	A	1	A
13	1	A	1	A
14	2	A	1	A
15	4	D	1	D
16	1	D	1	D
19	1	D	1	D
20	1	D	1	D
21	5	D	1	(A)
7	4	A	2	A
10	3	A	2	A
18	4	D	2	D
17	2	D	3	D

A = Posture change by the attacker.
D = Posture change by the defender.
○ = Posture change identified incorrectly.

We think the most enduring parts of this project are nos. 1 and 3, the general areas of importance in determining engagement outcomes and the method of obtaining parameter values. The next most enduring part is no. 2, the specific factors. We expect these to last only to the next major data collection effort. For example, the *distance advanced* is probably not the best representation of the tactical situation. We think that the *status of units in adjacent sectors* would be a better replacement for, or at least a valuable addition to, it.

**Figure C.21. Breakpoint Model (*Event* Version) Output:
Divisional Posture Changes vs History**

Eng	HISTORICAL		MODEL RESULTS	
Id	*Day*	*PC*	*Day*	*PC*
1	3	A	1	A
2	2	A	2	A
3	1	A	1	A
4	6	A	1	A
5	2	A	4	A
6	3	A	3	A
7	4	A	6	Ⓓ
8	5	A	4	Ⓓ
9	2	A	4	Ⓓ
10	2	A	3	A
11	2	A	5	Ⓓ
12	1	A	4	A
13	3	A	4	Ⓓ
14	1	A	2	Ⓓ
15	2	D	2	Ⓐ
16	4	D	4	D
17	4	A	3	A
18	3	A	2	A
19	4	A	3	A
20	2	A	3	A
21	3	A	2	A
22	1	A	2	A
23	3	D	3	D
24	2	A	2	A
25	12	A	2	A
26	1	D	3	D
27	1	A	2	Ⓓ
28	4	A	4	A
29	4	A	3	A
30	1	D	3	D
31	3	D	4	D
32	3	D	5	D
33	3	D	6	D
34	3	D	5	D
35	2	D	4	D
36	2	D	3	D
37	5	D	5	D
38	4	D	5	D
39	4	D	4	D
40	6	D	5	D

Figure C.21.   (*continued*)

Eng	HISTORICAL		MODEL RESULTS	
Id	Day	PC	Day	PC
41	2	D	3	D
42	2	D	3	Ⓐ
43	3	D	3	D
44	2	D	3	Ⓐ
45	5	D	4	D
46	2	D	2	D
47	2	D	3	Ⓐ
48	3	D	3	D
49	2	D	3	Ⓐ
50	3	D	6	D
51	8	D	3	Ⓐ
52	3	D	6	D
53	3	D	2	D
54	3	D	2	Ⓐ
55	3	D	3	D
56	3	D	3	D
57	11	D	4	D
58	1	D	5	D
59	2	D	4	D
60	4	D	4	D
61	3	D	6	D
62	2	D	3	D

**Figure C.22   Breakpoint Model (*Time-Step* Version)
Output:
Divisional Posture Changes vs History**

Eng	HISTORICAL		MODEL RESULTS	
Id	Day	PC	Day	PC
1	3	A	1	A
2	2	A	1	A
3	1	A	1	A
4	6	A	1	A
5	2	A	1	A
6	3	A	1	A
10	2	A	1	A
19	4	A	1	A
20	2	A	1	A
22	1	A	1	A
24	2	A	1	A

Figure C.22 *(continued)*

Eng	HISTORICAL		MODEL	RESULTS
25	12	A	1	A
27	1	A	1	Ⓓ
29	4	A	1	A
47	2	D	1	Ⓐ
52	3	D	1	D
56	3	D	1	D
60	4	D	1	D
7	4	A	2	A
8	5	A	2	A
14	1	A	2	A
15	2	D	2	Ⓐ
21	3	A	2	A
23	3	D	2	Ⓐ
28	4	A	2	A
31	3	D	2	Ⓐ
32	3	D	2	D
33	3	D	2	D
34	3	D	2	D
38	4	D	2	D
39	4	D	2	D
42	2	D	2	Ⓐ
50	3	D	2	D
53	3	D	2	D
54	3	D	2	D
58	1	D	2	D
59	2	D	2	D
61	3	D	2	D
9	2	A	3	Ⓓ
12	1	A	3	Ⓓ
18	3	A	3	A
26	1	D	3	D
30	1	D	3	Ⓐ
36	2	D	3	D
37	5	D	3	D
40	6	D	3	D
44	2	D	3	D
46	2	D	3	D
49	2	D	3	D
51	8	D	3	Ⓐ
55	3	D	3	D
62	2	D	3	D

Figure C.22   (*continued*)

Eng	HISTORICAL		MODEL RESULTS	
13	3	A	4	Ⓓ
57	11	D	4	Ⓐ
17	4	A	5	A
11	2	A	6	Ⓓ
35	2	D	6	D
43	3	D	6	Ⓐ
45	5	D	6	D
48	3	D	6	Ⓐ
16	4	D	7	D

The least enduring part is no. 4, the specific parameter values. We expect that these will have to be recomputed for the next set of engagements to which the model is applied.

The next step is to include some or all of the factors listed in Figure C.24 as model elements, and to test the model on additional cases—for example, World War II engagements not involving U.S. units or the recent Middle East conflicts. This would test our hypotheses about which parts, if any, of this project will make a useful contribution to the field of combat analysis.

Figure C.23.   Summary of the Breakpoint Model Results

Level	PERCENT OF POSTURE CHANGES CORRECTLY IDENTIFIED	
	Event Version	*Time-Step Version*
Regimental	86	95
Divisional	78	74

Figure C.24. Reasons for Model Inconsistencies

1. Physical obstacles favoring defense (terrain, fortification, urban environment)	6
2. Surprise	5
3. Armor imbalance	12
4. Artillery imbalance	5
5. Air-support imbalance	8
6. Relative combat effectiveness difference	10
7. National characteristics	4
Total	50 (or 2.1 reasons per inconsistency)

BIBLIOGRAPHY

Adkins, Richard D. *Analysis of Breakpoints in Land Combat.* Monterey, Calif.: Naval Postgraduate School, 1975.

Clark, Dorothy K. *Casualties as a Measure of the Loss of Combat Effectiveness of an Infantry Battalion*, ORO-T-289. Baltimore, Md.: Operations Research Office, The Johns Hopkins University, 1954.

Dupuy, Col. T. N. (USA, Ret). *Representing Battle Termination in Combat Simulations: The Modeling of Defeat Criteria.* Prepared for Sandia Laboratories. Fairfax, Va.: Data Memory Systems, Inc., 1987.

Fain, Janice, et al. *Forced Changes of Combat Posture.* Final report for a project sponsored by the US Army's Concepts Analysis Agency, Bethesda, Md., under Contract No. MDA903-87-C-0807. Fairfax, Va.: Data Memory Systems, Inc., September 1988.

McQuie, Robert. "Battle Outcomes: Casualty Rates as a Measure of Defeat," *Army* (November 1987), pp. 31–34.

Notes

CHAPTER 1

1. "Scotts Fixed Opinion," *Bugle Notes,* United States Military Academy, West Point, N.Y., 1934.

CHAPTER 2

1. None of Napoleon's great captains ever faced another in battle. Gustavus (1594–1632) and Turenne (1611–1675), were near-contemporaries, as were Frederick (1712–1786) and Napoleon (1769–1821). See Napoleon's "Notes sur l'art de la guerre," in *Correspondance de Napoléon Ier, publiée par ordre de l'Empereur Napoléon III*, XXXI:347, 1858–1870, 32 volumes.
2. The author of this book—T. N. Dupuy—has suggested that there have been eight Great Captains: Alexander, Hannibal, Caesar, Genghis Khan, Gustavus, Frederick, Nelson, and Napoleon. That list excludes two cited by Napoleon (Turenne and Eugene) and includes Genghis Khan, Napoleon, and Napoleon's great naval contemporary and adversary, Nelson. Genghis Khan was defeated twice in some twenty battles; Nelson, who commanded in only three great battles, was never defeated.

3. Livy, *The War with Hannibal* [Books XXI–XXX of *The History of Rome from Its Foundation*]. Tr. Aubrey de Sélincourt. (Baltimore: Penguin, 1965), XXX:30. Some allowance must be made for hyperbole.

4. Theodore Ayrault Dodge, in *Great Captains* (Boston: 1889) lists six: Alexander, Hannibal, Caesar, Gustavus, Frederick and Napoleon. T. N. Dupuy, in *Introduction to Military History* (Fairfax, Va.: Data Memory Systems, Inc., 1987), adds to these the names of Genghis Khan and Nelson.

5. Trevor N. Dupuy, *The Military Life of Gustavus Adolphus* (New York: Franklin Watts, 1969), xix. Dupuy summary is apt: "Mobile, coordinated firepower in a system of linear combat formations—that was the contribution of Gustavus Adolphus, the true father of modern warfare."

6. Ibid., 33.

7. Andrew Michael Ramsay, *The History of Henri de La Tour d'Auvergne, viscount de Turenne* (1735), II:303.

8. Ibid., II:358.

9. Gen. Maxime Weygand, *Turenne: Marshal of France*, trans., George B. Ives. (London: Harrap, 1930), 59.

10. *Ibid.,* 77–78.

11. Ibid., 78.

12. David G. Chandler, *The Art of Warfare in the Age of Marlborough* (New York: Hippocrene, 1976), 302–307.

13. Lt. Gen. Sir George MacMunn, *Prince Eugene: Twin Marshal with Marlborough* (London: Sampson Low, n.d.), 121.

14. In his *Kriegs-Lexicon* (Vienna, 1908), the Austrian analyst Gaston Bodart ranked Zerndorf the bloodiest in the period 1618–1905. He gave the total engaged as 85,000 and total casualties as 29,000 or 34.1 percent. Christopher Duffy, in *The Army of Frederick the Great* (New York: Hippocrene, 1974), 235, gives the total engaged as 79,300 and total casualties as 31, 297, or 39.5 percent.

15. As quoted in J. Christopher Herold (ed.), *The Mind of Napoleon* (New York: Columbia University Press, 1955), 229.

CHAPTER 3

1. Janice B. Fain and others, *Forced Changes of Combat Posture*, prepared for U.S. Army Concepts Analysis Agency under Contract No. MDA903-87-C-0807 by Data Memory Systems, Inc. (DMSi), Fairfax, Va., 30 September 1988. The study team also included Charles F. Hawkins, James T. Price, Richard C. Anderson, Gay M. Hammerman, and Trevor N. Dupuy.

2. Most of the men had fought in Europe in World War II, because the good condition of official records on both sides in that conflict made it most appropriate for archival research. Unfortunately no Vietnam War engagements could be studied; enemy records are not available, and U.S. records are not accessible in usable form.

3. There is no statistical significance in the number of factors cited for each division, and the strikingly large number of factors cited for the 106th Division probably reflects the large number of study participants from that division as much as it reflects the problems of the division.

4. Interview with General Bruce Clarke.

5. This was unquestionably an erroneous decision (T.N.D.).

6. Interview with James L. Fletcher.

7. Interview with Paul Elliott.

8. Interview with Oliver Patton.

9. Interview with Alan Jones.

10. Interview with Michael S. Davison.

11. See, for example, Operations Reports, 141st Infantry, 1 Jan 44–31 Jan 44, pp. 134–135, in RG 407, Box 9934, 336 INS(141)-0.3, Washington National Records Center, Suitland, Md.

12. Debatably, this was probably an erroneous decision (T.N.D.).

13. By interesting coincidence Jones, a battalion staff officer, was the son of the 106th Division's commanding general.

CHAPTER 4

1. J. F. C. Fuller, *The Conduct of War* (London: 1961), 124.

2. T. N. Dupuy, *Numbers, Predictions and War* (New York, 1979), 152–153.

CHAPTER 5

1. See T. N. Dupuy, *Elusive Victory; The Arab–Israeli Wars, 1947–1974* (New York: 1978), Appendix B.

CHAPTER 6

1. Alfred von Schlieffen, *Cannae* (Fort Leavenworth, Kan.: 1931), 305.

2. Heinz Guderian, *Panzer Leader* (New York: 1952), 101.

3. Attributed variously to Terence, *Phormio*, and to Pliny the Elder by Pliny the Younger, *Letters*, Book 6, Letter 16.
4. See T. N. Dupuy, *A Genius for War: The German Army and General Staff, 1807–1945, 143–147.*
5. *Ernest D. Swinton, The Defence of Duffer's Drift* (Wayne, N.J., 1986).
6. Maj. Single List (pseud.), *The Battle of Booby's Bluffs* (Washington, D.C., 1922).

CHAPTER 7

1. The defeats were Aspern-Essling, 1809; Leipzig, 1813; La Rothière, 1814; and Waterloo, 1815. The drawn battles were Eylau, 1807; Maloyaroslavets, 1812; and Laon, 1814. Using the method of calculation shown in Chapter 2, his percentage was 92 percent (48 victories, 4 defeats, not counting draws).
2. Louis Antoine Faunelet de Bourrienne, *Memoirs of Napoleon Bonaparte* (New York: 1890), Vol. II, 2.
3. Henri Lochoque, *The Anatomy of Glory* (London: 1978), 15.
4. Bourrienne, Vol. II, 13.
5. David G. Chandler, *The Campaigns of Napoleon* (New York: 1966), 296.
6. James Lawford, *Napoleon, The Last Campaigns, 1813–15* (New York: 1979), 69.
7. Maximilian Yorck von Wartenburg, *Napoleon as a General* (London: 1897), Vol. II, 398.

CHAPTER 8

1. These were: McClellan, Pope, Burnside, Hooker, and Meade.
2. Ulysses S. Grant, *Personal Memoirs of U. S. Grant* (New York, Charles L. Webster & Co., 1894), 429.
3. There is considerable debate about the relative strength and loss figures of the two armies in this campaign, particularly since Southern records are so sketchy. This debate, however, has arisen from low estimates Southerners have made of Lee's losses in the Wilderness and at Spotsylvania. Bearing in mind known losses on certain days and comparative losses in comparable but better-recorded conflicts (such as Malvern Hill, Antietam, Chancellorsville, Second Bull Run, Fredericksburg, and Gettysburg), the estimates of Southern casualties shown below are minimum figures. Proportionally, Lee's losses were greater than Grant's.

CHAPTER 9

1. The general history and the detailed account of this battle in the opening phase of the Russo-Japanese War is taken from two official sources. The account of the Russian defeat at the Yalu is based on the German general staff translation into German of the Russian official history, *Der Russisch–Japanische Krieg: Amthiche Darstellung des Russischen Generalstabes* (Vol. I, Pt. II; *Vorgeschichte und Geschichte des Krieges bis gum 20, Juli 1904*). The German version was augmented by notes and insertions in the text based on official reports sent to Berlin by German officers accompanying the Russian armies. The Japanese side of the story is taken from the British *Official History of the Russo-Japanese War, Part II* (prepared by the Historical Section of the Committee of Imperial Defense). This account is based on the official history of the war prepared by the Japanese general staff and is augmented by reports from British officers attached to the Japanese field forces (notably Sir Ian Hamilton, commander at Gallipoli, and Ernest Swinton, the armored fighting-vehicle pioneer). Additional reference was made to Hamilton's later book, *A Staff Officer's Scrap Book* (London: 1912). Also included are reports from American military attachés (notably John J. Pershing and Peyton C. March).

2. This was real shrapnel, not the shell fragments erroneously called "shrapnel" since World War I. The shrapnel referred to here was an artillery projectile, designed to burst in the air by means of a time fuse, from which were projected steel or lead balls, scattered with great destructive force on enemy personnel on the ground.

3. The account of this engagement is based on the official German history of World War I prepared in the absence of a general staff (forbidden in the Treaty of Versailles) by the Reichsarchiv in Berlin. The title of the appropriate volume is Reichsarchiv, *Der Weltkrieg 1914–1918, Vol. II (Die Befreiung Ostpreuszens)*. This history is very candid, well mapped, and quite detailed. There is no Russian counterpart to the German account, but reports taken from the large bag of Russian prisoners swept up in the following battle of Tannenberg were used by the Reichsarchiv.

4. What happened later is beyond the scope of this account, but Prittwitz' defeat at Gumbinnen led not only to his being replaced by Hindenburg, with Eric Ludendorff as his chief of staff, but also to the German victory over Samsonov at Tannenburg ten days later.

5. The German official story of the gas attack and the following days of bitter battle is found in the Reichsarchiv, *Der Weltkrieg 1914–1918, Vol. II (Die Operationen des Jahres 1915)*. The account from the German side squares well with the British recital in the *Official History of the War: Military*

Operations, France and Belgium, 1915, Vol. I. The British history is provided with very detailed maps that illustrate in a vivid manner the ebb and flow of this battle. The German account devotes several paragraphs to defending the decision to use poison gas.

6. The documentary coverage of this campaign is extensive and provides a wealth of detail on logistics, particularly transport and tonnages, seldom found in official military histories. Although there is no official German General Staff account and the so-called Italian General Staff publication is little more than the headquarters journal of the Italian commander, the British and American histories deal adequately with both the opposing camps in the Tunisian battles. The wholesale surrender of the German and Italian forces in May 1943 gave the Western Allies access to complete files of Wehrmacht and Luftwaffe documents, plus very extensive interrogation reports. The American volume in the official *U.S. Army in World War II: Mediterranean Theater of Operations: Northeast Africa: Seizing the Initiative in the West*, was written by the late George F. Howe, a well-known American historian. It is in many ways a model of its kind. The British official history, *History of the Second World War: The Mediterranean and Middle East, Vol. IV.* easily ranks alongside the American volume. The authors of the British series, J. S. O. Playfair and C. J. C. Molony, were both soldiers and historians.

7. See note 5, above.

CHAPTER 10

1. Maximilian Fretter-Pico, *Missbrauchte Infanterie* (Frankfurt: 1957), 114–119. See also Albert Seaton, *The Russo-German War, 1941–1945* (New York: 1972), 375.

2. Private communication from the respected Irish-German military historian Dermot Bradley, 23 March 1989. Dr. Bradley in turn received his information about this in a private conversation in 1983 with General Hollidt, who told him "Graf von Schwerin was a rather difficult subordinate."

CHAPTER 11

1. The commander of that division was Lieutenant General Count Gerhard von Schwerin (see Chapter 10).

2. The average losses for American divisions in intensive combat in Europe in World War II was about 1 percent per day; the 28th Division losses were an average of 3 percent per day for twelve days, and on at least one of those days the loss rate exceeded 6 percent. German loss rates were comparably high.

CHAPTER 12

1. Dorothy Kneeland Clark, "Casualties as a Measure of the Loss of Combat Effectiveness of an Infantry Battalion," Johns Hopkins University Operations Research Office (1954).
2. Indirect fire is fire delivered on a target which cannot be seen by the firer or aimer of the weapon. This is accomplished by registering the weapon on a base point or checkpoint on the battlefield which can be seen by an observer who then sends commands by telephone or radio to shift the fire to a target which he sees, but unlikely cannot be seen from the weapon. This permits the weapons to be placed behind hills or marshes where they cannot be seen by the enemy.
3. Slightly lower loss rates were incurred by the U.S. 99th Division on December 16, 1944, and the U.S. 101st Airborne Division on 22 December 1944 in its successful desperate effort to defend Bastogne, both in the Battle of the Bulge. For a discussion of the HERO Data Base see *infra*, p. 144.
4. Based on HERO Report: *German and Soviet Replacement Systems in World War II* (Dunn Loring, Va., 1974), 100–103.
5. The G-1 (personnel) records of the U.S. 12th Army Group are not always consistent. One set of records suggests that the loss of the 99th Division that day was less than 7 percent (still exceptionally high).

CHAPTER 13

1. So far as Clausewitz is concerned, this statement is an oversimplified misrepresentation of his ideas as to combat theory. See T. N. Dupuy, *Understanding War: History and Theory of Combat* (pp. 21–30), Chapter 3. Nonetheless, it is the conventional view of Clausewitz's theory by people who have rarely read his writings.
2. Thomas L. Livermore, *Numbers and Losses in the Civil War* (Boston: 1901).
3. Frederick William Lanchester, "The Principle of Concentration," *Engineering*, October 1914. A summary of Lanchester's concepts appears later in this chapter.
4. Antoine Henri Jomini, *Treatise on Grand Military Operations: Summary of the Art of War*, and many other works, from 1805 to 1837.
5. Charles J. J. J. Ardant du Picq, *Battle Studies* (New York: 1921).
6. See, for instance, T. N. Dupuy, *Numbers, Predictions, and War* (New York: 1977) and *Understanding War*.
7. Dorothy K. Clark, *Casualties . . .*; see p. 137 *supra*. The recent study, by Janice Fain, et al., is *Forced Changes of Combat Posture* (1988). A summary of the latter study report is in Appendix C.

8. Interestingly, approximately eighty years before the publication of Lanchester's first article on this subject, Clausewitz, using a very different approach, had shown a relationship between strengths, deployments, and casualties virtually identical to that of the Lanchester Equations. It is doubtful that Lanchester ever saw the Clausewitz statement of the relationship.

9. Many military operations research analysts, few of whom are familiar with military concepts and terminology, have erroneously made this comparison in terms of "aimed" fire and "indirect" fire. Direct fire is, ipso facto, aimed fired. Indirect fire can be either aimed or unaimed; Lanchester was without doubt making a distinction between aimed fire and unaimed fire, whether direct or indirect.

10. James G. Taylor, *Lanchester Models of Warfare* (Arlington, Va.: Operations Research Society of America, 1983).

CHAPTER 15

1. Perhaps the greatest of all Byzantine emperors, Heraclius, and almost certainly the greatest soldier of that durable empire, whose battlefield and organizing genius was comparable to that of the greatest Great Captains, had his place clouded in history by the following events. First, after the death of his first wife, he married his niece, Martius, a marriage condemned by many of his subjects as incestuous. Second, the loss of Syria, Palestine, and Egypt to the Arabs in his declining years has caused some historians to forget that these were but a fraction of the lands he regained for the empire in his years of vigor and glory.

2. The fifth and greatest king of the distinguished House of Plantagenet, the military genius of Edward I is often neglected in favor of his grandson, Edward III. It must be remembered, however, that the military system which brought Edward III and Henry V to glory in the Hundred Years War was that established by Edward I, who also bequeathed them a prosperous, well-administered Kingdom as the base for their successful campaigns in France.

3. The author was one of those "occasional American soldiers," with combat service in Burma longer than that of any other American—even Stilwell.

APPENDIX C

1. This is a summary of a 1988 study report—entitled "Forced Changes of Combat Posture"—by a team of scholars from Data Memory Systems, Inc.

(DMSi) under contract with the U.S. Army Concepts Analysis Agency. In addition to Dr. Fain, the team consisted of Richard Anderson, Gay Hammerman, Charles Hawkins, Lt. Col. James T. Price (USA, Ret.), and Col. Trevor Dupuy (USA, Ret.).

2. Chapter 3 of this book is based upon these structured group discussions.

Bibliography

Ardant du Picq, Charles J.J.J. *Battle Studies*. New York: 1921.

Bourrienne, Louis Antoine Fauvelet de. *Memoirs of Napoleon Bonaparte*, 4 vols. Ed. R. W. Phipps. New York, 1890.

Caulaincourt, Armand-Augustin-Lours de. *No Peace with Napoleon*. Westport, Conn.: 1875.

Chandler, David. *The Campaigns of Napoleon*. New York, 1966.

Charol, Michael (Michael Prawdin). *The Mongol Empire*. London, 1952.

Clark, Dorothy Kneeland. *Casualties as a Measure of the Loss of Combat Effectiveness of an Infantry Battalion*. Washington, D.C.: Operations Research Officer, 1954.

Clausewitz, Carl von. *On War*. Trans. Michael Howard and Peter Paret. Princeton, 1976.

Delderfield, R. F. *Imperial Sunset: The Fall of Napoleon, 1813–1814*. New York, 1890.

Dodge, Theodore Ayrault. *Great Captains*. Boston, 1889.

_____. *Alexander the Great*, 2 vols. Boston, 1890.

_____. *Hannibal*, 2 vols. Boston, 1891.

————. *Julius Caesar*, 2 vols. Boston, 1892.

————. *Gustavus Adolphus*, 2 vols. Boston, 1895.

————. *Napoleon*, 4 vols. Boston, 1904.

Dupuy, R. Ernest, and Trevor N. Dupuy. *The Encyclopedia of Military History*. New York, 1977.

————. *Military Heritage of America*. New York, 1956.

————. *Compact History of the Civil War*. New York, 1960.

Dupuy, Trevor N. *The Military Life of Alexander the Great of Macedon*. New York, 1969.

————. *The Military Life of Hannibal, Father of Strategy*. New York, 1969.

————. *The Military Life of Julius Caesar, Imperator*. New York, 1969.

————. *The Military Life of Genghis Khan, Khan of Khans*. New York, 1969.

————. *The Military Life of Gustavus Adolphus, Father of Modern War*. New York, 1969.

————. *The Military Life of Frederick the Great of Prussia*. New York, 1969.

————. *The Military Life of Napoleon, Emperor of the French*. New York, 1969.

————. *The Battle of Austerlitz*. New York, 1968.

————. *A Genius for War: The German Army and General Staff, 1807–1945*. Englewood Cliffs, N.J.: Prentice-Hall, 1977.

————. *The Evolution of Weapons and Warfare*. New York, 1980.

————. *Numbers, Predictions, and War*. New York, 1977.

————. *Understanding War: History and Theory of Combat*. New York, 1987.

Edmonds, Sir James (ed.). *Official History of the Great War*. London, 1922–1935.

Esposito, Vincent J., et al. *A Military History and Atlas of the Napoleonic Wars*. New York, 1965.

Fain, Janice B., et al. *Forced Changes of Combat Posture*. Fairfax, Va., 1988.

Freeman, Douglas S. *R. E. Lee*, 4 vols. New York, 1949.

Fuller, J. F. C. *The Generalship of U. S. Grant*. New York, 1929.

————. *Grant and Lee*. London, 1933.

————. *The Generalship of Alexander the Great*. New Brunswick, 1958.

————. *Julius Caesar*. New Brunswick, 1965.

German Reichsarchiv. *Der Weltkrieg 1914–1918*, 14 vols. Berlin, 1925–1933.

Grant, Ulysses S. *Personal Memoirs of U.S. Grant*, 2 vols. New York: 1895.

Hamilton, Ian, *A Staff Officer's Scrap Book*. London, 1912.

Historical Evaluation and Research Organization, *German and Soviet Replacement Systems in World War II*. Dunn Loring, Va., 1974.

Howe, George F., *Mediterranean Theater of Operations; Northwest Africa; Seizing the Initiative in the West (U.S. Army in World War II)*. Washington, D.C. 1957.

Jomini, Antoine Henri. *Traite des Grandes Operations Militaires*, 4 vols. Paris, 1830–1831.

Lachouque, Henry, and Anne S. K. Brown. *The Anatomy of Glory*. London, 1978.

Lamb, Harold. *Genghis Khan: The Emperor of All Men*. Garden City, N.Y., 1927.

Lanchester, Frederick William. "The Principle of Concentration," *Engineering*, October 1914.

Lanza, Conrad H. *Napoleon and Modern War*. Harrisburg, PA, 1943.

Lawford, James. *Napoleon, The Last Campaigns*. New York, 1979.

Livermore, Thomas L. *Numbers and Losses in the Civil War*, Boston, 1901.

Manceron, Claude. *Austerlitz*. London, 1966.

Meneval, Baron C. F. de. *Memoirs of Napoleon Bonaparte*, 3 vols. New York, 1910.

Napoleon, Emperor. *Maximes*. Paris, 1874.

Petre, F. Loraine. *Napoleon's Last Campaign in Germany—1813*. London, 1974.

————. *Napoleon at Bay—1814*. London, 1977.

Playfair, I. S. O., and C. J. C. Maloney. *History of the Second World War: The Mediterranean and Middle East*, 4 vols. London, 1954–1966.

Russian General Staff, *Der Russisch-Japanische Krieg*. Translated by the German General Staff. Berlin, 1910.

Taylor, James G. *Lanchester Models of Warfare*. Arlington, 1983.

U.K., Committee of Imperial Defence. *Official History of the Russo-Japanese War*. London, 1910–1920.

U.S. Army. *Field Manual 100–5, Operations*. Washington, DC, 1986.

Williams, Kenneth P. *Lincoln Finds a General*, 5 vols. New York, 1959.

Yorck von Wartenburg, Maximilian. *Napoleon as a General*, 2 vols. London, 1897.

Index